DATA
*
WISE
in
ACTION

DATA *WISE in *ACTION*

Stories of Schools
Using Data to
Improve Teaching
and Learning

**Edited by Kathryn Parker Boudett
and Jennifer L. Steele**

Harvard Education Press
Cambridge, Massachusetts

Third Printing, 2010

Library of Congress Control Number 2007932209

Paperback ISBN 978-1-891792-80-9
Library Edition ISBN 978-1-891792-81-6

Published by Harvard Education Press,
an imprint of the Harvard Education Publishing Group

Harvard Education Press
8 Story Street
Cambridge, MA 02138

Cover: YAY! Design

The typefaces used in this book are
Palatino, Helvetica Neue, and Bureau Grot Seven Nine.

CONTENTS

Preface

What does it look like when a school uses data wisely? As researchers at the Harvard Graduate School of Education and as current and former K–12 teachers, administrators, and consultants, we have been lucky enough to work with many leaders—both teachers and administrators—who are committed to using data to measure, understand, and improve student learning in their schools. The stories of a few of those leaders form the heart of this book. These individuals have worked to foster school cultures that support a collaborative process of inquiry, planning, and reflection. Still, they are not superheroes—just caring educators who, despite real challenges, use evidence and collaboration to improve student learning. If you are such an educator pursuing similar goals in your own school, we hope the stories in this book will provide insight and inspiration to guide your work.

In 2005 we shared a collaborative process for using data in *Data Wise: A Step-by-Step Guide to Using Assessment Results to Improve Teaching and Learning.* The nineteen authors of that book, which was edited by Kathryn Boudett, Elizabeth City, and Richard Murnane, included faculty members and doctoral students from the Harvard Graduate School of Education (HGSE) as well as school leaders from the Boston Public Schools. The book offered a practical, step-by-step approach that would provide busy teachers and administrators with a comprehensive model for using data—including but not limited to standardized test data—to identify common student learning needs, to generate and implement instructional solutions, and to measure those solutions' effectiveness at raising student achievement within a department, grade-level, or school.

Data Wise incorporated vignettes about two fictional schools, Clark K–8 School and Franklin High School, to illustrate the steps of the process. The fictional schools were composites of real schools in which the book's many authors had worked. The vignettes illustrated typical issues, dilemmas, and conversations that arise within schools at each stage of the Data Wise improvement process.

Since its publication, *Data Wise* has been read by tens of thousands of school leaders, many of whom have shared the book with colleagues and staff. It has also become the core text of the graduate, summer, and online Data Wise courses offered at HGSE. Students from around the world have told us that they have found it a valuable and practical resource.

However, the success of *Data Wise* has generated a new demand among school leaders: to hear real stories from schools that are implementing the process. Over and over, people who have read the book have told us that they wished there were a real Clark or Franklin from whose experiences they could learn. With *Data Wise in Action*, we hope to grant this wish.

In deciding to develop this book of case studies, we knew of a number of schools that had been implementing the Data Wise improvement process for several years.

Those who had been doing the work longest had participated in the early years of a graduate Data Wise course sponsored jointly by HGSE and the Boston Public Schools. We also knew of schools that, after participating in HGSE's Data Wise summer institute or reading the book, had begun implementing the process more recently. We chose eight schools to feature in this book and talked to staff members at each school about how they had implemented one or more of the eight Data Wise steps. Through these case studies, we attempt to illuminate the leadership challenges schools face and the strategies they use to overcome those challenges.

This book is intended first and foremost for educators who are interested in implementing—or are already working to implement—the Data Wise improvement process in their schools. Current and potential "Data Wise leaders" work in a wide variety of schools and hold a wide range of positions, including classroom teachers, principals and headmasters, assistant principals, instructional directors, and peer coaches. Some Data Wise leaders are seasoned teaching veterans; others are enthusiastic educators new to the field. Some have little experience with data analysis, while others are longtime data explorers. What unites them all is an interest in working with colleagues to use data to improve student learning.

A key goal of this book is to present examples and concrete suggestions about how to implement the Data Wise improvement process, while also illustrating the complexity (and messiness!) of the work. A second goal is to demonstrate how the schools we profiled adapted the Data Wise process to fit their particular needs. We hope that showing the variety of ways in which schools used the process will help drive home the point that there is no one "best way" to do this work. Our final goal is to illustrate that Data Wise school cultures often start with a single leader and spread outward. In your school, that single leader could be you.

In writing this book, we have been extremely fortunate to have the support of many individuals. Kathleen McCartney, Dean of the Harvard Graduate School of Education, and Bob Fogel, Dean for Administration, have been steadfast supporters of the Data Wise project since its inception. Their dedication to fostering a community that informs the nexus of practice, policy, and research has been a major source of inspiration for our work. We are grateful for the financial support they provided for this research through the Dean's Dissemination Fund, which was made possible by a generous grant from Al and Kate Merck. We are also particularly indebted to Keith Collar, Executive Director of Research, Innovation, and Outreach at HGSE, who has accompanied us every step of the way on this journey. Keith helped us sharpen our overall vision for the book, regularly attended writers' group meetings, read and commented on drafts, and provided advice throughout the process. The final product owes much to his ideas and commitment.

In addition, we are deeply indebted to our editors at Harvard Education Press, Caroline Chauncey and Douglas Clayton, who have been involved with Data Wise since the idea for the first book began to take shape. We have been incredibly fortunate to have Caroline at our side throughout the planning, writing, and editing processes. Her creative thinking about this work has never flagged, her insights guided our planning, and her keen eye helped us chisel out crisper, sharper, more compelling versions of each draft that we produced. We are also grateful to Dody Riggs and Jeffrey Perkins, who guided us through the book production and design processes, respectively, and to Daniel Simon, whose finely tuned copyediting added polish to our work.

Richard Murnane and Elizabeth City continued their pioneering involvement with Data Wise by serving as valued advisors to our work. We greatly appreciate their guidance about how to coordinate a case-based project and craft a compelling book as well as their willingness to help us improve preliminary drafts. We also appreciate Mary Grassa O'Neill for all that she and her colleagues at HGSE's Principals' Center have done to support the Data Wise Summer Institute, through which we were introduced to several schools profiled in this book. In addition, Rachel Becker and Virginia Eves offered valuable comments on preliminary drafts, Daniel Koretz provided sage technical and editorial feedback, and Kimberly Steele gamely proofread chapters at the eleventh hour. During the project's planning and research phases, Kerry Herman, a senior researcher at the Harvard Business School, met with our writing group and provided expert, step-by-step guidance on both the logistics and the art of case writing. Susan Moore Johnson and Stacey Childress also provided insightful perspectives on the case-writing process. And throughout the project, Melita Garrett offered vital administrative assistance when we needed it most.

Finally, this book would not exist without the administrators and teachers who invited us into their schools, shared their strategies for data use, and told their stories of carrying out the Data Wise improvement process. With gratitude, then, we extend our lasting appreciation to the staff of Pond Cove Elementary, Newton North High, McKay K–8, West Hillsborough Elementary, Murphy K–8, Two Rivers Public Charter, Mason Elementary, and Community Academy, and to the principals who allowed us to profile these schools: Tom Eismeier, Jennifer Price, Almi Abeyta, Anthony Ranii, Mary Russo, Jessica Wodatch, Janet Palmer-Owens, and Lindsa McIntyre. We were continually impressed by the commitment and creativity these principals and their staff members bring to their work, and we hope we have done justice to the incredible efforts underway in these schools. We are honored to share their stories.

INTRODUCTION

Kathryn Parker Boudett and
Jennifer L. Steele

In a widely lauded, urban K–8 school, a second-year principal gives a presentation to faculty showing declines in student test scores and is met with stunned disbelief . . . followed by a desperate effort to find someone to blame.

*

In a suburban elementary school, teachers are dismayed to realize that in spite of their many efforts to work together to improve instruction, some students are still performing below expectations.

*

In an up-and-coming charter elementary school, the administrative team realizes that, despite an enthusiastic push to create action plans for instructional improvement, some plans do not directly address instruction.

*

In a small, alternative high school, a school-wide action plan for raising student achievement is nearly derailed due to high student mobility.

If you are like many K–12 educators with whom we have worked, these scenarios of good intentions gone bad may sound all too familiar. Have you ever resolved to harness your school's data in the service of large-scale instructional improvement and then ended up confused or disappointed? For many of us, pressure to show evidence of continued growth in student achievement is greater than it has ever been. Yet political pressure to meet accountability targets can pale next to the moral imperative to help *all* students achieve at high levels. In an increasingly complex world, our children's access to future opportunity depends on it.

The good news is that, challenging as it is, using data to improve teaching and learning *is* possible. In our experience, the key lies in building a school culture in which faculty members collaborate regularly and make instructional decisions based on evidence about students' skills and understanding. This book tells the stories of eight schools that have committed to building this kind of culture. It also lays bare the leadership challenges this work involves and offers concrete strategies for addressing such challenges head on.

The schools we profile are alike in that they have embraced the spirit of *Data Wise: A Step-by-Step Guide to Using Assessment Results to Improve Teaching and Learning*, a book we wrote with colleagues two years ago that offers school leaders a systematic approach for using data. That book made no claims of having discovered the *only* way to do this work. Instead, it laid out a concrete set of eight tasks embedded in a process that we

had seen successful schools employ when using data effectively. A diagram of the Data Wise improvement process (exhibit 0.1) and a brief overview of each of the eight steps (exhibit 0.2) appear at the end of this chapter. In this companion book, we illustrate what the eight Data Wise steps look like *in action*. Each chapter tells the story of how a Data Wise leader or team of leaders tackled a different step of the process.

THE DATA WISE LEADER

In practice, we have found that school leaders who are most successful in using data to improve instruction are those who engage their faculty in collaborative decisionmaking. As it happens, there is also a substantial research base supporting this view (see the selected readings at the end of this book for some helpful sources). In particular, researchers studying schools and other workplaces have found that leaders who are most successful at transforming their organizations are those who know how to frame important questions and then engage their colleagues in finding creative answers. In other words, they do not presume to have a monopoly on good ideas, and they wisely invite the insights of the people who carry out the work of the organization. Data Wise leaders typically do not try to solve problems for others. Rather, they harness the energy of the whole faculty and bring teachers' collective wisdom to bear on issues of student achievement. This collaborative approach to problemsolving is powerful, but it also involves several challenges. You will see many of these challenges, and how schools have dealt with them, in the pages of this book.

CHALLENGES DATA WISE LEADERS FACE

Building an atmosphere of trust is perhaps the greatest challenge that Data Wise leaders face. You may have experienced careless use of student achievement data, such as hearing someone draw the conclusion—without taking any other factors into account—that teachers at a top-scoring school are more skilled than those at a low-scoring school. Because achievement data are often presented as hard numbers and graphs, they may seem impervious to critique even when used poorly, and that can leave teachers feeling skeptical.

It doesn't have to be that way. When schools create a collaborative culture around data use—when they use data not to point fingers but to inform collective decisions—something powerful can happen. Teachers begin to "own" the student learning challenges they unearth. They become dedicated to finding creative ways to address them. Perhaps most important, they begin to feel responsible to one another for carrying out the instructional improvements they helped design. As a result, teachers often become intensely curious about whether the changes they have made in their classrooms are reflected in students' classroom and test performance. In fact, once a collaborative, evidence-based culture has been established, teachers can become the biggest constituents for collecting solid evidence of student learning; they start asking for more and better data.

Though building trust is critically important throughout the improvement process, we have found that Data Wise leaders also face specific challenges connected to each of the eight steps in the process. For instance, in the *Prepare* phase, schools must gather the staff members, resources, and expertise they need to proceed with later phases of the work. Common challenges schools encounter in this phase are finding the right people to lead the work and ensuring that those people have the skills they need to lead others in interpreting data.

In the *Inquire* phase of the improvement process, educators examine both test-score data and student work to identify a target area—called the *learner-centered problem*—in which they would like to see student achievement improve. Then they examine their own teaching to identify a *problem of practice*—a way in which changing their instruction might increase student learning in the target area. Common challenges Data Wise leaders face in this phase include learning to manipulate, interpret, and present a wide range of student data as well as building school-wide consensus around what good teaching looks like.

Finally, in the *Act* phase of the improvement process, Data Wise leaders face several new challenges. First, they must work with colleagues to arrive at a consensus around an instructional action plan. Subsequently, they must hold themselves and their colleagues accountable, not only for implementing the plan, but also for examining whether it seems to be raising student achievement. In addition, they must sustain the school's commitment to the plan over time.

MEET OUR DATA WISE LEADERS

Our work with schools has taught us that the most powerful tool we have for helping schools is sharing the experience of leaders who have attempted, struggled, and persevered in this work. We have also learned that the work looks a bit different in every school. Therefore, in choosing schools and leaders to profile in this book, we sought schools that were diverse with respect to grade level, demographic profile, and type of community. As a result, our case studies include two high schools, two K–8 schools, and four elementary schools. Four schools are part of the Boston Public School system, one is located in a Boston suburb, and the other three are located respectively in Washington, D.C., northern California, and coastal Maine. Some schools serve affluent communities, and others serve communities that are economically disadvantaged. Some have trouble meeting federal accountability requirements, while others do not. Finally, some have recently begun to use the Data Wise improvement process, and others have been doing so for several years. Because of their differences, these schools' stories illustrate how the Data Wise improvement process can play out in schools facing a wide range of goals and challenges.

Phase I: Prepare

Highlighting the initial step in the improvement process, *Organizing for Collaborative Work*, chapter 1 introduces Principal Tom Eismeier and Media Specialist Shari Robinson, who seek to reinvigorate data use in their suburban elementary school after an unsuccessful data initiative left some teachers data-wary. Tom and Shari must choose a data team with not only the skill but also the sensitivity and persistence to reengage their colleagues in using data to improve instruction.

Chapter 2 examines *Building Assessment Literacy*. Here, you will meet Jennifer Price, the first-year principal of a suburban high school known for academic excellence, who wants her staff to understand and address the school's achievement inequities. In pursuit of that goal, she must generate staff members' interest in data and help them learn to use data responsibly.

Phase II: Inquire

Chapter 3 highlights *Creating a Data Overview* and tells the story of Principal Almi Abeyta, who, after assuming leadership of an award-winning, urban K–8 school, must learn to share student achievement results with her faculty in a way that triggers collaborative learning and problem-solving and enhances their commitment to raising student achievement.

With a focus on *Digging into Data*, chapter 4 shows what happens in a suburban elementary school when Principal Anthony Ranii and his teachers realize that their collaborative culture is not resulting in improved student achievement. Their mission to boost student learning leads them to expand the kinds of data they examine and to engage students in using data to monitor their own learning.

In chapter 5, which focuses on *Examining Instruction*, you will meet veteran teacher Tricia Lampron, who, when first hired into a highly successful urban K–8 school, is a bit daunted by the school's practice of frequent peer observations. Principal Mary Russo and her staff find that in order to sustain their collaborative culture, they must create an environment in which newly hired teachers like Tricia can soon feel at ease with the practice of examining instruction with their colleagues.

Phase III: Act

Chapter 6 investigates *Developing an Action Plan*. In this chapter, Jessica Wodatch, Jim May, and Jeff Heyck-Williams, administrators at an urban charter school, find that without a school-wide structure for action planning, teachers' action plans sometimes lack a measurable outcome or a clear instructional focus. They must respond by creating a new structure for action planning that encourages a school-wide commitment to each plan.

Chapter 7 addresses *Planning to Assess Progress*. It introduces Hilary Shea, a fifth-grade teacher in an urban elementary school, who leads her colleagues to discover that they may not be maximizing the instructional potential of one of their strategies for building students' reading comprehension. Determined to help students write effectively about what they read, Hilary and her colleagues modify their instruction and devise a plan for measuring how well their new approach actually improves students' learning.

Finally, chapter 8 focuses on *Acting and Assessing*. It recounts the story of Lindsa McIntyre, a principal at an alternative urban high school, who works with her staff to choose an action plan that will enhance rigor and help the school overcome its beleaguered history. She and her leadership team must then investigate how well the action plan is being implemented and determine how to modify the plan when external circumstances threaten its long-term success.

An Ongoing Process

Due to its cyclical nature, we see the Data Wise improvement process not as a short-term initiative but as an ongoing approach to instructional decisionmaking and professional growth. For that reason, you may find it helpful to look at schools that have been using the Data Wise improvement process for various lengths of time to understand the different challenges they face.

Because *Data Wise* was published so recently, this work is still new to many schools that we profile, especially to those depicted in the *Prepare* phase. If your school is also new to the work, you may find stories of Data Wise leaders' early struggles and successes especially helpful. If you are interested in the longer-term outlook for schools using the Data Wise improvement process, you may be drawn to the profiles of two schools that have used the process consistently for several years: Murphy K–8 School, whose pioneering success with this approach helped inspire and shape *Data Wise*, and Mason Elementary School, a school that has served as an inspiration in many Data Wise courses. We view the widely recognized success of these two Boston schools in raising student achievement as testament to what a collaborative, evidence-based school culture can achieve.

As you read the cases in this book, you may find that you learn as much from Data Wise leaders' dilemmas and false starts as from their unqualified successes. We say this because many of the questions with which they struggle arise repeatedly among schools we have worked with. For instance, the question of when it is time to stop planning and start inquiring arises at both Pond Cove Elementary and Newton North High School, just as it does unfailingly in our courses. Similarly, Two Rivers administrators' questions about how prescriptive their action plan should be and how broadly it should be applied are questions that never seem to go away, perhaps because there is never just one right answer. Context matters. School culture and history matter. Thus, we suggest that you read these cases as instructive examples of what other schools have done rather than as foolproof recipes for success. That being said, we suspect you may discover in these pages some creative ideas that you may be eager to apply in your own school. Knowing what did and did not work for other schools can often yield useful insights . . . it is data, after all.

HOW TO USE THIS BOOK

We wrote this book with three types of readers in mind; how you approach this volume depends on why you are reading it. If you are an educator or policymaker who is determined to figure out what using data to improve instruction really entails, we recommend that you simply curl up and read the book from cover to cover. If you are a school leader, professional-development provider, or university professor charged with teaching others who are new to using data, you may want to form a working group that learns about one step of the Data Wise improvement process each time you get together. The team could begin by reading the chapter in the original *Data Wise* book that describes the step in detail, and then go on to read the corresponding chapter in this book to see how that step plays out in practice. Finally, if you are part of a team that is already implementing the Data Wise improvement process in your school, then your team—or even your whole faculty—could read and discuss the particular chapters that best inform the work you are currently doing.

Each chapter in this book contains three sections: a case narrative, a set of lessons from the case, and a series of discussion questions. The "lessons" section distills some important take-away messages from each story and offers additional suggestions drawn from other schools we have worked with. If you are using this book to spark conversations with your colleagues, you may wish to ask them to hold off on reading this section until after the group has had a chance to talk together about their impressions of what some of the most important lessons might be. The list of questions for discussion at the end of each chapter offers some possible jumping-off points for such conversations and is intended to help you think about how to apply what you learned in the chapter to your own setting.

As a current or potential Data Wise leader, your school and your circumstances are no doubt unique. Nevertheless, we hope that you may begin to see yourself, your colleagues, and the challenges you face reflected in many of the stories shared in this book. Our wish is that you will engage with the Data Wise improvement process clear-eyed, armed with insights and inspiration gleaned from schools that have gone before you.

N.B. Demographic information about each school appears in a sidebar near the beginning of its chapter. The demographic data come from district and state websites and pertain to the 2005–6 school year. In cases where data were not available online, we requested the information from principals, whose answers came from the 2006–7 school year.

EXHIBIT 0.1. *The Data Wise Improvement Process*

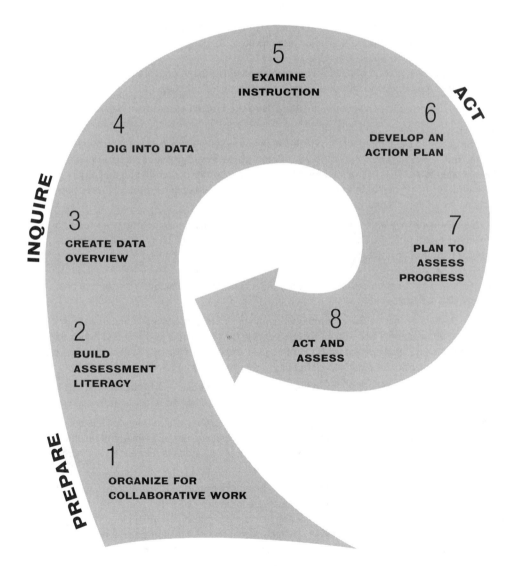

EXHIBIT 0.2. *Overview of the Data Wise Process*

The Data Wise improvement process is an eight-step model for instructional improvement involving three phases: *Prepare*, *Inquire*, and *Act*. Each phase plays an important role in building a school's capacity to use data to improve instruction.

During the *Prepare* phase, educators lay a foundation for evidence-based decision making, developing the processes and skills they need to invite whole-faculty collaboration in the next two phases.

- **In step one,** *Organize for Collaborative Work,* schools create a data team and then organize data and schedules in a way that will later facilitate the collaborative examination of data.

- **In step two,** *Build Assessment Literacy,* educators learn basic principles of educational assessment that will help them interpret test results responsibly.

During the *Inquire* phase, groups of educators work together to explore data from a range of sources in an effort to understand students' learning and teachers' practice.

- **In step three,** *Create a Data Overview,* educators use standardized assessment data to ask, "What are our students learning, and what are some of their major gaps in understanding?"

- **In step four,** *Dig into Data,* members examine a wider range of student performance data—including projects, quizzes, class work, and homework—to gain clarity about the challenges they identified in step three. The goal of step four is to identify a *learner-centered problem:* a gap in skill or understanding common to many students that, if corrected, would have far-reaching implications for students' continued academic growth.

- **In step five,** *Examine Instruction,* schools begin to investigate how teaching practice is contributing to student performance. The objective of this step is to identify a *problem of practice:* an instructional challenge that teachers believe to be worth tackling collectively.

During the *Act* phase, educators develop and carry out a plan for addressing the problem of practice and improving student learning.

- **In step six,** *Develop an Action Plan,* members identify an instructional strategy that, if widely implemented, would stand a good chance of addressing the problem of practice and improving student achievement. Teachers and administrators also decide together on professional-development strategies to support the planned instructional improvements.

- **In step seven,** *Plan to Assess Progress,* educators set short-, medium-, and long-term goals for improved student learning and plan how they will determine whether those goals have been met.

- **In step eight,** *Act and Assess,* schools implement the action plan, monitor how well it is being carried out, and execute their plan for assessing progress. By carefully examining the results of their actions as they unfold, educators can make midcourse adjustments and engage in increasingly sophisticated cycles of inquiry and action.

At the end of the *Act* phase, a new cycle of inquiry begins, bypassing the *Prepare* phase, where the groundwork has already been laid. Thus, in the Data Wise improvement process graphic shown in exhibit 0.1, the arrow curves back to the *Inquire* phase. As the process of ongoing inquiry and reflection becomes ingrained in a school, faculty members gain proficiency and learn to ask tougher questions, set higher goals, and involve more faculty members in using data wisely.

The eight steps described here are explained at length in *Data Wise: A Step-by-Step Guide to Using Assessment Results to Improve Teaching and Learning* (Harvard Education Press, 2005).

Phase I: **PREPARE**

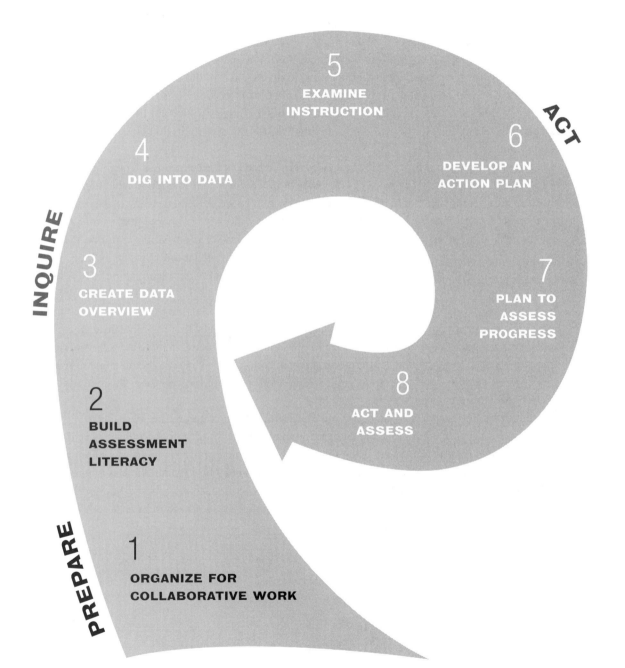

The *Prepare* phase of the Data Wise improvement process is about mobilizing your forces. It involves finding the right people to lead the work, providing structures that help them work together, and preparing them to use data responsibly. Just as a solid foundation is essential for building a durable house, so is thoughtful preparation necessary for building a collaborative school culture around effective data use.

Schools that are just beginning to use data to improve instruction sometimes feel they do not have time for the prepare phase—they want to dive right into the data. The temptation is understandable. Teachers and administrators often tell us there is no time to waste in working to raise student achievement, and they are right. There *is* no time to waste, but the prepare phase is not about wasting time. Rather, it is about laying the groundwork that will help sustain effective collaboration and data use.

The prepare phase comprises the first two steps of the Data Wise process. The first step, *Organize for Collaborative Work*, involves choosing a data team of staff members who, ideally, are enthusiastic about instructional improvement and well respected by their peers. It also includes the team's preparatory efforts to establish a meeting schedule, a set of shared goals, and a time-line for achieving those goals. The more the team is able to build rapport and a common vision among themselves, the more effective the step of organizing for collaborative work will be.

The second step, *Build Assessment Literacy*, involves helping the data team gain the fundamental skills to lead others in examining data. In other words, building an all-star data team does not depend on having a staff that is already well versed in analyzing test score data or in communicating with data displays. These skills can be learned, and that the more educators engage in this work, the more sophisticated they become. The process of building assessment literacy involves helping the data team master the core concepts they need to begin analyzing test data in a responsible way. It also involves learning about common misuses of assessment data that schools would be wise to avoid.

In essence, the prepare phase focuses on distributing leadership among several staff members and helping them build the knowledge they need to support their colleagues in using data to improve instruction. By ensuring that this work is collaborative from its inception, your school can establish a precedent of looking at data collectively. The prepare phase is where you start to build the kind of team-driven, instruction-focused culture that leads to school-wide instructional improvement. Smart, collaborative preparation is the foundation on which your evidence-driven school culture will stand.

Chapter 1

ORGANIZING FOR COLLABORATIVE WORK

Pond Cove Elementary School Lays the Groundwork

David P. Ronka

As you prepare to use data to improve instruction, how do you choose a team to lead the work? And how should the team members prepare to engage their colleagues? In this chapter, Pond Cove Elementary School works to recover from a disappointing data initiative that narrowed the curriculum and provoked teachers' anxiety. Not wanting to give up on data altogether, the principal assembles a data team and encourages members to think about how to start from scratch with a collaborative, nonburdensome approach. As the team prepares to help teachers take ownership of data, they must heed the lessons of the past. They must also balance the tension between thoughtful preparation and the desire to move forward with implementation.

SEEKING A FRESH START

Pond Cove principal Tom Eismeier was per-plexed. How could a well-intentioned data initiative have caused his staff such frustra-tion and anxiety? Two years earlier, the state had developed a comprehensive formative assessment system for informing instruction and holding schools accountable for student achievement. In the fall of 2004, Pond Cove Elementary had begun administering the formative assessments as prescribed—nine times a year in first grade, three times a year in second grade, and seven times a year in grades three and four. The rigorous assess-ment schedule was meant to guide instruction by giving teachers frequent feedback about student learning.

At Pond Cove, hopes for the new formative as-sessments had been high. Eager to receive more fre-quent feedback about their students' learning, teach-ers had taken the assess-ments seriously. Too seriously. It wasn't long before Tom started to see cracks appear in the system. Teachers were consumed by the frequent assessments, and rather than using the results as one of many ways to inform instruction, the tests had become the focal point. One culprit was the way in which the tests had to be administered—the staff had to double-score a certain percentage of the tests in order to assess their level of inter-rater reliability. Tom complained to colleagues that the system was "more about doing the assessment the right way than using the assessment to figure out where kids are," and he worried that "if this keeps up, we're just going to be teaching to the tests." The approach had become overly burdensome and time consuming, and teachers' anxiety had skyrocketed as they struggled to keep up with the system's administrative demands.

Gradually, teachers grew suspicious of the for-mative assessment system. Were the data meant to help them teach better, or were they really meant for administrators to use for their own purposes? Tom had tried to ease the pres-sure teachers were feeling by reminding them that the tests weren't everything. But in the end, the system's high stakes and stringent administrative requirements were overwhelming. What had started as a chance for teachers to receive regular feedback about student learning had left them too busy to contemplate meaningful instructional change.

Fortunately, Tom wasn't the only educa-tor expressing concern. The state realized what was happening and imposed a mora-torium on the new system for the following school year. Now, however, with the experi-ence behind him, Tom was unsure how he could possibly reintroduce data to the faculty of Pond Cove.

Pond Cove Elementary School
Cape Elizabeth, ME

Type: **Public**

Setting: **Small Town**

Grades: **K–4**

Number of Students: **650**

Number of Teachers & Administrators: **50**

Students Qualifying for Free or Reduced-Price Lunch: **5%**

Students' Race / Ethnicity Distribution:

Asian **4%**

Black **1%**

Latino **1%**

Native American **0%**

White **94%**

FINDING A BLUEPRINT

Pond Cove is located in Cape Elizabeth, Maine, a small, affluent town overlooking the beautiful, rocky north Atlantic shoreline south of Portland. The school is housed in a newly renovated building on a campus that also hosts the town's middle and high schools. The hallways of Pond Cove are clean, orderly showcases for colorful student work, including a giant papier-mâché rooster students made in honor of an annual visit from a well-known children's book author. Even after serving as principal of Pond Cove for the past thirteen years, Tom continued to be impressed by the school's faculty and students. The teachers were passionate about their work and eager to improve their practice. Parents were very involved in the education of their children and had correspondingly high expectations for the faculty of Pond Cove.

Teachers at the school typically rose to the occasion. Tom often saw faculty members trying innovative teaching strategies or developing ways to improve school-wide initiatives like writers' workshops. What worried him in the wake of the recent, unsuccessful data initiative was that teachers lacked a systematic way to measure whether their strategies seemed to be improving student achievement. Now that the formative assessment pressure was off, Pond Cove seemed in danger of tossing the baby out with the bathwater when it came to using data to guide instruction.

The lack of a systematic approach to data was especially troubling because state test results had identified areas in which there was room for growth. "We were doing well," Tom acknowledged, "but we knew we could do better." For instance, he had recently learned that in 2005–6, 21 percent of the school's fourth graders had scored below *meets the standard* in reading (that is, in the bottom two of four performance categories), and 22 percent had scored below *meets the standard* in mathematics. As far as Tom was concerned, the school simply had to do a better job of equipping those students with the skills they would need to succeed in middle and high school. To do that, teachers needed a systematic way to identify and target gaps in students' understanding. Put simply, they still needed data. What they *really* needed, though, Tom thought, was a way to use data that would support rather than supplant good teaching.

An opportunity to try a new approach to data analysis came when Cape Elizabeth superintendent Alan Hawkins chose *Data Wise* as a book that all administrators would read and discuss during the summer of 2006. As Tom read through the beginning chapters of the book, his interest was piqued by the emphasis of the Data Wise improvement process on using data to influence instruction. He wondered whether Data Wise could foster instructional improvement in ways that prior initiatives had not.

Glimpsing a window of opportunity, Tom offered to lead a district-wide Data Wise initiative, and the superintendent readily agreed. However, Tom soon realized that the challenges of forming an effective data team would be magnified if he tried to include staff from all three schools in the district. He reasoned that a district-wide team might get bogged down in trying to find a common meeting time or in highlighting the differences between schools rather than actually carrying out the Data Wise improvement process. Better, he thought, to start at the building level, where teachers could build upon their existing collegial relationships. He realized that the initiative would have to be collaborative in order to have any serious, long-term impact, and that it would therefore be critical to choose team members who commanded peers' respect and could facilitate collaboration. Tom wondered whom he would find to take on the challenge.

BREAKING GROUND

As the new school year began, Tom realized that the ideal person to help him spearhead the Data Wise initiative would be Dr. Shari Robinson, the media specialist at Pond Cove and one of the district's two professional development facilitators. Shari had recently finished a dissertation exploring ways to increase faculty collaboration in order to improve instruction, so when Tom asked her to help him lead the initiative, she quickly agreed. Tom felt that the convergence of Shari's enthusiasm for collaborative school improvement and Data Wise's structured approach to data analysis might create just the right conditions for a school-wide data renewal.

As Tom and Shari set out to assemble a data team, they already perceived that the Data Wise improvement process was different from what had preceded it. Building a group of like-minded leaders and designating time at the beginning to "organize for collaborative work" struck Tom as obvious but missing elements of past efforts. As he thought about who might make up the team, he understood that if Data Wise were to catch on with the wider faculty, the data

team had to include members who were trusted and well respected within the school and who, together, brought a range of skills and interests to the work. Although Tom could think of particular teachers he wanted to recruit, he first extended an open invitation to all the grade-level instructional team leaders. If building a data team was one of the differences between past initiatives and this one, Tom wanted to cast the net widely and let everyone who was interested jump in. "I wanted to make sure," he explained, "that team leaders felt involved in the process but not pressured to join the core team." Tom also thought that inviting the team leaders' involvement would help spread the word that a new, collaborative approach to data was getting underway.

There were also certain faculty members who seemed obvious choices for the data team. For instance, because Pond Cove had a longstanding focus on literacy, Tom invited two reading specialists, Becky Swift and Suzanne Hamilton, to join the team. Both Becky and Suzanne were well respected and regarded as experts by their peers. Tom also asked Sarah Simmonds, Shari's fellow professional development leader for the district. To round out the group, Tom recruited the district's technology director, Gary Lanoie. He suspected that Gary would be able to provide the team with any technical expertise that their data work required.

Finally, Tom purchased copies of *Data Wise* and distributed them to the new team with an assignment to read the book before their first meeting. The last step before moving forward was the christening of the data team. They decided to call themselves the "Data Enthusiasts."

BUILDING A SOLID FOUNDATION

As the Data Enthusiasts gathered for their first Data Wise meeting, there was a feeling of anticipation and nervous excitement. Most of the Enthusiasts had read the book by that point and had a good idea of what they were getting into. Shari believed the improvement process held great potential, which she hoped to see realized at Pond Cove: "The Data Wise process made so much sense to me when I read the book, but now that we were putting it into action, I didn't want it to end up as just another failed initiative." She realized that there was a lot at stake: "Data's always been here and it's here to stay. Teach-

> ## "The Data Wise process made so much sense to me when I read the book, but now that we were putting it into action, I didn't want it to end up as just another failed initiative."

ers need to own it." Yet she also recognized that the Data Enthusiasts would be asking the teachers to trust them at a time when the previous data initiative still stung for many like an open wound. For Tom, Shari, and the rest of the data team, strengthening school-wide trust was a central goal. Many on the team were administrators, and Tom knew that "as an administrator, you lose your credibility the longer you're out of the classroom. There's no way around that." Sarah agreed, noting she had heard one colleague say, "Data are for the administrators. It's not going to change what I do. It's to make them look good." Not only would the team have to earn teachers' trust, but they would also have to remind teachers that effective data use was really about addressing students' learning needs.

The team reasoned that if they were going to "open up the classroom" by analyzing and discussing student achievement data, then they should try to cultivate a data culture that was supportive, nonpunitive, and collaborative. Although the Pond Cove faculty had already demonstrated openness toward observing and sharing instruction, the team believed that one of the worst mistakes they could make would be to roll out a half-baked initiative and see teachers turned off to future use of data. Having seen the discouraging impact of the last initiative, they did not want to be the ones to repeat it.

As the team reflected on previous curricular and assessment initiatives, they noticed a common theme. Pond Cove faculty were always looking for ways to improve, so much so that they sometimes rushed into a solution without spending time looking at the problem. As Tom put it, "We had to be careful not to go too quickly and jump to the answers before we had a chance to ask the questions. We needed to restrain ourselves." Tom knew that he was fortunate to have such a willing faculty, but he also knew that their eagerness to jump ahead meant that the Data Enthusiasts needed to take time to lay a solid foundation before they asked the faculty to start building on their work. While he wanted to introduce all teachers to the Data Wise improvement process before the end of the school year, he also knew that patience would be essential.

Realizing that they would always face a tension between preparing thoroughly and advancing the work, the Enthusiasts got down to the business of creating a "data inventory." Not only was developing the inventory one of the first tasks in the Data Wise improvement process, but it also made sense logically that the first step in supporting teachers to use data would, indeed, be to look at the big picture and determine all the types of data that were available in the school. Using a model from *Data Wise*, Tom and Shari had created blank data inventory templates, which they distributed to the team. Team members then brainstormed all the data types available in the school while Shari took notes and generated the inventory shown in exhibit 1.1.

"As we started to dig into the data inventory," Shari later remembered, "we were all very overwhelmed by the task." It took some time and patience, but accumulating all the information in the data-inventory format encouraged the team as they realized how much data existed at the school. But as they reviewed the list, they also realized that just having the data on-site would not be enough. What mattered was that teachers have easy access to the information they needed. Shari recounted how big an obstacle data accessibility had been when she was working on her thesis. She remembered combing through paper records weekend after weekend just to aggregate data from the state assessments. Putting herself in the teachers' shoes, she wondered how they could be expected to use data if they had to hunt for them. The team realized that making data accessible to teachers would be their next significant challenge.

To address this challenge, the Enthusi-asts turned to Gary and asked him about the feasibility of getting some of the data from their inventory into the electronic student information system. Gary explained that report cards were already in the system, and of the nine remaining data sources, the annual state assessment, the twice-yearly math and language arts assessment, and the twice-yearly reading assessment were the only ones available electronically such that they could conceivably be imported into the system. If the other data were to be used, they would have to be entered by hand. Knowing that hand entry would be too burdensome, the team decided that the three electronically available data sources would be a great starting place. In preparation for the next meeting, Gary offered to develop a prototype of what a student profile would look like with the three data points.

Becky also had an idea for making some of the data even more accessible. She was already researching a grant to pay for the online data-management component of the school's reading assessment. She explained that it would allow teachers to enter the results and analyze them in detail directly online. She promised to give an update at the next meeting.

Though team members were impressed by Gary's and Becky's ingenuity, they also raised some concerns about the accessibility solutions that were being considered. Would all teachers be willing (and able) to use a computer system to analyze data? Tom believed that if the data were made available in a timely manner and were relevant to the teachers' work, then teachers would see the benefit and be motivated to learn the skills required. But there was some lingering skepticism: Wouldn't online student data be

EXHIBIT 1.1. *Pond Cove's Data Inventory*

Data Source	Content Area	Dates of Collection	Grade Levels	Accessibility	Current Data Use
State Accountability Test	Reading Math Science	Spring Spring Spring	3, 4 3, 4 4	District, Principal, Teachers, Parents	State and federal accountability, Inform instruction
Twice-Yearly Individualized Reading Test	Reading	Fall & Spring January & Spring	1– 4 K	Teachers, Literacy team, Principal	Inform instruction, Evidence of growth
Twice-Yearly Standardized Test	Reading Math	Fall & Spring Fall & Spring	4 4	District, Principal, Teachers, Parents	Inform instruction, Evidence of growth
Report Cards	All content areas and social growth	January June	K–4 K–4	Parents, Teachers	Report classroom progress
Mathematics Curriculum Unit Assessments	Math	Throughout the year	K–4	Teachers	Inform instruction
Formal Student Writing Samples	Writing	End of writing units/topics	K–4	Teachers, Parents	Inform instruction, Evidence of growth
Informal Writing Assessments	Writing	Ongoing throughout the year	K–4	Teachers	Inform instruction, Evidence of growth
Hearing and Recording Sounds	Writing	Fall Spring	1 1	Teachers	Inform instruction, Evidence of growth
Developmental Spelling Assessment	Spelling	Fall Spring	1 1	Teachers	Inform instruction, Evidence of growth
Reading Observation Survey	Reading	Fall	1	Teachers, Literacy team	Inform instruction, Select Reading Recovery students

vulnerable to security breaches or privacy violations? Gary assured the team that security and privacy would not be an issue, given the available technology. As they wrestled with these issues, the team realized that this was just a taste of the concerns that teachers were likely to raise, especially those teachers who might feel threatened by data. They would have to be sensitive to this dynamic and have answers ready.

Team members also wondered who would be responsible for analyzing the data—the Enthusiasts or the whole faculty? On one hand, the team felt strongly that it was their job to lay the groundwork and distill information for the teachers. On the other hand, they understood that for the initiative to be successful, teachers had to own the process. Shari and Sarah both recounted how previous initiatives had failed because they were perceived to have come from the top down and were seen by the teachers as "add-ons"—one more thing that took time away from instruction. This, in fact, had been another pitfall of the most recent initiative, in which, as Sarah noted, the assessments were seen as "top-down, external, too formal." Again, more questions emerged: How do you make data analysis an organic and sustainable part of teachers' work? And who has the final responsibility for analyzing data— the data team or the teachers? The process seemed to be bringing up more questions than it was answering.

MAKING DATA ACCESSIBLE

In the two weeks that followed, Gary worked hard to develop a way for teachers to view students' annual and twice-yearly test results at a glance through the district's intranet. Since the district's student information system allowed for customization, he did not need to do any complicated reprogramming. But he did need to build user accounts that would give teachers access only to the records of their current and prior students.

At the next meeting, Gary was greeted by a group of anxious Data Enthusiasts. They wanted to see the student data tool he was working on! He showed the team a new screen in which each row represented a student and each column displayed students' scores on one of the tests the team had asked him to include. The team was again impressed by Gary's swift work and felt that having this information so readily accessible could transform their ability to use data. As before, however, concerns began to emerge as the Enthusiasts realized that the technical challenge of getting the data into the student information system was only the first barrier to effective data use. Even more daunting were questions about what teachers should *do* with the data once they became available for downloading. Tom reminded the team that with the prior initiative, teachers had been given access to students' performance data, but they had lacked an understanding of the data's uses or limitations. In some cases, instruction had actually been *weakened* as teachers worried more about doing the assessments right than about preparing powerful lessons for their students.

Still, they concluded that the difference between the prior approach to data and this one was that the former had not helped teachers understand the inferences that could be made from the data, and thus the results of the prior system were often blown out of proportion or misused. This brought forth a barrage of questions: When teachers looked at the data, how would they know what they were looking for? How would looking at data translate into improved instruction? What questions should teachers bring to the data? What kinds of conclusions would they be able to draw? And what were they going to do with the conclusions? As Tom and Shari listened, they noticed that the team's questions seemed to boil down to two overarching concerns: How could the data team frame Data Wise as fundamental to instruction rather than an add-on to the things teachers were already doing? How could the team ensure that data were being used appropriately and that data use was helping teachers improve instruction?

One key to answering these questions was to find out what the teachers were already doing in their classrooms, and this was, in fact, the next task in the Data Wise improvement process—preparing an inventory of instructional initiatives. The team knew from reading *Data Wise* that an instructional initiative was any program the school had consciously put in place to improve teaching and learning. They further understood that it was important to document these initiatives in order to acknowledge what was already happening before planning any improvements.

This time, Tom had made blank instructional inventory templates, which he distributed at the end of the meeting. The Enthusiasts were to ask the grade-level team leaders to complete the inventory prior to the Data Enthusiasts' next meeting in two weeks. Shari, who also used a note-taking template to record decisions and hold the group accountable, recorded the inventory as a "next

step" for the group. A copy of the template and notes appears in exhibit 1.3 at the end of this chapter. Tom was particularly eager to see the completed school-wide inventory, as it was a key element for tying the Data Wise improvement process to instruction. He knew that many positive instructional initiatives were already happening at the school, which the inventory would confirm. It also might be a first step in helping the team understand why Pond Cove kids were mastering some content areas better than others.

MAKING DATA MATTER

In between meetings, Becky and Suzanne held a workshop with the reading teachers to introduce a new version of the school's twice-yearly reading assessment. The reading teachers were frustrated when they heard that there was a lack of alignment between the old and new versions of the assessment. Because the new assessment results would not be comparable to the old results, teachers would lose the ability to compare new results to historical trends. What followed was a passionate discussion about the strengths and weaknesses of the reading assessment data and about how data, if not used appropriately, could be dangerous.

Later, Becky pulled Shari aside to tell her about the meeting. She thought Shari should know that teachers had voiced serious concerns about inappropriate uses of assessment data. As Becky described the teachers' concerns, Shari said that she sympathized with their point. She told Becky about a particularly negative data experience she had once observed in another school. Data from the state assessment had been projected onto a screen at a faculty meeting without any introductory framing. The person giving the presentation had simply gone through the display, pointing out all the problem areas. Thinking back on the incident, Shari said, "Data can wound. The faculty were really turned off by how they were being chastised by data. It set such a negative tone for data use."

In contrast to that experience, Shari said it sounded like Becky and Suzanne had been able to turn a potentially negative data discussion with the reading teachers into a positive one by listening to their concerns and inviting honest feedback. Shari drew a parallel to the Japanese practice of Lesson Study. "In Japanese Lesson Study," she said, "no single teacher owns the lesson that is being critiqued." Extending this idea to Pond Cove, she added, "Just as no one owns the lesson, no one owns the data." Shari thought that the Lesson Study idea of depersonalizing the data might help teachers view data not as a reflection of themselves but as a valuable feedback mechanism for understanding what students were learning and not learning, and why. Becky and Shari realized that the frank discussion the teachers had had about the reading assessment's limitations was actually an important step in building a positive data culture.

MAKING DATA MANAGEABLE

When the data team gathered at the next meeting, they compiled their instructional inventories by content area. As shown in exhibit 1.2, they realized they were managing eleven initiatives in language arts alone.

Never before had they seen on paper a list of everything they were trying to do in the school for language arts, and the inven-

EXHIBIT 1.2. *Pond Cove's Inventory of Instructional Initiatives in Language Arts*

Lower Grades (K–2)
- Units of Study for Primary Writing
- Handwriting without Tears

Lower/Middle Grades (K–3)
- Word Study/Spelling

Upper Grades (3–4)
- Constructed Responses
- No-nonsense Writing
- Teaching the Qualities of Writing (TQW)

School-wide (K–4)
- Guided Reading
- Leveled Books
- Comprehension Toolkit
- Writing Workshop
- End-of-year, Grade-level Writing and Reading Expectations

tory gave them mixed feelings. On one hand, they felt that the number of initiatives reflected their commitment to giving students the best education possible, and they believed that each of the initiatives had value. On the other hand, they realized that the school was full of many important but uncoordinated programs running simultaneously. How did they know which programs were effective?

Their inventories for math, science, and social studies were almost as expansive as the language arts inventory, and the breadth of their initiatives revealed the potential scope of the Data Wise process. Were they going to use data to drive instructional improvement in all these areas? They quickly realized that if they were going to be able to tackle the process, they would have to narrow their focus. As they discussed this dilemma of where to start, they realized that their efforts would pay the biggest dividends if they concentrated on initiatives that already had momentum. As Tom put it, "We need to make a connection to what is most relevant to what the teachers are doing." They didn't have to look long for this focus.

For starters, prior state and local assessment results had shown that reading comprehension was a consistent area of weakness at Pond Cove. In reading, over 20 percent of fourth graders scored below *meets the standard* on the state accountability test, and only 7 percent exceeded the standard, as compared to 17 percent who exceeded the standard in mathematics. The teachers were pleased that most students met the standard, but they were deeply concerned about the 20 percent who did not, and they also wanted to help a larger share of their students attain reading excellence. Given these concerns, the school had put considerable emphasis on reading intervention and remediation. As reading specialists, Becky and Suzanne reflected on how the literacy intervention program used at Pond Cove for the past fifteen years had been helpful both in increasing student reading achievement and in getting teachers involved in examining instruction, sharing best practices, and regularly looking at student achievement data. Given that literacy was a fundamental "gateway" skill for students and that there was a lot of positive momentum around the literacy program, the data team decided to use reading comprehension as their springboard.

To add to the positive momentum, Becky announced that the grant was approved and

that classroom teachers would now be able to enter and analyze the reading assessment data directly online. With the inventory of instructional initiatives memorialized on paper, the team acknowledged they were making progress. However, there was a lingering feeling that they were up against deadlines that were beginning to outweigh the importance of going slowly.

TIMING THE IMPLEMENTATION

The Data Enthusiasts turned their attention back to the steps laid out in the Data Wise improvement process. They felt they had successfully organized for collaborative work by establishing the data team, creating their data inventory and inventory of instructional initiatives, and making the grade-level team leaders aware of the work. They believed they had made forays into step two, building assessment literacy, by meeting with the teachers about the differences between the old and new versions of the reading assessment. Becky and Suzanne had even moved toward the *Inquire* phase of the process by recently asking the teachers to analyze students' reading test results for strengths and weaknesses. But as the team looked more closely, they realized that they needed to circle back and be more intentional about step two, building assessment literacy. They considered scheduling a faculty discussion about the uses and abuses of data that would give faculty a chance to express their hopes and fears about data analysis. By doing so, they would be providing the whole faculty with their first taste of the Data Wise improvement process.

As the team discussed how a faculty meeting might be organized and what sort of response they'd get from the teachers, more questions arose: Should they introduce data with fanfare or quietly and subtly slip it in? How would they inspire teachers to think about instructional change when many of them (rightfully) felt they'd been doing a good job for years? Would there be enough resources in place to support the initiative when the lightbulbs went off and teachers started "getting it"?

To Shari, these questions were starting to produce some anxiety. Her firm belief in the importance of using data, coupled with the investment the data team had made so far, were raising the stakes, and she still wasn't sure that Data Wise would be any different from other reform initiatives. "I feel like I'm at the edge of a cliff," she thought as she considered the risks associated with getting the whole school involved—risks for both the faculty *and* the administration. She knew the grade-level team leaders had been told about Data Wise early in the fall, but she wondered just how much the rest of the faculty knew. Had the team leaders told the teachers about the Data Enthusiasts' work, and if not, how would the teachers react?

The question of how to formally "kick off" Data Wise to the greater faculty in the data overview presentation was looming

large on the horizon and beginning to take on a life of its own. It was already December, and the relevance of the fall reading assessment was diminishing. Should the team rush the process in order to get data into the hands of teachers while it was still "hot"? Or would this short-circuit the Data Wise process? There were no easy answers to these questions. They decided that if they did present a data overview early in the new semester, they would need to think carefully about how to plan a nonthreatening, objective discussion protocol and avoid conjuring the ghost of data initiatives past.

The team adjourned knowing that when they met next after the holiday break, they would need to move quickly on their new plan so the Data Wise process could still have an impact that school year. Although Tom was convinced that patience was still critical, he was confronted with the uncomfortable reality that the year was almost halfway over and they were still in the preparation phase. The needs addressed by Data Wise would surely be there in the future when the initiative was in full bloom at Pond Cove, but he didn't want to risk losing the momentum the data team had gained by waiting much longer.

✳ LESSONS FROM THE CASE

The experiences of Tom, Shari, and the Pond Cove data team highlight the tension in the Data Wise process between the preparation and inquiry phases. Like all school leaders seeking to do something different with data, Tom and Shari both brought with them lessons learned from their past experiences. For Tom's part, he didn't want to have a repeat of the formative assessment system debacle. For her part, Shari had seen many initiatives come and go with little impact on instruction. Tom wanted to craft the Data Wise experience in a way that would protect teachers as much as possible from the kind of misguided pressure they experienced with the prior data initiative. His strategy to accomplish this was threefold:

1. **Patiently prepare.** Tom fought the urge to launch right into the *Inquire* phase of the Data Wise improvement process, knowing that if he did so he would again find his teachers on the receiving end of a hastily implemented data initiative. Instead, he encouraged everyone on the data team to go slowly. This decision involved certain tradeoffs. On one hand, it ensured that the improvement process would be well thought out and that supports would be in place when data were rolled out to the greater faculty. On the other hand, Tom had to wrestle against the clock. As fall turned into winter, he saw the relevance of the fall reading assessment data slipping away, and with it the clear entry point that it provided into Data Wise.

   This is a common tension that school leaders face when they undertake the Data Wise improvement process, and it brings up a larger question about how to match the improvement cycle with the school calendar. Is there a "right" way to do this? Should the data overview be done at the beginning of the year, or is it an iterative process that happens many times throughout the year?

   The answer varies from school to school. For instance, as you will see in the profile of McKay K–8 School in chapter 3, the principal initially viewed the data overview as an annual event, but she later began to use "mini data overviews" to facilitate small-group professional development throughout the school year. When a school first begins using the Data Wise improvement process, it may be more effective to time the rollout to the faculty with the results from a major assessment, as Tom had hoped to do at Pond Cove with the fall reading assessment results. This allows the faculty to focus on specific assessment results, but it has the downside of possibly limiting the overview to one data source, when a rich data overview often draws on multiple sources. Another consideration is the current climate of the school. If teachers are feeling beaten up by state assessment data, for example, it may be wise to start the improvement process with something less volatile. What is important about the step of organizing for collaborative work is that it encourages patience and preparation, two things that are often forgotten amid the throes of daily work.

2. **Choose the right data team.** Tom was very intentional in the selection of Pond Cove's data team. He knew that the success of the improvement process would depend on the people leading the work. In selecting a balanced team, he tried to keep several considerations in mind. First, he wanted to make sure that the data team would help him capitalize on existing momentum in the school. Choosing respected literacy leaders Becky Swift and Suzanne Hamilton accomplished this and connected the work of the Data Enthusiasts to the data-driven work that Becky and Suzanne were already doing with the reading teachers. Second, Tom needed talented professional-development leaders who commanded the respect of their colleagues. He found that in Shari Robinson, whose background in collaborative decision-making and enthusiasm for data use made her perfect to co-chair the team, and in Sarah Simmonds, another ace professional-development leader with insight on how to transform teachers' practice. Finally, Tom needed someone who would take responsibility for the technical ins-and-outs of data organization and accessibility. He was fortunate to have a district

technology director like Gary Lanoie who could bring both expertise and commitment to the role.

But what do you do if your school does not have a diligent database builder like Gary at your disposal, or a grant writer like Becky to procure money for data analysis software? While we would encourage school leaders, in whatever ways they can, to support staff members who want to take on these kinds of responsibilities, the truth is that you do not need a technological guru to make data accessible to teachers. For instance, chapter 7 describes the work of Mason School in Boston, where the data coordinator organized hard copies of school-wide test data into easily accessible binders, and where teachers maintained classroom-level data binders tracking each student's performance on multiple measures. With this decidedly low-tech system, teachers could quickly locate a wide range of information about the performance of a particular student or class.

Although Tom was careful to recruit certain members, he also wanted to create a buzz around the work of the data team and invite as many stakeholders as were interested in the work. Thus, he extended an open invitation to all the grade-level team leaders at Pond Cove. What resulted was a separate group of interested instructional leaders who did not wish to be Data Enthusiasts per se but who still shared in the decisionmaking and communication network.

It is worth noting that, while they weren't involved in the first few meetings, two Pond Cove parents later joined the Data Enthusiasts. They volunteered at a parent association meeting after hearing Tom talk about the Data Wise improvement process. Many schools, busy simply managing teacher involvement, might not choose to go this route, but the parents in Cape Elizabeth were very involved with the school, and Tom understood that the implications of effective data use extended beyond the school's walls. If Data Wise caught on as he hoped, he knew that parents would need to be involved in deciding how data would be made publicly available and in helping the community understand responsible data use.

3. **Focus on what's relevant.** How do you decide where to focus your efforts? As mentioned, Tom decided to focus the Data Wise efforts where there was already momentum in the school—reading comprehension. But how did Tom and the other school leaders realize that reading comprehension was a need? Becky and Suzanne had spent considerable time analyzing literacy data and identifying areas of need in the context of the reading remediation program. Also, state assessments indicated that there was a problem with reading comprehension at Pond Cove. To add to this, the entire faculty of Pond Cove had collectively decided at their end-of-year planning session (prior to Data Wise) that this would be the focus for the next school year.

The reality is that choosing a focus can be a particularly difficult aspect of the Data Wise process. The point of Data Wise is to help school leaders identify areas of need. But in order to identify areas of need, you need to know where to look. Pond Cove's answer to this dilemma was very organic—they simply started with Data Wise where the school had already identified a need during the previous year's planning process. Similarly, you will read in chapter 2 how the new principal of Newton North High School chose an area of focus—the school's achievement gap—that was a pressing community concern and could motivate teachers to learn to use data to improve instruction.

For other schools, the choice of focus may not be as straightforward. For instance, you will read in chapter 6 how administrators at Two Rivers Public Charter School, even after directing their attention toward particular content areas (reading and mathematics), initially struggled with the question of how specific their focus should be. It's natural for educators to want to tackle all of their school's challenges at once, because leaving any need unattended feels wrong. However, the danger in casting the net too wide is that resources and attention become diffuse, and nothing of importance gets accomplished in any one area. It is worth remembering that some schools may decide on a school-wide focus *after* they present a comprehensive data overview to the faculty, particularly if, through the data overview, they identify a content area or general skill in which students seem to have the greatest need for support.

Continuing in the vein of Tom's threefold strategy, Shari's experiences and reflections from organizing for collaborative work highlight additional lessons:

4. **Share ownership.** After reading and rereading *Data Wise,* Shari felt the process had the potential to reach teachers and help them improve the way they taught. The Data Wise improvement process emphasized building a system with which teachers could regularly assess what content students were and were not mastering and then use that knowledge to evaluate and change instruction in the classroom. But how would the data team be able to succeed where other initiatives had failed? As Shari thought about past initiatives, she identified a common theme in how they were rolled out to the faculty—from the top down. Shari felt that teachers must have a sense of ownership in the process if they were to be willing to examine their own teaching and become open to change.

   Shari also concluded that there was danger in presenting data analysis as an "add-on"—just one more requirement that teachers must endure so they can do what they really want to do—teach students. Instructional time is already so vulnerable to outside imposition that faculty may see Data Wise as just one more demand on their time. Thus, you may find it helpful to convey to teachers in your school that Data Wise is not so much a discrete initiative as a systematic way of looking at the initiatives in place in your school. In other words, the Data Wise process can provide rich information about whether an instructional initiative— what the process terms an *action plan*—seems to be working, and why. One administrator in a school that we worked with put it this way: "We don't always need to work harder. In fact, Data Wise helps us learn how to work smarter."

   Shari wrestled with how to introduce Data Wise to the faculty in such a way that it wouldn't be perceived as a top-down initiative. On one hand, she recognized that the data team was in place to provide support and direction to the teachers. On the other hand, however, she knew that in order for teachers to really engage with the data, they had to be a part of the struggle and the learning process. She and Sarah talked about this tension between the work of the data team and the work of the teachers. This is a very important consideration when moving from the preparation to the inquire phases of Data Wise. We have seen data teams handle this many different ways, but those that have created a sustained culture of data use often strike a balance in which the data team does the support and infrastructure work—such as scheduling meetings, collecting and organizing data, and creating data displays and templates—while the whole faculty focuses on work that is closer to the classroom, such as looking at student work, examining instruction, and developing and implementing an action plan.

The work of Data Wise belongs to the whole school, but not everyone in the school has to do each part of the work. Where do the strengths and interests of your faculty lie? If you have teachers who are particularly skilled at analyzing and presenting data, you might recruit them to help prepare the data overview or to help the data team understand how to analyze data. Other teachers might be interested in facilitating groups and helping instructional teams use protocols to engage in fruitful data discussions, and still others who are pedagogy experts might eventually help facilitate the process of choosing or implementing the action plan. The goal is to respect and draw upon the diverse talents of your faculty as you progress through the improvement process.

To help put teachers at ease with the Data Wise improvement process, you may find it helpful to engage them in discussions about their hopes and fears around data use. Humility on the part of the data team can go a long way here. Faculty may be more open to data discussion and analysis when they see leaders who are willing to hear questions and doubts, and who themselves have hopes and fears. Becky and Suzanne found this to be true when they facilitated the discussion with the classroom teachers about their concerns regarding the reading assessment. The "Fears and Hopes" protocol, which prompts each person to share a hope and a fear about a new undertaking, is particularly good for guiding this sort of frank discussion.* For their part, the Data Enthusiasts worked hard to create an internal culture where they could speak openly with one another about how each new idea would actually contribute to better teaching and learning, and they hoped to model this approach for the faculty.

5. **Establish productive routines.** Perhaps an obvious but nevertheless important lesson from Pond Cove is the need for order and structure during team meetings. A reading of the meeting notes from the first several data team meetings reveals a strict adherence to procedure. Each meeting was thoroughly documented with a list of attendees, the minutes from the meeting, and action items for the next meeting (see exhibit 1.3). Each subsequent meeting's minutes was almost a mirror image of the "next steps" from the past meeting, with each action item having a corresponding progress report in the subsequent meeting. It is important that each meeting move the team forward in the Data Wise improvement process, not only because there is much to accomplish but also in order to build and maintain momentum.

Every school enters the Data Wise work from its own unique place. From past history to present climate, it is important to adapt the Data Wise improvement process so that it will fit the school culture while also gradually fostering a more collaborative, evidence-based culture. As different as schools are, however, we have yet to see a setting where the preparation phase could be skipped successfully; having a collaborative data team with productive routines is just too important. The work that Pond Cove did during the preparation phase set them up for future success throughout the improvement process, and this, after all, is what preparation is about.

✳ QUESTIONS FOR DISCUSSION

1. What kinds of leadership challenges have you faced, or do you think you would face, in establishing an effective data team at your school? What qualities would you tap into in choosing people for your team?

2. What are your faculty members' attitudes toward looking at data, and what is their level of skill? Is there a legacy of prior data initiatives at your school, and if so, is it mostly positive or negative?

3. Where do you have "momentum" at your school? Are faculty members rallying around a particular instructional initiative or learning problem?

4. Describe a success that you have had with team-building at your school or in your professional experience. How was the team chosen, and what kind of task was it undertaking? What do you think made the experience successful?

---

* For the "Fears and Hopes" protocol, see McDonald, J. P., Mohr, N., Dichter, A., & McDonald, E. C. (2007), *The power of protocols: An educator's guide to better practice* (2nd ed., p. 23). New York: Teachers College Press.

EXHIBIT 1.3. *The Data Enthusiasts' Note-taking Template and Meeting Notes*

Meeting Date:
October 30, 2006

Present:
Tom Eismeier, Suzanne Hamilton, Gary Lanoie, Shari Robinson, Sarah Simmonds, Becky Swift

Notes:
Gary presented the technology he developed to record student data. The format is standardized so that all three schools will be able to use it. The student records will be read-only. Gary agreed to include the reading assessment scores for two students for the next meeting. The team agreed that when teachers look at the numbers, they need to have some direction as to what they are looking for. In a discussion of the three assessments that Pond Cove will use, Becky reminded the team that she has written a grant to pay for the data entry for the reading assessment scores. Data from the twice-yearly math and language arts assessment and the state assessment are accessible electronically, but the reading assessment online data management system costs $3,500.

Next Steps:
Inventory of instructional initiatives. We need to get the data out to teachers and have conversations about the reading assessment. We can demonstrate that we are a good school, willing to work on areas of weakness. What questions do we have? What conclusions can we draw? What are we going to do about it? Tom has given a brief overview of the Data Enthusiasts' work to the Pond Cove Team Leaders. On Nov. 8 fourth-grade teachers will have a chance to debrief about the reading assessment process. Work on the inventory will be done by grade level, and team leaders will provide feedback. Parent feedback could come from the parent association. Gary requested a couple of weeks before our next meeting to add the reading assessment student scores to the template. The next Enthusiasts' meeting will be held on Nov. 13 at 2:30 p.m.

Chapter 2

BUILDING ASSESSMENT LITERACY

Newton North High School Gets Smart about Data

Rebecca A. Thessin

How do you build educators' fluency in the language of assessment? And how can you allay staff members' fears about data by helping them learn to interpret test scores responsibly? This chapter describes how a culture of collaborative data use begins to take shape at Newton North, a high school in Newton, Massachusetts, known for strong academic achievement among most of its students. Backed by a community mandate to better serve the school's struggling learners, the new principal and the math department chair create a data team and prepare its members to lead their colleagues in using data to improve instruction. This chapter highlights the challenge of making data seem relevant to faculty who are unaccustomed to collaborative data analysis. It also illustrates how schools can use the prepare phase of the Data Wise improvement process to invest time in building skills and building trust.

In her opening-day speech to the faculty of Newton North High School, new principal Jennifer Price, known to her staff as Jen, explained that one of her top priorities as principal would be to define and ultimately close the achievement gap between students who flourished at Newton North and those who floundered. As a former teacher and school administrator but first-time principal, Jen was committed to making Newton North a supportive environment for *all* students; as a contributing author of *Data Wise*, she believed that the faculty could begin to identify and reach out to struggling students by working together to analyze a wide range of data sources.

Located in a prosperous suburb of Boston, Newton North High School enjoys a longstanding reputation for academic excellence. The school offers a host of competitive honors and Advanced Placement (AP) classes, a television production studio, a prolific theater department, and a full-service, student-run restaurant. Each year, over 80 percent of graduates go on to four-year colleges, with many attending highly selective institutions. Its staff includes over 250 teachers and administrators, many of whom are experienced educators with masterful command of their content areas.

When Jen assumed the principalship, a number of these teachers expressed excitement about the arrival of a young, enthusiastic principal who was determined to improve equity without sacrificing excellence. Jen, too, was eager to take the helm of such an impressive school. Still, having worked in other high-achieving schools, she knew that in organizations where success was the norm, the idea of using data to improve instruction could easily be seen as beside the point. She believed that even the best teachers could use data to leverage their talents more efficiently, by focusing their instructional innovations on areas where students struggled most. Jen knew, however, that building a more collaborative, data-driven culture would take time. So she set two immediate goals for promoting data use at Newton: finding a cadre of staff members willing to carry the data initiative forward, and building their capacity to do this work well.

To accomplish her first goal—recruiting busy teachers to volunteer for a data team—she needed to think strategically. Because the faculty did not yet know her and because data had not been widely used at Newton North prior to her arrival, she needed to help staff understand how the school could use data to improve instruction. When they hired her, Newton's superintendent and school committee had made it clear that achievement inequity among students was a major community-wide concern. Jen believed the concern was urgent and that it

---

Newton North High School
Newton, MA

Type: **Public**

Setting: **Suburban**

Grades: **9-12**

Number of Students: **1,973**

Number of Teachers & Administrators: **256**

Students Qualifying for Free or Reduced-Price Lunch: **6%**

Students' Race/ Ethnicity Distribution

Asian **10%**

Black   **6%**

Latino **9%**

Native American **<1%**

White **75%**

should drive the school's use of achievement data. "I knew," she explained, "that launching a data team not for its own sake, but as a group committed to studying a topic that resonated with people in this community, would contribute to the team's success."

FRAMING THE CHALLENGE

During her opening-day speech, Jen reminded the staff of a fact they already knew—not all students at Newton North were thriving. She presented them with the data: 13 percent of students had scored in the bottom two of four categories—*needs improvement* or *failing*—on the state accountability tests in both math and language arts, and many of these students were earning mostly D's and F's in their classes. In a school where two-thirds of students scored *advanced* (the highest of four performance categories) in mathematics and just under a third did so in language arts, it was striking that a substantial portion of the student body was struggling on the test they would need to pass to earn a high school diploma.

Jen explained in her speech that the faculty must address this situation by doing a better job of reaching those students who were falling behind. She suggested that the school engage in a deliberate effort to analyze data from a range of sources in order to understand who these students were and why they were struggling. Again, Jen highlighted some facts that teachers already knew: enrollment rates in Newton North's honors and AP classes were lower among students of color than among white students. Moreover, the share of students scoring in the *needs improvement* or *failing* categories on

the state test was disproportionately high among low-income students, students with limited English proficiency, students with disabilities, and African American students. However, Jen noted that these categories partially overlapped with each other and pointed out that the patterns might look different on achievement indicators other than the state accountability test, such as course grades or college entrance exam scores. In short, Jen argued that the immediate question facing faculty was how to define Newton North's achievement gap. Was it primarily a racial or socioeconomic gap or something else? Was there a difference in the performance of students who entered Newton North after being educated in other districts and those who had attended Newton schools for many years?

FORMING A DATA TEAM

Leaving those questions for her audience to contemplate, Jen announced her plan to form a multidisciplinary, school-wide data team. Team members, she explained, would work collaboratively to lead the school in defining the achievement gap and finding strategies to close it. She encouraged faculty and administrators who were interested in that effort to join the team, explaining that multiple teachers from each department were welcome and that data-analysis experience was not required.

One of the administrators listening to Jen's speech was Cindy Bergan, the school's math department chair. She felt inspired by Jen's call to action and perceived a common feeling among other staff members: "It's hard not to become engaged," she said, "when you care about your students, and you see that some students are really successful, but there are also kids who are not." That summer, Jen had approached Cindy and some other department heads, including science department chair Amy Winston, about developing a data team. Both Cindy and Amy had expressed strong interest, and Cindy had even agreed to lead the team as it took shape. She shared Jen's conviction that a systematic focus on data would help teachers make better instructional decisions, and she was excited to help push the school in a new direction:

> We've never had a coherent approach to looking at data and understanding how multiple data sources inform each other. Everybody gets their charts, their graphs, and they go in the drawer. We've never pushed ourselves to go the next step. So when Jen said, "Let's do this with a process," I got on board.

Cindy felt that Jen's excitement and knowledge about data use would help the work catch on and generate results. "She has a lot of energy and a lot of interest in this area, which is very enticing," she said. "And I knew her enthusiasm and personality would encourage others to contribute as well."

Cindy's sense that faculty were inspired by Jen's opening-day speech was borne out by the fact that thirteen staff members subsequently volunteered to be part of the data team. Jen and Cindy were delighted by the response but knew that it wasn't quite enough. In terms of academic departments and perspectives toward data, they wanted the team to represent as broad a constituency as possible so all faculty members would feel that someone on the team represented

their interests. Jen explained that she "really wanted people who initially would not have signed up for the data team. Even people you might classify as 'data phobes.'" Having the viewpoints of skeptics, Jen thought, would enhance the team's attentiveness to general faculty misgivings.

To attract skeptics to the team, she and Cindy realized they would deliberately have to recruit them. Cindy helped Jen identify staff members who were well respected by peers but who were likely to be wary of test-data analysis. Jen approached them transparently, saying, "I really need you to be part of this," and explaining that their questions and concerns would make the team's work that much more thoughtful. "In the end," she told them, "the team will have to present its findings to the faculty, and there are a lot of teachers who share your concerns. We want those concerns to be represented throughout the process." In many cases, this direct appeal worked. For instance, although English department chair Nancy Kranes said she considered herself to be "a math phobic person," she agreed to join the team and expressed her willingness to learn.

To ensure that the school's use of data extended beyond just state assessment results, Jen and Cindy also wanted to include faculty whose content areas did not appear on the state test. With that in mind, Jen approached Adam Brown, the chair of Newton North's high-profile theater program. Adam, it turned out, had been intrigued by Jen's opening-day presentation and was happy to join the team. Given the rigorous teaching he saw happening throughout the school, he could not understand why some students were not achieving at high levels. Having heard Jen talk about the discrepancies in student performance, he was interested in figuring out the reasons for the gap: "I wanted to be a part of studying those numbers and finding those kids so that we could individually help them."

By the time the data team held its first meeting in early October, it had grown to include twenty-four members, including representatives from nine academic departments, the guidance and registrar's offices, and the district data analyst's office. Reflecting on how she and Cindy were able to recruit such a large, diverse team, Jen explained that the gap between successful and struggling students was a reality that teachers confronted daily. "Here at Newton North," she said, "every department sees the achievement gap manifested in one way or another. By focusing the work of the data team on the achievement gap, the use of data becomes connected to why people come to work."

LEARNING TO TALK ABOUT DATA

Within a month, Jen and Cindy had accomplished their goal of assembling a large and varied data team. Because many team members were new to data analysis, Jen began thinking about how she could develop their assessment literacy. Also, although she planned to take an active role on the team, she wanted to equip other staff members to feel comfortable holding leadership roles as well. Thus, at Jen's urging, Cindy had attended the Data Wise Summer Institute at Harvard three months earlier. Also, Amy Winston and science teacher Michael Hazeltine had enrolled in the Data Wise course at Harvard that September. Jen reasoned that

by pursuing external professional development, Cindy, Amy, and Michael would develop enough familiarity with the Data Wise improvement process to be able to lead the data team—and, eventually, the whole faculty—through its eight steps.

Most team members, however, arrived at the first data team meeting with no outside preparation and little idea of what to expect. Some staff members with limited data-analysis experience felt apprehensive. For instance, Adam was no stranger to standardized test results, but because he had not received formal training in assessment or data analysis, he feared that the team might move too fast for him. He also perceived similar worries among some of his colleagues: "I think, at first, a lot of us had a fear of realizing 'I don't know what I'm doing.'" Nancy, too, said she felt unprepared but held out hope that she would learn more through participation on the team. "Rather than being the deer in the headlights with data, I want to become a data queen by the end of the year," she said.

Jen and Cindy recognized that if they were going to sustain teachers' interest in the team, they would have to create a safe learning environment where people felt comfortable asking questions and not knowing all the answers. Josepha Blocker, a math teacher on the team, recalled that everyone was made to feel that their contributions mattered: "Jen made a point of saying, 'Team members who don't already know a lot about data are as valuable as those people who do.' She indicated that it was important for these individuals to speak up to help the team prepare a data analysis that the entire faculty could understand."

At the first meeting, the team decided to meet every other Friday for an hour after school. They also decided on a meeting format: Jen, Cindy, or another staff member would spend part of each meeting explaining a data-analysis concept. The group would spend the remainder of the meeting discussing the data they wanted to collect or (eventually) the analyses they had conducted. Prior to the first meeting, Cindy had prepared "assessment literacy" folders for all the team members. The folders included copies of the school's state accountability test results printed from the state department of education's website, as well as "language of assessment" templates on which team members were encouraged to keep track of vocabulary they learned during the meetings.

From the first meeting onward, Jen made a deliberate effort to teach the language of assessment by making sure that important terms entered the conversation. She integrated words like *cohort*, *sample size*, *cut score*, *predictor*, and *outcome* into the team's discussions and either explained these terms herself or prompted other staff members to do so. (These terms are defined and applied in the appendix to this chapter.) She also encouraged staff members to ask questions about the terms and to suggest relevant examples.

In learning the language of assessment, staff members made a concerted effort to support one another. At one of the team's first meetings, as Jen defined an "outcome" variable, Amy jumped up to write the word and its definition on a large flip chart. "*Outcome: A characteristic or behavior that you want to predict or explain.*" Jen clarified that at Newton North, the team was interested

in explaining differences in student achievement, so their outcomes of interest would be student-achievement variables like state test scores. She asked for examples of other achievement indicators they could use as outcome variables, and team members suggested grade-point averages, college entrance examination scores, and AP test scores. Amy listed these examples on the flip chart, while several data team members wrote the term and its definition on the handouts they had received at a previous data team meeting.

Jen then explained that a big part of their work to understand the achievement gap would be to figure out which student characteristics were associated with differences in achievement outcomes. As Jen defined the term *predictor*, Amy wrote it on the chart paper: "*Predictor: A characteristic or behavior that predicts or explains differences in the outcome variable.*"

Once team members had a clear understanding of outcomes and predictors, Jen and Cindy invited them to brainstorm a list of data sources that they could explore to better understand the nature of the achievement gap at Newton North. Team members called out a wide range of data sources they had at their disposal, which were captured on chart paper. Cindy offered to type the list and bring it to the next meeting to guide the team in assembling a data file they could analyze. Exhibit 2.1 shows the data sources the team identified for measuring outcomes and predictors, organized by type.

By the end of the team's third meeting, the team members had divided up the outcomes and predictors and assigned them to small groups responsible for addressing

EXHIBIT 2.1. *Data Team's Brainstormed List of Potential Outcome and Predictor Variables*

Name	Description	Source
OUTCOMES: High School Achievement		
High School Grades	Final grades for all courses taken at Newton North High School	School-based Electronic Data Record
SAT	All SAT I and SAT II scores	School's Career Center
State Accountability Test	All available scores from grades 3 through 10	District's Central Office
PREDICTORS: Elementary and Middle School Achievement		
Course Grades	Middle school grades for all courses taken	Students' Cumulative Folders (or middle school electronic records)
National, Norm-referenced Test	Given at elementary level	Students' Cumulative Folders
PREDICTORS: Academic and Extracurricular Engagement		
Attendance	Record of current year and past years' data	School-based Electronic Data Record
Curriculum Level	For all courses taken at NNHS: Regular, Honors, or Advanced Placement	School-based Electronic Data Record
Discipline	Multiple behavior codes: Yes/no	School's House Offices
Sports	Multiple participation codes: Yes/no	Physical Education Department
Theater	Participation: Yes/no	Theater Ink (School Theater Records)
PREDICTORS: Demographic Characteristics		
Bused from City	Yes/no	School-based Electronic Data Record
Country	Country of birth	School-based Electronic Data Record
English-Language Learner or Limited English Proficient	Yes/no	School-based Electronic Data Record
Free/Reduced-Price Lunch	Yes/no	School-based Electronic Data Record
Gender	Male/Female	School-based Electronic Data Record
Language	Other language spoken at home	School-based Electronic Data Record
Race/Ethnicity	Federally reported racial/ethnic codes	School-based Electronic Data Record
Special Education	Has an Individualized Education Plan? Yes/no	School's Special Education Department
Zip Code		School-based Electronic Data Record

four key questions: What data are available? What format are they in? Who is in charge of keeping track of these data? How can we gain access to these data? They agreed to investigate these questions and come to the next meeting prepared to share what they had learned. Momentum was building; having many hands involved in the work gave the group a shared sense of mission.

As team members acquired fluency in the language of assessment, many of the fears they had harbored during their first meetings dissipated. For instance, Adam found that the team's focus on building a common language helped put everyone at ease:

> You're bringing in all these different people—counselors, English teachers, and world language teachers—so everyone's coming from a different place. I think what's important is to mainstream the language to a point where it makes sense for everybody. Once we all understood the terminology, everyone got more excited about our work, and we started moving at a faster pace. Once we understood the language, it wasn't as hard as it originally seemed.

Reflecting on Jen's role in this process, he said, "She's encouraging meaningful conversations in a safe setting where no one has to worry about what someone else will think." Although a team member might fear momentarily that he or she did not say something right, Adam explained that, "in the end, everyone shared the same purpose in wanting to help kids."

PUTTING DATA IN THEIR PLACE

Jen and Cindy were heartened by the team's embrace of the language of assessment and

their eagerness to start looking at data. During the weeks that it took Amy and Cindy to obtain and clean the student data files the team had requested, Jen set aside time for explicitly teaching team members about the uses and misuses of data. Both Jen and Cindy had noticed in the past that teachers' resistance to the idea of using data to improve instruction often stemmed from the fact that they had seen data—and especially standardized test data—used carelessly or punitively. Jen believed that addressing this issue head-on would prepare team members to conduct their own data analyses and, down the line, share their work with the larger faculty. To teach this material, Jen developed a list of scenarios that she hoped would engage her colleagues in conversation.

In preparation for one of their fall meetings, Jen asked the data team to read chapter 2 of *Data Wise*, which she had co-authored with Harvard psychometrician Daniel Koretz and which introduced such concepts as *validity* and *reliability*, which were important to understand when interpreting standardized test results. Then, to facilitate a discussion during the meeting, she handed out a list of eight scenarios she had developed to illustrate errors people sometimes make when trying to use test data to draw conclusions about teaching and learning. This handout, together with a handout containing the explanations that Jen distributed at the end of the meeting, can be found in the appendix to this chapter.

Jen started by reading the first scenario: "A town decided to use an IQ test to rank firefighter applicants. Those with the highest scores were given the job first." She then asked team members to talk with the person next to them about what was "good" and "bad" about this particular use of data. The room was soon filled with animated conversation as team members began to converse. After a few moments she broke in and asked people what they thought. Adam, for one, was shocked to hear that a town might actually use IQ tests to award jobs to firefighters,

> ## "Once we all understood the terminology, everyone got more excited about our work, and we started moving at a faster pace. Once we understood the language, it wasn't as hard as it originally seemed."

since a person's IQ score seemed unconnected to his ability to fight a fire. Jen told him that she had indeed read in an education class about data being used in this way. She was starting off with an extreme case of data misuse just to get them warmed up.

Jen pointed out that the town was probably right to try to establish some objective, transparent criteria for screening and hiring public servants. However, she agreed with Adam that IQ test scores—though perhaps not entirely irrelevant—were probably not the best indicator of firefighting ability. Jen used this example to teach the team that "validity" referred to how well an inference drawn from a test score was warranted. She acknowledged that IQ tests were subject to controversy even as measures of intelligence, but that an inference about a person's intelligence based on an IQ score was probably much more valid than an inference from the same score about the person's firefighting

skills. "So, whenever you hear the word 'validity,' think 'firefighters' and remember this example," she said. "Validity may seem like a tricky concept in the abstract, but you all seemed to have a lot to say about it today."

After going through a similar process for the second scenario, which concerned value-added measures of teachers' effectiveness, Jen introduced the day's first take-away lesson: *Consider to what extent the skills you're measuring are the skills you care about.* In other words, she reminded team members to always consider whether the inferences they were drawing from a test score were warranted by the score itself.

Next, Jen led a discussion of scenario three, in which a school was placed on "probation" because its fourth-grade pass rates had declined. When she asked team members for their thoughts, one teacher asked whether it was typical to put schools on probation for a single year's decline. Jen tossed the question back to the group, at which point another teacher chimed in that she believed probation only happened under No Child Left Behind after a two-year decline. Jen and Cindy concurred, and Jen asked the team why such a rule might exist. "Because there's not enough data?" one teacher asked. Jen again agreed but asked why. Finally, one teacher pointed out that comparing fourth-grade scores from one year to the next meant comparing different groups of students—that is, different cohorts, and the two cohorts might not have started with the same skills. "That's right," Jen said, explaining that there were, in fact, several things that could have changed from one year to the next . . . the baseline skill level of the fourth graders (which the teacher had noted and which Jen defined as a source of *sampling error*) and various sources of *measurement error*, including the particular items included on the test, the harshness of the graders of open-response items, and particularities of the testing conditions. For instance, Jen asked, what if there was a cold snap on the test day this year, and the heater wasn't on, and the suboptimal testing conditions depressed students' average score for the year? Such problems could account for short-term fluctuations in test scores that would be expected to wash out over multiple years of testing. For this reason, Jen noted, conclusions about test score trends drawn over the long term were more trustworthy than those drawn in the short term.

Jen used this scenario and scenario four—a flawed comparison of third-grade and fifth-grade pass rates in a particular school—to highlight the day's second take-away: *Know whom or what you're comparing.* In summarizing the take-away, she reminded team members to ask themselves to what extent two groups whose scores they were comparing actually started from a comparable point.

Jen went on to ask team members to confer about scenario five, in which a principal claimed that his school had not served its low-income students as well in Year 2 as in Year 1. When asked what was good about this use of data, team members pointed out the benefits of looking at changes over time and focusing on subgroups about which the school is concerned. They were quick, however, to point out something they found

troubling. According to the graph Jen had distributed with the handout, 0 of 11 low-income students scored in the *proficient* or *advanced* category in Year 2, as opposed to 1 out of 10 in Year 1. By stating that the school's low-income students were performing worse this year than in the previous year, this principal had made a sweeping statement about performance based on the scores of only 11 children, which represented a very small sample. The consequence, Jen explained, was that the results were not likely to be statistically significant, and could easily be due to accidents of group composition.

Reflecting on this example, Nancy said, "One of the things I've picked up with the data team is how data can be manipulated. For instance, one school might show a 10 percentage-point improvement in pass rates, but with a very small sample, those 10 percentage points could be only one student!" She even recalled seeing an administrator make this kind of assertion at a recent presentation she had attended—a memory that only served to remind her and the rest of the team how commonplace and easy it could be to use data in slightly misleading ways. In response to Nancy's story, a teacher said that it sounded like the administrator wasn't exactly *lying* when he said there had been a 10 percentage-point difference in pass rates—he simply was not presenting all the information people needed to evaluate the importance of the gain. Nancy and Jen both agreed.

Jen then presented scenarios five and six, in which principals focused on test score differences that might not have been statistically significant, as well as scenario seven, in which teachers were asked to make curricular decisions based on individual test items, and scenario eight, in which teachers were asked to give extra attention to students scoring just below passing on a single high-stakes test. She used each of these scenarios to illustrate take-away number three: *Try not to draw sweeping conclusions from small amounts of data or small differences.* In emphasizing this message, Jen stressed the need to look at multiple outcome measures to determine if student learning is occurring, and if not, where improvements should be made. However, she acknowledged that the danger of this take-away was that it could lead people to feel that they never had enough data to draw conclusions. The point, she explained, was to be prudent, and to take conclusions based on small amounts of data with a big grain of salt. For important decisions, she said—such as defining the achievement gap at Newton North—her advice was to use multiple measures, which is exactly what the data team had chosen to do.

Jen's examples of uses and misuses got everyone in the room talking about data. By giving people an opportunity to discuss their thinking after each scenario, Jen ensured that people would stay engaged with the topic. Even those team members who had found chapter 2 of *Data Wise* to be slow going felt a boost of confidence when they learned that, in many cases, developing "assessment literacy" involved applying their own common sense and then learning what specific terminology they should use to express it. Reflecting on what the team had learned, Amy said, "The experience of looking at the cases Jen shared and the conclusions people try to draw from different sets of data really makes data team members think twice about what they might try to show in a data analysis themselves."

By spring semester, after soaking in several months of assessment-literacy training, self-professed "math-phobe" Nancy Kranes was well on her way toward becoming the data queen she had envisioned the previous fall. In one meeting, for instance, she inquired about how the confidence interval on standardized tests might affect the team's ability to define a meaningful gap in achievement. And during a discussion of cohort-to-cohort comparisons, she reminded the team that consecutive cohorts might not have started with the same baseline skills. As she explained, "Now, when a presentation is being made, or when someone mentions the word qualitative or quantitative, I know what that means."

LOOKING BACK AND MOVING FORWARD

During much of the fall and winter of Jen's first year at Newton North, an unsigned teachers' contract became an obstacle to the data team's work. During this time, the team was not always able to meet every other Friday as planned. Despite the importance of moving forward with the Data Wise improvement process, Jen did not want to ask teachers to meet when the union was encouraging them not to fulfill any responsibilities beyond teaching their required classes. At other times, the team met without Jen, since having the principal present would also have broken the teachers' "work to rule" regulations.

Challenges like contract negotiations and data gathering may have slowed Newton North's progress through the prepare phase of the Data Wise improvement process. Nevertheless, Jen recognized the benefits of letting the new concepts soak in over a period of months. She knew it was important to take the time to build assessment literacy so school faculty would understand how to conduct effective data analysis. She also felt it was important to dedicate time to gather a substantial amount of data on the students that the team had selected to study. If they did this work well, Jen knew they could create a high-quality data analysis that the faculty at large would be less likely to question or poke holes in:

> If we're serious about understanding the achievement gap, a problem that has plagued the Newton schools for a long time, we should take an extra four or five months to do it right. Then we can find the right solutions. We're spending the additional time so we can be really confident about what we find . . . before we spend limited resources on remedies that don't fix the problem.

By spring, data team leaders had successfully assembled a detailed student record on a subset of Newton North's students. To facilitate the process of data gathering, they had decided to focus only on eleventh graders. Unlike freshmen and sophomores, most eleventh graders had scores from both the state accountability test and a pre-college entrance examination test (PSAT) on file, and because these students would be in the school one more year, the data team could still use its findings to take action on the students' behalf. The data file Cindy and Amy created contained a row for each student as well as a column for each outcome and predictor variable listed in exhibit 2.1.

Once the data became available to them, team members who were so inclined were encouraged to "play with the data" by creating charts and graphs in Excel that addressed questions that interested them. They were able to ask questions of the data and look for correlations between the predictors that interested them and the outcomes they cared about. Cindy and Jen expected that the data team's assessment literacy would continue to grow as they proceeded to conduct hands-on data analysis and exploration.

The team felt good about what they had accomplished in their first months together. They had created a clean data file that they could analyze, and they were beginning to identify which students were struggling most when achievement was measured with three different outcomes: state test scores, grade-point averages, and PSAT scores. They were also poised to dig into other data, including student work, as they moved through the inquiry stage of the improvement process. Cindy and Jen felt that the time they had invested in assembling a data team, building assessment literacy, and building trust among team members would begin to pay dividends the following year. Newton North was well on its way to defining the achievement gap and engaging its faculty in deciding what to do about it.

✳ LESSONS FROM THE CASE

1. Use data to tackle a problem people care about. Jen realized that increasing teachers' collaborative use of data was not an end in itself but a means to an end. On behalf of the larger Newton community, her mission was to find a way to ensure that all students were well served at Newton North. That would mean closing the school's achievement gap so that not just most but *all* of its students developed the skills they needed for success beyond high school. Jen then made the case that the collaborative examination of data was ideally suited to defining the gap as well as working to close it.

In calling attention to such an important issue, Jen and Cindy were able to pique the interest of colleagues who might not otherwise have been interested in examining data. Faculty members who joined the data team felt they were supporting the school's mission to provide all students with equal access to a rigorous and high-quality education. Furthermore, because the data team's work was so closely tied to the school's mission, Jen and Cindy hoped that the work of the team could be sustained over time. As a result of their deliberate focus on an issue of great importance to the whole school, they were able to gather a multidisciplinary team that transcended departmental boundaries. While other schools profiled in this volume, including Two Rivers Public Charter School (chapter 6) and Community Academy (chapter 8), also made the decision to choose school-wide foci for their data analysis, they were both small, nontraditional schools. The fact that a comprehensive high school like Newton North took this path and felt that it was the right one demonstrates that even a large secondary school can benefit from an interdisciplinary data-use initiative.

By focusing the school's initial data work on the school-wide achievement gap, Jen and Cindy not only generated large-scale interest in data but also provided the data team with a clear starting point for their work. The team then worked collaboratively on defining the *nature* of the gap, which they could eventually present to the entire school in the form of a data overview—thereby completing step three of the Data Wise process. From there, the data team members and their departmental colleagues planned to define what the Data Wise improvement process calls the *learner-centered problem* by digging into a wider array of qualitative and quantitative data, including student work, interviews and focus groups with students, and so forth. Unlike the broad idea of an achievement gap, a learner-centered problem would be a statement about a particular skill or concept with which many students were struggling and which the faculty could take action to correct. In time, teachers might even engage in peer observation among classrooms in an effort to identify ways for the school to change instructional practice. Examples of how these steps played out at other schools appear in chapter 4, which describes how West Hillsborough Elementary School went about digging into a broader range of student achievement data, and in chapter 5, which describes the approach to examining instruction used at Murphy K–8 School in Boston.

2. **Support colleagues in learning how to use data responsibly.** When beginning an examination of data for the first time, it is important for the data team to be aware of the uses and misuses of data. In some cases, a school's faculty members may be experienced in examining and acting upon student test scores. However, data can be used carelessly even by educators who have experience and good intentions. Thus, it is always worthwhile to review proper and improper uses of data so team members can come to a collective understanding about this issue.

Jen and Cindy recognized the benefits of including faculty members from all subject areas and all levels of experience on the data team. They then dedicated the better part of a school year to the process of developing team members' ability to talk to one another about data. They also saw the importance of taking time to create a dataset that would eventually allow them to produce a relatively clear picture of the achievement gap at Newton North.

But what if your school does not have someone on staff who would feel comfortable teaching assessment literacy to colleagues? We suggest looking to other resources for support in this area. For instance, it may be possible to bring in an outside data specialist or consultant to spend time with your data team or even your entire school staff. Another option is to send members of your faculty to an outside workshop or training that focuses on this topic, as Jen did when she asked Cindy, Amy, and Michael to attend Data Wise offerings at Harvard. Teachers who receive outside training could then become responsible for offering professional development to others at your school.

Regardless of the method you choose, building awareness of data's uses and misuses is an important step in allaying educators' misgivings about data. The fact that Jen and Cindy understood common misuses of data helped reassure the data team members that looking at test scores was not going to be an exercise in teacher humiliation or punishment. As data team members eventually took steps to include more faculty from outside the data team in this work, assuaging those fears would be an important first step.

3. **Appreciate the importance of building trust.** You will notice that this theme comes up again and again throughout this book. Trust is simply essential to every step of the process! At Newton, Jen first began building trust by asking Cindy, a respected, data-savvy department head, to lead the data team, and by tapping Amy to lend further support. By distributing leadership and then serving as the team's chief supporter instead of as its director, she could allow the process to become the work of the team rather than the work of the principal.

At Newton North, a feeling of trust developed among the data team members as they worked together to develop a common vocabulary. Although Jen realized that some data team members already understood key assessment terms, she believed it was vital to define terms publicly and create a shared body of knowledge among the group. By jointly defining terms such as *outcome* and *predictor*, all faculty members on the team, regardless of their prior experience, could soon engage in the data team's conversations. These professional-development efforts also cultivated a safe environment in which all data team members felt free to ask questions without being looked down upon for doing so. Members were applauded for asking questions and incorporating vocabulary words just learned rather than being chastised for not already knowing the answers. The trust that data team members gained for one another, for Cindy, and for Jen only fortified their commitment to the group and its Friday-afternoon meetings.

4. **Recognize that patience can be a virtue.** Jen understood that forcing change too quickly would only undermine trust and long-term progress. Thus, she allowed the Data Wise improvement process to unfold at a rate that made sense within the culture of the school. Given

Jen's role as a first-year principal at a well-regarded high school, she realized that insistence on sudden, dramatic changes in the school's approach to data would not be well received. Implementing any new initiative, especially one aimed at increasing collaboration and evidence-based decisionmaking, was not a task to take lightly. She felt that if enduring change was to take root within the school, it would have to be led simultaneously by data-savvy teachers in many academic departments. She and Cindy assembled a large, diverse data team in the hope that its members would sow the seeds of change widely.

Still, the process demanded great patience. Like the Pond Cove "Data Enthusiasts" profiled in chapter 1, the data team members at Newton North were eager to move forward with the work. The achievement gap weighed on them; they wanted to define and start correcting it. However, they also realized that the initiative's success would depend on whether they had the skills to lead it with confidence, and for that reason, they knew that the time they had devoted to assessment literacy was crucial. By refusing to rush or shortchange the process of building capacity, they took steps to ensure that the seeds of change would be deeply planted.

✳ QUESTIONS FOR DISCUSSION

1. What steps does your school currently take to build staff members' assessment literacy? What additional steps could you take to ensure that faculty members are equipped to use data responsibly? What internal and external resources could the school draw upon to support teachers in becoming more data literate?

2. Review the "Using Data Wisely" handout and the accompanying explanations in the appendix to this chapter. Would it be productive to have staff members at your school discuss these scenarios as the Newton North data team members did? Who would be the right person at your school to review the explanations document ahead of time and facilitate the discussion?

3. Are there ways in which you have seen assessment data misused? Describe a scenario that you considered to be a misuse, describe why it was a misuse, and suggest how a data-savvy educator might take steps to correct it.

4. Describe a successful attempt you have experienced or witnessed on the part of a school to prepare its staff members to increase their data literacy. Explain who was involved, the lesson or concept that was communicated, and factors that you think made the endeavor successful.

APPENDIX A: *Newton North High School's Handout on Using Data Wisely*

USING DATA WISELY:

Understanding Common Uses and Misuses of Achievement Data

What Strengths and Weaknesses Can You Identify in Each Example?

1. A town decided to use an IQ test to rank firefighter applicants. Those with the highest scores were given the job first.

2. A state decided to link teacher pay raises to the average "value-added" scores for their students in each class, asserting that doing so would reward the most effective teachers.

3. A school was placed on "probation" because the fourth-grade pass rates on the state tests declined "significantly" from 2006 to 2007.

4. In District X, the fifth-grade pass rates were lower than the third-grade pass rates on the state mathematics test. A policymaker examining the data concluded that the district's fifth-grade teachers must be less effective than its third-grade teachers.

5. A principal presented district staff with the graph in exhibit 2.2 and commented that the school had not served its low-income students nearly as well this year (Year 2) as last year (Year 1).

6. A principal told his staff to look at any student with at least a ten-point change in scaled scores on the state mathematics exam from sixth to eighth grade and to determine what had caused those changes.

7. A department head asked teachers to identify specific questions on which their students scored below the state average and to decide what the department should do to address students' weaknesses on those questions.

8. A principal directed teachers to determine which students were within one or two questions of passing the state test, and then to dedicate extra time to ensuring that those students passed in the future.

EXHIBIT 2.2. *Percentage of Low-Income Fourth Graders Scoring Proficient on the State Language Arts Test*

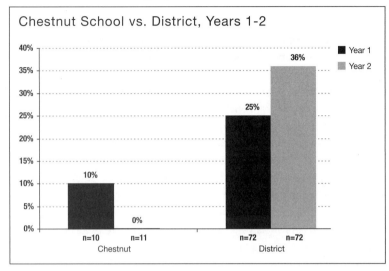

Chestnut School vs. District, Years 1-2

■ Year 1
▨ Year 2

- Chestnut: n=10 (Year 1) 10%, n=11 (Year 2) 0%
- District: n=72 (Year 1) 25%, n=72 (Year 2) 36%

EXPLANATIONS OF DATA USES AND MISUSES

Take-away 1: Consider to what extent the skills you're measuring are the skills you care about.

1. **A town decided to use an IQ test to rank firefighter applicants. Those with the highest scores were given the job first.**

   There is merit in the town's willingness to set transparent criteria by which potential fire-fighters will be selected for this position. The town is sending a clear signal that to get a job as a firefighter, applicants will need to do more than be politically connected to the department.

   The problem lies not with their intention but with the criterion they have chosen. Towns-folk want to use a cognitive test to allocate firefighting jobs to the most capable individuals. But what if people with the highest IQ scores are not the most capable firefighters? In other words, what if the measure the town is using to assess a potential firefighter's quality is not well matched to his or her ability to fight fires effectively?

   It stands to reason that a talented firefighter should be physically strong, determined, courageous, and a team player. IQ tests simply do not purport to measure those qualities. This is not to say that intelligence doesn't matter for a firefighter, but that it is just one of many traits a good firefighter will possess.

   This example illustrates the concept of *validity*, which is a property of the conclusion you wish to draw from a measurement. When you use a test score to draw a conclusion about a person's underlying trait or skill, the validity of your conclusion will depend on how well the score captures the trait you care about and wish to measure. In this case, any conclusion you draw from an individual's IQ score about his or her ability to put out fires may not be particularly valid.

2. **A state decided to link teacher pay raises to the average "value-added" scores for their students in each class, asserting that doing so would reward the most effective teachers.**

Unlike cohort-to-cohort comparisons, value-added measures of teacher or school effectiveness track individual students longitudinally. They attempt to estimate the effects of individual teachers (or schools) on students' test scores from one test administration to the next. Value-added *incentives*, like the program described in this example, aim to reward teachers who are most effective at raising student achievement in their classrooms. To the extent that these teachers are highly skilled at what they do, rewarding their efforts is an admirable intention.

However, whether value-added incentives actually reward the most effective teachers is still an open question. In part, this is due to the difficulty of measuring growth over time. First, there is the problem of linking tests vertically to allow grade-to-grade comparisons. Putting test scores on the same scale from grade to grade (known as vertical linking) becomes increasingly precarious when there are wide gaps between the grade levels being compared, because content taught in a given subject area changes markedly as one advances through the grades. Second, when curricula differ among classrooms, the test may capture students' growth in some classes more than others. For instance, if a high-stakes mathematics test emphasizes Algebra I skills, it will better capture the effectiveness of an Algebra I teacher than of a geometry teacher, though both teachers may be equally effective. Third, not all grades and subjects are tested annually. The consequence is that language arts or mathematics teachers might be eligible for value-added incentives, while history or computer science teachers might not be. This problem is especially limiting in secondary schools.

Beyond the challenge of measuring growth, value-added incentives are also limited by the difficulty of attributing differences in students' achievement growth to the effectiveness of their teachers. First, because test scores contain measurement error, it is difficult to obtain value-added estimates that are precise enough to make fine distinctions among teachers, especially when teachers are responsible for a relatively small number of students. Another problem is defining a comparison condition (what economists call a counterfactual) for what you think students would have learned, had they not been assigned to a particular teacher or school. A third problem lies in statistically disentangling the teacher's effectiveness from the larger classroom dynamics, including the relationships among students in the classroom as well as the external events and conditions that may affect the class as a whole.

Some educators also worry about the perverse incentives that come from paying teachers to raise test scores. Any time disproportionate incentives are linked to a single test, teachers may allocate too much time and emphasis to raising scores on that test (by ethical or unethical means) at the expense of other important areas of emphasis. In other words, putting too much weight on a single test score can make it a less valid measure of teaching quality than it might otherwise be. While the problem of perverse incentives arises in any high-stakes testing environment, some argue that it is especially serious when considerable monetary incentives are tied to a single test score. Consequently, a better measure of teacher effectiveness might take numerous criteria into account, including a range of both teacher and student performance indicators.

Take-away 2: Know whom or what you're comparing.

3. **A school was placed on "probation" because the fourth-grade pass rates on the state tests declined "significantly" from 2006 to 2007.**

   Tracking schools' academic performance can help states identify schools that need resources, professional development, or other support in order to better serve their students. Helping schools that need support and ensuring that their students are well served are laudable goals.

   However, one limitation of this scenario is that, like Adequate Yearly Progress (AYP) calculations under No Child Left Behind, it is based on cohort-to-cohort comparisons. Even if the change in pass rates and the sample sizes were large enough for the difference to be statistically significant (which is what the term "significantly" implies), what you do not know is whether the 2006 cohort of fourth graders had the same baseline skills upon entering the school as the 2007 cohort. In other words, the limitation of cohort-to-cohort comparisons is they presume that students in each grade-level cohort entered the school with the same average skills. To the extent that this is not true—for instance, if cohorts are very small or if a school experiences notable demographic changes—cohort-to-cohort trends may not accurately reflect a school's effectiveness.

   Besides cohort-to-cohort differences in baseline samples, various sources of measurement error can also result in year-to-year data fluctuations that would wash out in the long run. Sources of measurement error would include item selection on a particular test, the harshness of open-response graders on a particular test, or specific conditions under which a particular test was administered. To the extent that these details vary randomly from year to year, one or more of them could disadvantage a school in one year, but its effect would be expected to wash out over multiple years of school-wide testing.

   This is why, when making decisions that can cause resources to be reallocated, it is important to evaluate a school's performance over a longer period of time than a single year. These are also reasons why No Child Left Behind requires schools to be identified as needing improvement only after failing to make AYP for two consecutive years, and not based solely on a one-year trend.

4. **In District X, the fifth-grade pass rates were lower than the third-grade pass rates on the state mathematics test. A policymaker examining the data concluded that the district's fifth-grade teachers must be less effective than its third-grade teachers.**

   The policymaker in this example was attempting to compare the performance of students in the third and fifth grades, which might be useful if the third- and fifth-grade content standards were comparable and the tests were vertically aligned. In reality, however, comparing pass rates in two different grades, which typically cover different mathematical content, is probably no more illuminating than comparing pass rates in different subject areas.

In another sense, this scenario is analogous to the third scenario. Why? Because on average in the district, this year's cohort of fifth graders may have entered the grade less academically prepared than this year's cohort of third graders. Without baseline data on these students' scores from before they were exposed to their current teachers, it would not be wise to make claims about teachers' effectiveness, even if the standards were comparable and the tests were perfectly aligned.

Take-away 3: Try not to draw sweeping conclusions from small amounts of data or small differences.

5. **A principal presented district staff with the graph in exhibit 2.2 and commented that the school had not served its low-income students nearly as well this year (Year 2) as last year (Year 1).**

This principal's intention to compare student performance across years is good, as is his attention to the needs of economically disadvantaged students. By disaggregating data, a school can obtain a better picture of how specific groups of students are performing and determine if interventions are needed to support them.

As in scenario three, there is a cohort-to-cohort limitation in this scenario, since the low-income students in Year 1 may or may not be the same low-income students in Year 2. However, in this scenario, there is an even more serious problem. To find it, look at the sample sizes. How many low-income students scored *advanced* or *proficient* in Year 2? Zero out of eleven. How many in Year 1? There were only ten low-income students, so the 10 percentage-point decline in the share of low-income students scoring *advanced* or *proficient* was due to a difference of *only one student*. Given that year-to-year differences in pass rates (even differences of *more* than one student) are not going to be statistically significant in such a small sample of low-income students, it is somewhat misleading for the principal to state that the school is serving low-income students less well than in the previous year. In other words, with such a small sample, the difference between this year's performance and last year's could easily be due to baseline differences in group composition. (Another way of stating this is that the principal's conclusion is vulnerable to *sampling error*.)

Perhaps what the principal should be calling attention to is the fact that in both years, almost none of the school's low-income students scored *advanced* or *proficient*, whereas a large share of low-income students performed at those levels across the district. Even though the school serves only 10–11 low-income children in grade 4, they do not appear to be flourishing as well as other poor students across the district. (Of course, it remains possible that the low-income students at this school are more disadvantaged than those in the district as a whole.

Low-income status, usually designated as eligibility for federally subsidized meals, is by itself a coarse measure of socioeconomic background.)

6. **A principal told his staff to look at any student with at least a ten-point change in scaled scores on the state mathematics exam from sixth to eighth grade and to determine what had caused those changes.**

    There is merit to this principal's desire to "personalize" test scores. Focusing on the students behind the scores helps prevent their individual academic needs from being overlooked. Also, when a student's performance drops from one year to the next, it may be helpful to take into account the student's life circumstances during that year, including his or her classroom placement, family situation, health concerns, disabilities, and so forth. To the extent that this was what the principal has in mind in this scenario, his suggestion seems well intended.

    However, one problem with focusing on a ten-point change is that it is an arbitrary number—why not a twenty-point change, or a five-point change? The principal might address this question by asking himself, "Is a ten-point change substantively meaningful, and why?" One benchmark for estimating the importance of a ten-point change is the test's standard error of measurement, which is often available in the test's technical report. If the standard error of measurement is larger than the arbitrary ten-point interval, the principal should probably choose a wider interval.

    A final problem with the principal's approach is that, even if the ten-point difference were larger than the standard error of measurement, and teachers were to identify students who had made ten-point gains, they still would only be able to speculate about the reasons for those changes. They would have no way of systematically determining the causes. In fact, it is possible that the differences could simply result from the way the two tests were scaled.

7. **A department head asked teachers to identify specific questions on which their students scored below the state average and to decide what the department should do to address students' weaknesses on those questions.**

    Looking at specific types of questions and at performance in specific subject-area topics or strands can help a school determine where students and teachers may need additional support. This department head was probably hoping to identify target areas for improvement and to encourage teacher dialogue about successful teaching strategies. However, the department head's focus was too narrow.

    Individual questions on the state test are just samples from a larger domain of content knowledge that students need to acquire if they are to succeed academically (and economically) after high school. Thus, focusing on individual questions misses the point of standards-based instruction. First, it is unlikely that the exact same question would appear again on the next year's test. Second, while it is true that test questions sometimes follow predictable patterns, drilling students on patterns in test questions rather than focusing on the larger body of knowledge that the questions aim to assess may shortchange students' acquisition of content that they will need in the real world.

Finally, it is difficult to say why students miss a particular question; in some cases, wrong answers may result not from a question's content but from the way it is asked—its format, linguistic complexity, and so forth. Thus, to begin drilling students on factoring polynomials because they underperformed on a single polynomial question is to draw sweeping conclusions from a very small data point. More powerful insight can be gleaned from looking at clusters of items rather than looking at one item independently. One way to focus on meaningful clusters of items is to examine how students performed on content strands such as plane geometry, systems of equations, and so forth. It can also be useful to compare performance in a given subject area across different kinds of assessments, including district tests and classroom-based assignments.

8. **A principal directed teachers to determine which students were within one or two questions of passing the state test, and then to dedicate extra time to ensuring that those students passed in the future.**

As noted in scenario six, it is admirable for teachers to use achievement data to understand individual students' needs and to personalize instruction. However, all students who are currently not meeting standards should have access to extra resources and tutelage, not just students who scored just below the cut score (i.e., minimum passing score) on the prior test administration. Moreover, teachers should not ignore the academic needs of students who have previously passed the test.

Students who score just a few points below the passing score are often referred to as "bubble kids." Focusing disproportionate time and resources on these students has become a popular school and district strategy in response to the intensifying federal pressure to increase the number of students passing state accountability tests.

Unfortunately, a focus on bubble kids is problematic for at least two reasons—one technical, the other ethical. From a technical standpoint, the fact that test scores contain measurement error makes it inefficient to focus time and resources on students who scored just below a cut score. Due to measurement error, it is possible that the underlying skills of students scoring just below the cut score are considerably lower or higher than their most recent score would indicate. In addition, there may be other students in the class whose underlying skill levels actually do fall just below the cut score, but measurement error in their test scores might obscure that fact.

From an ethical standpoint, it clearly is unfair to students who are *not* "in the bubble" to devote additional time and resources to those who are, simply because of where the latter group happened to fall in the distribution of scale-score performance. All students, regardless of their scores on prior test administrations, deserve to be treated equitably and to have access to the resources and support needed to improve their academic achievement.

Phase II: **INQUIRE**

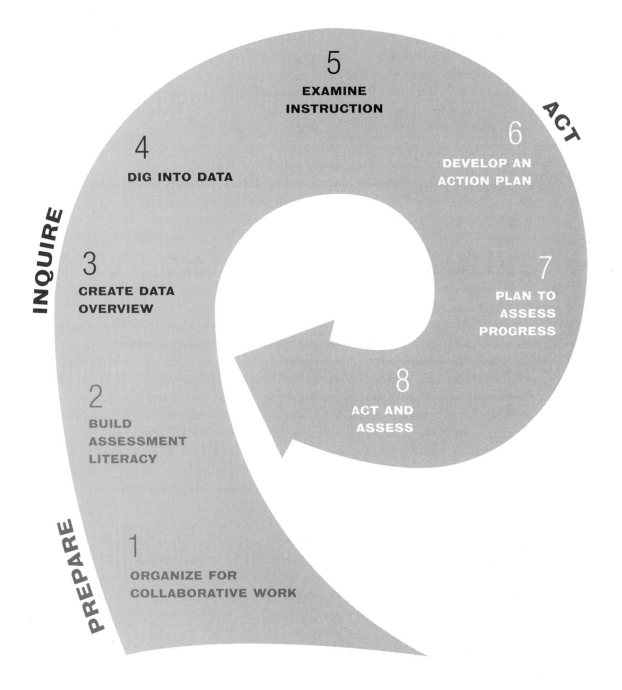

5
EXAMINE INSTRUCTION

ACT

4
DIG INTO DATA

6
DEVELOP AN ACTION PLAN

INQUIRE

3
CREATE DATA OVERVIEW

7
PLAN TO ASSESS PROGRESS

2
BUILD ASSESSMENT LITERACY

8
ACT AND ASSESS

PREPARE

1
ORGANIZE FOR COLLABORATIVE WORK

After you have built a foundation for collaborative data use in the *Prepare* phase of the Data Wise improvement process, it is time to turn to your data to explore questions about instruction and student achievement. This is the work of the *Inquire* phase, which is the part of the process in which schools begin to look to the data for answers. A common misperception of this phase is that examining data means focusing just on students' scores on annual, statewide tests. The truth is, while state tests provide a useful starting point, the work of the inquire phase goes well beyond examining results on any single measure of proficiency. It includes looking at students' class work and homework as well as their performance on district and school-wide assessments. This phase also includes an exploration of instruction throughout the school, a process that may incorporate classroom observations, teacher or student surveys, and informal conversations. In other words, the phase of *inquiring* is about tapping a broad range of data sources to identify steps the school can take collaboratively to improve student learning.

The inquire phase comprises steps three, four, and five in the Data Wise improvement process. Step three, *Create a Data Overview*, is the step that focuses most explicitly on examining standardized test score data, including but not limited to results from annual, statewide tests. As you will read in chapter 3, this step is about presenting a snapshot of student achievement that suggests fruitful directions for further exploration. Creating a strong data overview means marshalling achievement data to tell a coherent story, communicating with clear graphs and tables, and facilitating productive conversations about what the data reveal. An effective data overview suggests future lines of inquiry into what students know and are able to do.

In step four of the improvement process, *Dig into Data*, schools follow those lines of inquiry by examining student achievement on a range of measures. This may mean looking at quarterly or midyear standardized assessments, but it also means looking closely at students' projects, class work, and homework. Digging into data allows faculty and administrators to zero in on an important skill with which many students appear to struggle. We call this skill the *learner-centered problem*. A central goal of step four is identifying a widespread learner-centered problem that, if corrected, would have powerful ramifications for student achievement in many areas. For example, if many students in the school have a weak grasp of how to use evidence to support a written argument, then focusing on that skill across the school (or even across a grade level) may improve students' work in content areas as diverse as language arts, the natural and social sciences, history, and the arts.

Step five of the Data Wise improvement process, *Examine Instruction*, is about gaining a better understanding of teaching practices across the school. Once teachers have identified a learner-centered problem that they believe is important for the school to tackle, they face the question of what they might do differently in their classrooms to address the problem. This instructional challenge is called the *problem of practice*, and identifying it is the central objective of step five. It is important to realize that the "problem" of practice does not presuppose that teachers are currently doing something wrong. As with all teaching decisions, the "problem" is intrinsic to the work: *Given that many students are struggling with a particular skill, what can we as teachers do instructionally to ensure that they learn this skill?* Collaboratively examining instruction helps answer this question and prepares your school to take informed action to improve student achievement.

Chapter 3

CREATING A DATA OVERVIEW

McKay K–8 School Learns to Lead with Data

Mark B. Teoh

Most schools have more data than they know what to do with. What is the best way to distill all that information and paint a clear portrait of school-wide student achievement? And how can you highlight students' struggles and strengths in a way that inspires rather than overwhelms your colleagues? Presenting faculty with a data overview—a concise summary of student achievement results—can be a powerful way of sharing information, tapping teachers' insights, and suggesting directions for deeper inquiry. As with any powerful tool, however, wielding a data overview wisely requires careful consideration and planning. In the following case, a new principal seeks to use student achievement data as a call to action for faculty but finds that data sometimes have a voice of their own. Fortified by that insight, she assembles a data team and leads her school on a journey of understanding and improving student achievement results.

Armed with a decade of elementary school teaching experience and a newly minted school-administrator license, Almudena "Almi" Abeyta took on the principalship of East Boston's Donald McKay K–8 School in 2004. The year before Almi became principal, "the McKay," as it was known, had achieved striking increases in student achievement as measured by the statewide accountability test. As a result, the school had not only made Adequate Yearly Progress (AYP) under the federal No Child Left Behind Act, but as a school serving 91 percent low-income students, it had also received numerous public accolades, including recognition as a National Title I Distinguished School. Teachers at McKay expressed a commitment to improving student achievement, and they felt good about the academic progress their students were making. District and school personnel believed that Almi was taking over a school that could not fail.

As a novice principal, Almi knew that her first year would include its share of bumps in the road; when challenges did confront her, she did her best to address them head-on. While the pace of running a 600-student, K–8 school was intense, Almi's relationships with colleagues and her commitment to raising student achievement fueled her passion for the job. When her first year at the McKay School drew to a close, she felt that she had learned a tremendous amount, established bonds of trust with her staff, and laid the groundwork for a productive future. As with any new principal's first year, there had been good days and bad days, but on balance, she believed the year had been a success.

Thus, immersed in summertime planning for the school year to come, Almi was not prepared for the news she received from the district about McKay students' performance on the state accountability test. Poring over the data, she quickly saw the good news, which was that average test scores in mathematics had improved from the previous year. However, the story looked very different in language arts, where average test scores had dropped markedly. Almi found that the portion of students scoring in the top two out of four performance categories—*proficient* or *advanced*—on the third-grade language arts assessment had dropped from 39 percent to 24 percent. The same pattern emerged in the fourth grade, where the portion of students scoring at or above language arts proficiency had dropped from 47 percent to 24 percent. Finally, in the seventh grade, the share of students scoring *proficient* or *advanced* in language arts had dropped from 81 percent to 59 percent. Almi was stunned by

---

Donald McKay K–8 School
Boston, MA

Type: **Public**

Setting: **Urban**

Grades: **K–8**

Number of Students: **609**

Number of Teachers & Administrators: **45**

Students Qualifying for Free or Reduced-Price Lunch: **91%**

Students' Race/ Ethnicity Distribution
Asian   **1%**
Black   **3%**
Latino **89%**
Native American **0%**
White   **7%**

these results and wondered how this could have happened when everyone had seemed to be working hard:

> The results were a shocking blow. Fortunately, we made great gains in math, but with the drops in language arts, I knew we would not make Adequate Yearly Progress. Once I discovered this, I cried for a few days. Needless to say, this did not boost my confidence as a novice principal.

Almi found it difficult not to take the performance declines personally and spent a fair amount of time asking herself what, as an instructional leader, she should have done differently. After racking her brain to try to understand where things had gone wrong, she finally realized that the best thing she could do would be to stop dwelling on the past and start looking toward the future. She reasoned that it was her job as a leader to be resilient and address the problem in her usual head-on style. "Once I got over the initial shock," she recalled, "I had to pick myself up off the floor, dust myself off, and move forward." But how, she wondered, was she going to share these test results with teachers at McKay, and what was the school going do to turn things around?

THE FIRST DATA OVERVIEW: BREAKING THE NEWS

For what remained of the summer, Almi fretted over the question of how she was going to break the news of the school's poor test scores to her teachers. How would they react? Would they be surprised by the results? Would they blame her for the school's performance? She decided that what mattered most was that they have access to the information as quickly as possible once the school year

began so they could rapidly start working to get back on track. With that goal in mind, she planned to inform teachers about the performance decline in her opening presentation of the school year, then to follow the presentation with a discussion of possible reasons and remedies for the decline. Almi believed in a collaborative approach to leadership, and she felt that giving teachers an opportunity to share their insights with one another would help generate a collective quest for solutions. "I wanted to share the data with staff," she said, "because I felt the need to create a sense of urgency—we needed to improve." She hoped that presenting the test results at the opening meeting of the year would spark an animated discussion from which actionable steps for improving student learning would naturally emerge.

In addition, Almi was an advocate of using data to improve instruction, and she felt that the language arts results—discouraging as they were—could function as a powerful catalyst for school-wide instructional improvement. "Looking at data," she said, "is imperative to school improvement, because one cannot change without recognizing the need to change." Her challenge would be to help her teachers see this need, and she felt that "a data overview seemed the perfect place to start." Although Almi had not yet been introduced to the Data Wise improvement process, her principal licensure program had exposed her to the idea of using a series of data displays—what the Data Wise improvement process refers to as a *data overview*—to present a snapshot of student achievement in the school. This was how she planned to share the statewide accountability test results at the opening meeting of the year.

Once Almi had made the decision to present the assessment results to teachers at this meeting, she had to make choices about which specific data she would include and how she would make them easy to read and understand. The state test data that arrived during the summer did not come in a format that could be electronically manipulated, so Almi spent time perched in front of her computer entering the aggregate data into easy-to-read tables. She then incorporated these tables into a PowerPoint presentation that she could project on a screen, and she printed handouts of the presentation to distribute at the meeting.

The final data overview consisted of nine slides: two welcome slides and a meeting agenda were followed by three tabular slides highlighting the declines in language arts test scores in grades three, four, and seven. The language arts results were followed by a slide about upcoming math department activities, but the heartening upswing in average mathematics scores from the prior year was not mentioned. The final slides contained closing remarks and wished everyone a good year. Each slide used the same simple, decorative template and a large, easy-to-read font. Several slides included visual images, but on substantive slides, the images were small, thematically relevant, and unlikely to distract from the message. The tone of the data overview slides was cheery and upbeat, save for the disappointing test results sandwiched in the middle of the presentation.

On the day of the meeting, the excitement and buzz of a new school year filled the room. Over bagels, fruit, and doughnuts, teachers chatted about summer travel and welcomed new staff members. Once teachers had taken their seats, Almi warmly welcomed them back to school and launched into her well-rehearsed slide show. She glided through her first few slides, including the inspirational welcome and the carefully planned agenda. The presentation, she felt, was running smoothly. Then she arrived at the third-grade language arts results shown in exhibit 3.1.

EXHIBIT 3.1. *First Data Overview, Slide 4: Third-Grade Language Arts Test Results*

State Test Data Grade 3

- Students performed lower than the state on all questions.
- Overall, we dropped in third-grade language arts. What does this tell us?

Language Arts	2004	2005
Advanced	NA	NA
Proficient	39%	24%
Needs Improvement	44%	41%
Warning	17%	35%

The room fell absolutely quiet as Almi explained the declines in average language arts scores for each tested grade. "You could hear a pin drop," Almi said. "I was not prepared for the silence—it felt like I had dropped a bomb. I remember one teacher gasping." As she progressed from grade to grade in her presentation, Almi sensed that something was amiss. She had anticipated that this moment would be akin to a coach giving a team a pep talk. Instead, the teachers looked as if they were in shock. Faced with evidence that the school's language arts gains of recent years seemed to have vanished in one fell swoop, some looked horrified.

When Almi opened the floor for discussion, she was not met with the creative brainstorming she had hoped for. While some teachers remained silent, others sought to locate the responsibility for poor student achievement with the students themselves, the families, the community, and the work of their colleagues. Almi had not intended to field such an outpouring of frustration and anxiety, nor had she expected the extent to which teachers would see her presentation as an attack on their performance and abilities. Having experienced her own self-doubt when she first saw the test results, casting blame or doubt upon her faculty (most of whom had raised test scores in recent years) was certainly not her intention. Though she did feel that it was her job as principal to "light a fire" under faculty and prompt them to take the test scores seriously, they now were taking them beyond seriousness and toward despair. Almi simply had not anticipated the force and tenor of their reaction.

One point that kept coming up during the discussion was that because of these results, McKay would not make Adequate Yearly Progress. This troubled some teachers because the failure to make AYP could lead to district- and state-level probation. However, amid the frustration and disbelief that teachers expressed during and shortly after the meeting, it became evident to Almi that many of the teachers were not well versed in how AYP was actually calculated or in which measures were included in the state's accountability policy.

Having discovered a number of misap-prehensions in this area, Almi waited until the difficult opening day ended and then went straight to the Massachusetts Department of Education website to brush up on AYP details so she could highlight them at the next whole-faculty meeting. In doing so, she realized she needed to remind her staff that AYP involved steadily increasing targets for school improvement. Had the McKay's students' 2005 performance exactly equaled their performance in 2004, they still would not have made AYP. Of course, this year's students *hadn't* performed equally to last years' students—language arts scores had dropped—but Almi still felt that the teachers needed to understand the intricacies of how the state's accountability system worked. She wanted to drive home the point that no matter how well they thought they were performing as a school, resting on past laurels was not going to be sufficient in the policy environment in which they found themselves. She recognized that if teachers were going to use data effectively to improve their instruction, she would have to support them in understanding the state assessment data and the intricate federal accountability rules.

Almi met with her assistant principal, Melissa Granetz, to debrief the staff meeting and discuss how they could help teachers understand the effort required to make AYP in the coming year. Melissa liked the idea of enhancing teachers' awareness of state and federal accountability policies, and she offered to provide a series of professional-development sessions for teachers during their grade-level common planning time that fall. In the course of this work, Melissa took AYP reports from McKay and similar Boston schools and blinded their identities. She then brought these reports to grade-level meetings and led teachers through a process of discussing the reports, noticing the variation in the schools' academic strengths and weaknesses, and considering, based purely on test score data, which school was most likely to be theirs. She also explained how two schools could have similar test scores, but one of them (having raised its profi-

> ## "You could hear a pin drop," Almi said. "I was not prepared for the silence—it felt like I had dropped a bomb. I remember one teacher gasping."

ciency rate across student subgroups and content areas) would achieve AYP, while the other (having a stagnating, falling, or barely increasing proficiency rate in one or more subgroups or content areas over a two-year period) would not.

The goal of these sessions was to make data and accountability policy more accessible to the faculty in a nontechnical, nonthreatening way. Afterward, several teachers said they had appreciated the chance to strengthen their knowledge of policies that had such important implications for the school. Almi and Melissa hoped that helping teachers understand the accountability system would intensify the staff's determination to regain the ground they had lost on the state test.

During her second year at McKay, Almi focused a large share of teachers' professional development time on understanding how their expectations for student performance were connected across grades and subject areas. After the school's language

arts test score declines, she was eager to engage teachers in conversations about curriculum alignment. In observing classes, she had noticed that students were not always challenged more rigorously at higher grade levels than at lower ones, and she wondered if a lack of consensus around grade-level expectations had contributed to the decline in language arts scores. She felt it was critical that all teachers, not just those whose grade levels were tested on the state assessment, feel a sense of shared responsibility for the school's achievement results. Thus, she worked with teachers to bring more consistency among classes and to help streamline the scope and sequence of their curricula from one grade to the next.

During the summer after her second year as principal, Almi nervously awaited McKay's results on the state test. Last summer's disappointing results remained an all-too-vivid memory, and although she was convinced that the staff had worked extra hard in the past year to focus on instructional quality, she harbored a lingering fear that the data would not reflect their efforts.

While awaiting the results, Almi cracked open a copy of *Data Wise*, which she had heard about from colleagues in the district and been planning to read for a while. Reading for the first time about the Data Wise improvement process, Almi realized that, regardless of how the state test results turned out, she wanted to spend more time in the coming year fostering a collaborative culture around the use of data to improve instruction. She recognized, for example, that while McKay's teachers incorporated multiple sources of data in their planning and teaching, there was not yet a school-wide effort to come together and examine what all the data were telling them. Such an effort would require help, and she realized that she could simultaneously share leadership and hone the skills of her staff by formally creating a data team. She started by inviting her assistant principal, Melissa, and a fourth-grade teacher, James Cleere, to serve on the team, both of whom worked hard, showed real excitement about data, and shared Almi's commitment to improving instruction.

When the state test results finally arrived, they indicated that McKay students had improved overall since the previous year, and that language arts scores had rebounded to some extent. Almi was disappointed to see that the school had still not made AYP, but she was deeply relieved to find that the pass rates had risen or held steady for all grade levels in language arts and for some grade levels in mathematics. The teachers' hard work seemed to be paying off, but much work still remained to be done. For instance, when she thought ahead to the opening faculty meeting of the school year, she realized that she wanted to expand the scope of the data overview to include other data sources besides state test scores. She also wanted to create opportunities for the faculty to discuss how the school could make better use of data to guide instruction.

THE SECOND DATA OVERVIEW: COOL HEADS PREVAIL

The data overview that Almi created to open her third year at McKay was more ambitious in scope than the one from the previous year. It consisted of twenty substantive slides drawing upon evidence from multiple data sources. Eight slides focused on the state accountability test, and three focused on district reading assessment results in grades K–2—grades that were not tested by the state.

This year, in the slides that focused on state test results, Almi included four rather than two years of historical data in order to provide a longitudinal context for the current results. She said she had briefly wondered whether adding the extra years would just clutter the slide, but she had decided that teachers needed to see the historical background data so they could examine trends over time and contextualize their conclusions. For instance, she felt that seeing the size of the proficiency-rate fluctuations over several years could help teachers put recent fluctuations into their proper context.

Another feature that had changed in Almi's second data overview was how she framed the data. Like last year, she included an agenda slide near the beginning of the presentation, but this year, she also provided a list of teacher learning objectives much like what she encouraged teachers to include in their lessons for students. In addition, Almi hoped to emphasize that the school's progress in raising test scores was just one of many pieces of evidence of teachers' hard work. To remind teachers of all they had accomplished the prior year, Almi followed her "objectives" slide with a slide that listed and celebrated McKay's successes.

This year, Almi once again hoped the data overview would prompt a discussion about the data. To help frame the discussion, Almi included a discussion prompt on a slide following all the data tables. It asked, "How can we use our data to meet the needs of our students and to drive instruction this year?"

Almi hoped it would provoke conversation about what these data indicated and about directions teachers could pursue for further data inquiry.

Wary of the reception the data overview received the previous year, Almi also sought to present the achievement data in a positive light. To do so, she actively pointed out areas of improvement instead of just presenting the data as raw numbers. For example, while McKay had not met AYP objectives for another straight year, Almi chose first to emphasize that the number of students receiving *proficient* or higher marks had increased in many grades. Later in the overview, building on the AYP lessons that Melissa led in the previous school year, Almi broached the subject of not making AYP and explained the specific areas in which they had fallen short. Almi "framed AYP as a moving target" and reminded teachers "that as the years pass the target gets higher and harder to reach." Given that fact, she also reminded teachers they needed to keep up or intensify last year's work pace in order to get back on track with AYP attainment. Happily, when she said those things this year, it felt more like the troop-rallying pep talk she had hoped to deliver the previous year. "This time," she said later, "the data overview was not as heartbreaking."

Indeed, the opening meeting of the year was a far cry from the one she had run the previous year. This year, teachers were engaged with the slides and asked provocative questions about what they could do to help students improve. One issue teachers discussed with interest was the discrepancy between second- and third-grade results shown in exhibits 3.2 and 3.3. The slide displayed in exhibit 3.2 presents second-grade results from the district reading assessment, on which 70 percent of students met the grade-level goal.

EXHIBIT 3.2. *Second Data Overview, Slide 8: Second-Grade Formative Reading Test Results*

2006 Language Arts Data

Grade 2 Formative District Reading Assessment	
Language Arts Grade-Level Goal	**Students Attaining Goal**
Scale score of 28	70%

In contrast, exhibit 3.3 depicts the state accountability test results in language arts for third graders, on which only 19 percent scored proficient or advanced.

EXHIBIT 3.3. *Second Data Overview, Slide 9: Third-Grade Language Arts State Test Results*

2006 Language Arts Data Grade 3 State Test Results

- 2.3% of students scored *Advanced*.
- Share of students in *Warning* dropped 11 percentage points.
- Share of students in *Needs Improvement* rose 16 percentage points.

Year	2003	2004	2005	2006
	Percentage of Students			
Advanced	–	–	–	2
Proficient	29	39	24	17
Needs Improvement	53	44	41	57
Warning	18	17	35	24

These slides caused teachers to ask a lot of questions: Were the skills tested on the district reading test and the state language arts test that different? Did the discrepancy stem instead from instructional differences among grades? Or did the explanation lie in the fact that the district reading assessment was administered individually by teachers, perhaps introducing subjectivity into its scoring? Almi was pleased by the conversation that ensued. These were exactly the kinds of questions for further inquiry that she had hoped the data overview would generate.

Teachers also talked about what to do when, based on their state test results, good students appeared to be falling behind. To Almi, the difference in faculty reception of the overview reflected a change that had occurred in the school culture itself. She saw teachers' increasing openness as evidence that they were receptive to and, in some cases, even friendly toward a collaborative, evidence-based model of instructional improvement. Time would tell whether her perception would hold up as the school year got under way.

CREATING MINI DATA OVERVIEWS: A TARGETED APPROACH

As the school year shifted into full swing, the newly formed data team of Almi, Melissa, and Jim team set up regular meetings to discuss how they should implement a Data Wise approach to improving instruction at McKay. They also enrolled together in the Data Wise course at the Harvard Graduate School of Education.

One realm in which they felt they could immediately implement Data Wise principles was in the grade-level meetings. Melissa and Jim liked how Almi's previous data overviews had focused the faculty's attention on particular data points, and the group jointly decided to use a similar structure—the data overview—to facilitate data analysis in grade-level team meetings throughout the year. The team decided that, instead of creating one long data overview, they would develop short, "mini data overviews" that could focus discussion on a few pieces of data during a grade-level meeting. They decided to try out their idea initially with the third- and fourth-grade teams.

Past practice during grade-level team meetings had been to conduct item-level analyses of the state test results. For example, team members would identify test questions on which their students had underperformed and then examine those test questions to determine how they could teach that content more effectively. As they became more familiar with the Data Wise improvement process, however, Almi, Jim, and Melissa realized that this focus on individual test questions was too narrow, and that students' responses to individual questions were unreliable indicators of their underlying skill levels. A better approach, the team decided, would be to aggregate responses by content standard so teachers could identify particular standards on which students needed extra help.

Using this opportunity to introduce some of their learning from the Data Wise course, the group decided to focus their mini data overviews on mastery of state content standards and to represent the data visually using bar graphs rather than tables. They also decided to use three prompts that would guide teachers' discussion of each graph. These prompts came from a protocol called "Visual Thinking Strategies," which Almi and the team had learned about through an education program at Boston's Museum of Fine Arts.* Originally a pedagogical approach to analyzing art, the strategies asked viewers first to observe what was in front of them, then to back up their observations with evidence, and then to make further observations, looking for details the team may have initially overlooked. Realizing that they could easily apply these strategies to the analysis of data displays, they included a slide with Visual Thinking Strategies discussion prompts near the beginning of each mini data overview. An example of the slide is shown in exhibit 3.4.

EXHIBIT 3.4. *Mini Data Overviews, Slide 3: Data Discussion Prompts*

Visual Thinking Strategies for Data Analysis

1. What is going on in the data?
(Focus only on making observations.)

2. What do you see that makes you say that?

3. What more can you find in the data?

When complete, the mini data overviews for both third and fourth grade consisted of a set of meeting objectives, the Visual Thinking Strategies prompts, a bar chart comparing McKay students' overall performance on the state test to district and state averages, and a series of bar charts showing the McKay students' item-by-item performance on

particular content standards. (To sustain a manageable length for grade-level meetings, each mini-overview emphasized just a few content standards.) Teachers could examine how well their students had fared on a particular standard by viewing a bar graph that showed the percentage of students who had answered each item correctly. The slides not only named the relevant content standard—in exhibit 3.5, "understanding a text"—but also included a clear summary of what the standard meant.

EXHIBIT 3.5. *Mini Data Overviews, Slide 10: Percent Answering Correctly on Standard Eight*

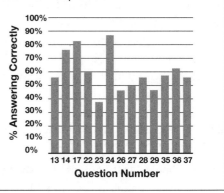

After viewing their students' performance on the standard, teachers would then examine a graph showing how well their students had fared on that standard relative to other students in the district. This type of slide is shown in exhibit 3.6. Again, the intention was not so much to focus on particular test items but to identify whole standards that they seemed to be teaching very well versus those that they needed to revisit or teach differently.

EXHIBIT 3.6. *Mini Data Overviews, Slide 10: Difference from the District in Percent Answering Correctly on Standard Eight*

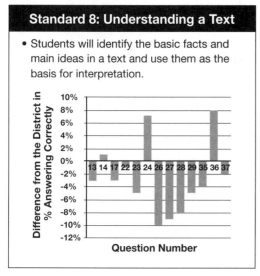

In previous years, grade-level teams had spent many of their precious hours together attempting to aggregate item-level data into standards, leaving them little time to discuss the results or to focus on implications of what they found. Thus, when Almi used these pre-prepared, mini data overviews with each grade level, the reception was encouraging. Teachers were glad that the laborious task of grouping data by standards was already done for them and that they could also see how their students fared against the district and state on each standard. As the data team had hoped, teachers were now able to devote more time to examining student work and discussing how they taught each standard. Eventually, they would use insights from these conversations to formu-

late grade-level action plans for instructional improvement.

PLANNING THE THIRD DATA OVERVIEW: A TEAM EFFORT

As the school year progressed, the data team considered how data could be further incorporated into the life of the school. Recognizing that momentum was building in the school around using data to inform and improve instruction, Almi invited other members of the teaching staff to join the team in planning the work of the upcoming school year. A seventh-grade math-and-science teacher and a third-grade teacher joined the group, as did the school's new principal intern. Together, they thought about the content and delivery of the data overview that would be presented at the opening meeting of the new school year. Their discussion uncovered a number of areas for future growth in McKay's approach to data.

First, they recognized that while teachers were being exposed to data regularly, their use of data to guide instruction was uneven. They were concerned that many teachers reacted defensively to data and decided they could use the data overview to address teachers' misgivings. Finally, they felt that while presenting information about student achievement should be a key focus of the data overview, the bulk of the three-hour time slot they were carving out for the opening meeting should be dedicated to small-group work. During this time, teachers could examine and discuss the data, engage in goal-setting activities, and consider which areas of student underperformance they wanted to investigate further.

In addition, the data team considered

other logistical issues, such as the availability of various assessment data as well as the question of who would generate and present the actual slides. One of the more critical decisions the team made concerned who would *deliver* the data overview. To minimize teachers' fears and defensiveness in response to data, someone floated the idea of having Melissa or one of the teachers actually present the slides to the faculty. This idea resonated with team members. They ultimately decided that one of the teachers on the team would present the state test results and another would lead the ensuing discussion.

They also discussed what types of data should be included in the data overview and in what formats the data should appear. The math-and-science teacher on the team volunteered to investigate different software packages for analyzing and presenting data, while the whole group would decide on data-presentation formats, such as when to use tables versus graphs to display achievement results. Besides the state test scores, other data that would be available for the data overview would include results from the district's end-of-year formative assessment and from a reading-and-literacy assessment administered by an external research group. The data team members wanted to present diverse data sources to the faculty because they recognized that one form of data alone could not tell a complete story about student achievement. Still, they hoped to balance that desire with the need to convey a succinct, coherent message that would provoke meaningful discussion.

The data group met regularly before the end of the school year and again in August before school started. Just knowing that she

had a whole team on her side to respond to the state test results felt like an enormous weight off of Almi's shoulders. She would continue to help shape the data overview, but she no longer would have the burden of doing it alone.

DELIVERING THE THIRD DATA OVERVIEW: ANTICIPATION AND VALIDATION

Two years after receiving her first set of student performance data from the state and just two weeks before the start of her fourth year as principal, Almi learned that the McKay School had at last made Adequate Yearly Progress in language arts. Her personal elation was exceeded only by her pride in the hard work of her students and faculty. The distance McKay's faculty had traveled over a two-year period could be measured only in part by students' academic progress on the state test. Teachers' professional growth was also evident in their enthusiastic use of data to inform instructional decisions. As the new school year approached, McKay teachers looked forward to finding out how their students had performed on the state test and were eager to discuss how those results could guide their practice.

Their eagerness was rewarded at the opening-day faculty meeting when Bruce Kamerer, a teacher on the data team, presented the data overview to his colleagues. Bruce beamed from ear to ear as he walked the faculty through the state test results, and when teachers saw their students' progress, the room filled with cheers and applause. The news confirmed their feeling that the school was moving in the right direction and that their collective hard work was paying off for students.

When the celebratory clamor died down, teachers' ensuing questions demonstrated their nuanced understanding of data and their commitment to let the test results inform their work. Some teachers inquired about longitudinal versus cohort-to-cohort trends, and others asked how their special-education students were faring. Still others asked how students had performed on particular grade-level standards and how closely the school's mathematics curriculum was aligned with state standards. Teachers clearly saw their moment of victory as a chance to recognize what they had accomplished while considering how to take their work to the next level.

As Almi watched Bruce deliver the data overview, she witnessed the power of shared leadership and knew she had reached a major milestone in her own development as a school leader. She also reflected with satisfaction on the strides her staff had made in their acceptance and use of achievement data. As Almi, the data team, and the whole faculty planned for the new school year, they could proceed with the confidence that they were indeed on the right track.

✳ LESSONS FROM THE CASE

Almi's experiences creating and presenting data overviews highlight the many complexities of what may first appear to be a fairly straightforward task. Creating a data overview is more complicated than it seems because good data overviews do more than summarize and inform—they also act as catalysts for the rest of the *Inquire* phase. In other words, they must marshal data to tell a coherent story about students' successes as well as struggles, and they must prompt teachers to pursue meaningful questions about instruction and achievement.

In her first three years as principal, Almi learned a lot about how data overviews could be used with teachers at the McKay School as a step toward improving instruction. Almi's story not only chronicles her growth as an instructional leader in focusing teachers' attention on data but also offers several important lessons for schools undertaking this step of the Data Wise improvement process.

1. **Effective data overviews are succinct, well organized, and aimed at the faculty audience.** The way in which the data team organizes the data overview—including the choice of data to highlight—will influence the kind of questions teachers ask and the kind of future inquiries they are likely to pursue. This fact places tremendous responsibility on the team to create a data overview that tells a coherent story, celebrates strengths as well as weaknesses, and emphasizes one or two key areas in which academic improvement is most needed. A data overview that attempts to be too comprehensive may not connect with an audience as well as an overview that sacrifices some detail for a succinct, clear message.

    Almi's first data overview was actually quite effective in its succinctness (it contained only nine slides) and in its uncluttered, easy-to-read slide layouts, of which exhibit 3.1 is representative. These are important elements of a powerful overview. What this first data overview overlooked, however, was the importance of celebrating students' and teachers' successes. This lesson was not lost on Almi, and her future data overviews included clear attention to students' growth and success.

Almi also came to understand the value of giving teachers time to come to terms with disappointing results. During the first data overview, teachers were stunned to see students' test scores drop suddenly in language arts. Surprised and disappointed, they were not prepared, in that moment of vulnerability, to engage in reasoned discussion about what the results signified or what they themselves should do next. To a large extent, their initial reaction mirrored Almi's own reaction to the test scores when she had received them from the district a few weeks earlier: she too had needed to overcome her shock and disappointment before she could, as she said, "dust [her]self off and move forward." Though she had wanted her data overview to "light a fire" under teachers, she also realized after the first attempt that they needed a period of time to come to terms with results. If faced with a similar situation in the future, she thought that she might distribute the slides to her teachers ahead of time and ask them to come prepared with questions they thought the faculty should try to address. Even if their questions involved questioning the results themselves, they would have had time to think them through rather than offering them as gut reactions to difficult news.

Over time, Almi learned that another trick for targeting her presentation toward her faculty audience lay in presenting data as graphs rather than tables. This change, when executed by the data team in the mini-overviews, made it easier for faculty to grasp the central message of a slide without doing on-the-spot numerical calculations in their minds. While tables can be very useful when comparing single data points, graphs often have the advantage when comparing patterns or trends, including trends over time. When deciding how to display data, it is often true that a picture is worth more than a bunch of numbers.

Also, more often than not, the time available to educators for discussing data is limited. Frequently, the time goes by faster than expected, so that the discussion has to end just when it is really getting started. When preparing the data overview, data teams can take steps to avoid this problem by asking themselves what they want teachers to spend time doing during the meeting and what insights they want teachers to take away from it. They can then use these goals to design their agenda and objectives. For example, at McKay, each of Almi's data overviews included a clear agenda listing the meeting's activities and the amount of time that would be allocated to each. Including the agenda showed respect for teachers' time and gave them a clear sense of what to expect. By the second data overview, Almi had also begun incorporating a separate "objectives" slide, which clarified what she hoped teachers would take away from the discussion. Almi had worked with her staff on how to write learning objectives for students; writing them for teachers was a powerful way of modeling that practice.

2. Effective data overviews draw upon more than one data source. While the data overview is meant to provide a big-picture snapshot of student achievement in the school, including multiple data sources in the presentation may help reduce the pressure teachers feel to focus all their energies on the state accountability test. It may also paint a more compelling and nuanced picture than focusing solely on the results from a single test. Almi's second data overview illustrates this point. In it, she not only presented longitudinal trends in mathematics and language arts on the state test, but for grades not tested by the state assessment, she included results from the district reading assessment. The discrepancy between the results from these two sources provoked interesting discussion among the faculty and suggested a possible direction for further inquiry.

We have seen other schools use multiple data sources to explore interesting discrepancies as well. For instance, chapter 8 describes how Community Academy's data overview highlighted a discrepancy between grades and state test scores that helped motivate the staff's examination of their homework policy. Other schools have also examined multiple data sources in interesting ways. As we saw in chapter 2, Newton North High School decided to use a variety of student achievement indicators—including SAT and PSAT scores, grades, and course-taking behavior—to strengthen staff members' understanding of the achievement gap. Another school we have worked with used students' state test scores and district reading scores to identify and address an achievement gap between students who entered the school as kindergartners and those who entered in later grades. Effective data overviews frequently allow teachers to think about how and why students' performance on different types of assessments might differ. As was the case with Almi's second overview, this question can lead to important conversations.

3. Effective data overviews foster discussion and further inquiry. From the beginning, Almi intended for her data overview presentations to serve as jumping-off points for meaningful faculty conversations. Although her first data overview may have triggered more frustration than problem-solving, Almi learned from that experience. Over time, she became increasingly skilled at building thoughtful discussion prompts into her presentations. Her second data overview, for example, asked teachers to brainstorm ways in which they could use data to enhance their instructional decisionmaking. Subsequently, she and the data team used Visual Thinking Strategies to guide the faculty in carefully observing data before drawing conclusions. In doing so, they provided a simple but powerful structure for focusing teachers' attention and curiosity on particular information about student achievement.

Using the data overview to generate effective discussion and inquiry is not as easy as it sounds. In our work with schools, we have often seen discussion prompts that were too broad to generate focused conversations. For instance, after showing a sequential series of five graphs, each of which makes a different point, a presenter might ask, "What do you conclude from the data?" Prompts that are this broad are not very useful because they do not clarify on which displays the discussion should focus. Providing handouts of the presentation—an excellent idea with any data overview—and allowing time after each data slide for participants to share observations can help ensure that everyone stays engaged in the discussion.

We have also seen discussion prompts that jump too quickly from the data overview to action planning, such as, "What can we do in the classroom to raise our reading comprehension proficiency rate?" While a prompt like this *may* lead teachers to hypothesize reasons for students' underperformance, it is nevertheless helpful to look more closely at student work and instructional practice in the school (steps four and five, respectively, of the Data Wise improvement process) before deciding what instructional actions to take. In fact, the Data Wise improvement process is organized so that most questions about action planning arise not in response to the data overview but in response to the follow-up inquiry that it generates. In other words, within the Data Wise improvement process, the role of the data overview is to alert teachers to broad areas of students' underperformance, which they can then explore collaboratively with additional data and inquiry.

What kinds of discussion prompts *do* spark conversations that lead to further inquiry? The Visual Thinking Strategy questions used by Almi and her data team offer one example, because they ask teachers *first* to focus on the data, and *then* to speculate on what the data suggest about teaching and learning in the school. In the course of these speculations, teachers may arrive at hypotheses they want to explore further. As *Data Wise* suggests, you can also assign teachers to small groups and engage them in a protocol such as the Question Formulation Technique. In that protocol, participants write on chart paper all the questions they have about a particular data display and then work together to narrow their questions— first to three top questions, and then to one priority question they would like to investigate further as a group. Yet another effective strategy we have seen school leaders use is to ask teachers to collect and turn in "exit slips," or small index cards on which they enumerate and submit their lingering questions to the data team at the end of a faculty meeting. By capturing questions that teachers didn't have time to ask in a group or were hesitant to share, exit slips can provide useful information for the data team in planning follow-up sessions for data inquiry.

4. **Creating a data overview is a collaborative process.** As Almi became more skilled at preparing and delivering data overviews, she also became more comfortable sharing the work with her data team, and the process became increasingly collaborative. Thinking back on this process, Almi acknowledged that "It's not always easy to share leadership, especially during a principal's first year on the job, but ultimately, it is worth it." Over time, she realized that inviting multiple perspectives into the process enriched both the experience of assembling the overview and the product itself, because it came to include not only her own vision but also that of her assistant principal and teaching staff. The resulting mini-overviews also modeled a process of data-driven collaboration and ensured that teachers' viewpoints were represented.

As Almi's experience suggests, there are a number of ways in which educators benefit from collaboration in preparing and delivering the data overview. The most obvious is that they can divide the labor of creating the requisite slides, which often include title and agenda slides, an objective or purpose slide, several graphical data slides, as well as summary and discussion slides. Particularly when team members vary in their proficiency with graph-making and slide-show design, dividing the labor to capitalize on individuals' skills and talents can boost efficiency considerably, as when the math-and-science teacher on Almi's expanded data team offered to investigate software for displaying data. Similarly, at Pond Cove Elementary School, profiled in chapter 1, the Data Enthusiasts jointly chose the student achievement results that their data overview would highlight, but their technology director was the one who manipulated the datasets and created the actual graphs.

Another benefit of collaboration is that the data overview can reflect the insights of a wider range of stakeholders, each of whom may view the data in slightly different ways or have different thoughts about which data to highlight. The resulting conversations about which data to emphasize—and how best to do so—often yield a higher-quality product than any one individual could have generated alone. Moreover, having multiple stakeholders preparing the data overview means having multiple perspectives on how well it is likely to resonate with faculty members. When the data overview is a team effort, aspects of the presentation that may confuse or alienate teachers are more likely to be flagged and changed before they make it into the final version.

Finally, when teachers play a role in preparing and presenting the data overview, the faculty as a whole are more likely to feel that their concerns and perspectives have been taken into account. Indeed, the next step of the Data Wise improvement process—digging into data—invites all teachers' collaborative inquiry into a range of data sources. The data overview can be viewed as the first step in setting them on that path.

✳ QUESTIONS FOR DISCUSSION

1. If you were in Almi's shoes after giving her first data overview, what would you do at the next staff meeting to start channeling teachers' frustration in a constructive direction?

2. If you were to create a data overview to present to your colleagues, which parts of the task would you find easiest? Which parts would you find most challenging? Can you think of colleagues with whom you could collaborate? How would you divide the work among yourselves?

3. What data sources would you include in a data overview at your school? What prompts might you use to generate a constructive discussion?

4. Describe a success you have had in presenting or explaining student achievement results to others. What were the circumstances? Who was the audience? What do you think made the experience successful?

---

* More information on Visual Thinking Strategies is available from Visual Understanding in Education at www.vue.org.

Chapter 4

DIGGING INTO DATA

West Hillsborough Elementary School Dives Deep

Thomas Tomberlin

How can teachers support all students in reaching their potential?
This chapter describes what happened when the faculty of West Hillsborough Elementary School in Hillsborough, California, found that their carefully honed culture of collaboration was not translating into gains in student achievement. To get past this "stuck point," they decided to focus their energies on using data more effectively. Although they had been working with data for years, the faculty realized that they had not fully integrated data into the core work of the school. They also determined that they had not been taking full advantage of all the different kinds of data available. This is the story of how they worked together to devise creative strategies for digging into data at the school, grade, classroom, and student levels in hopes of unlocking the learning potential of every child.

Anthony Ranii felt good about the school that had just hired him as principal. He liked the atmosphere in the very halls and breezeways of West Hillsborough Elementary School, where students and parents could often be found reading books or solving math problems together. When he visited classrooms, he enjoyed the buzz of productivity and the profusion of student work displayed on crisscrossing clotheslines. He appreciated how much of this work reflected the school's commitment to celebrating and accommodating the diverse learning styles of all students, a priority that he shared wholeheartedly. It seemed no wonder that the school had for many years posted strong performances on state assessments and had often been recognized as a California Distinguished School. West Hillsborough Elementary School, he reflected, was quite a place.

Although Anthony and the faculty were pleased with the accomplishments of the students, as they looked ahead to their first year together, they still saw room for improvement. "We have a really good start, but there is a long way to go," he said. "It's the tip of the iceberg—we have a lot more work to do." West Hillsborough's "good start" stemmed in part from many years of school improvement efforts that had focused on fostering a school environment in which teachers worked together, learned from one another, and shared effective instructional practices. Karen Lloyd Wolff, the district's information systems manager, recalled that schools in the district had taken many different avenues in their improvement efforts, but West staff had worked hard to "really focus on enhancing the culture of their school—the role of the teachers in the school, what it means to collaborate—and on further defining a common vision for the school."

In general, West teachers reported high satisfaction with their working environment and felt they were respected as professionals by the school and district administration. They appreciated how the atmosphere of trust and professionalism they had created allowed teachers to share their successes and stumbling blocks with equal candor. No one was made to feel inferior for expressing difficulty with their instructional practice, and no one was treated as a braggart for sharing instructional methods they'd found particularly effective. Third-grade teacher Shelby Van Doren described how the school culture had supported teachers in working together to improve their practice. "There isn't a lot of ego here," she explained. "No one thinks that she has got it all figured out. If you know or have found something that works, people want to hear about it and are willing to give it a try."

West Hillsborough Elementary School
Hillsborough, CA

Type: **Public**

Setting: **Suburban**

Grades: **K–5**

Number of Students: **375**

Number of Teachers & Administrators: **34**

Students Qualifying for Free or Reduced-Price Lunch: **0%**

Students' Race / Ethnicity Distribution

Asian **43%**

Black **1%**

Latino **1%**

Native American **0%**

White **55%**

AN UNANTICIPATED ISSUE

As successful as cultural reform at West Hillsborough Elementary School had been, however, the school faced an issue that no one in the school or district had anticipated: the strong culture was not translating into gains in student achievement. A few students were just squeaking by on the state tests, while others scored a comfortable *proficient* but might have been capable of more. "What are we doing to help those kids who aren't at the 99th percentile?" Anthony wondered. "Our teachers look at these testing summary sheets and see all blues and greens [*proficient* and *advanced* status]. But when you look deeper at these graphs, you might see students who are just barely making it into these categories. Are we doing enough for those students?" As for those students who aced the state tests, the faculty sometimes wondered if they were doing all they could to challenge them to go beyond standards and, as one teacher put it, really "be all they can be."

As Anthony took over the reins at West Elementary, he and his staff found themselves ready to reframe the school's central challenge not as one of meeting performance goals on the state assessment but as one of helping each child in the school live up to his or her full academic potential. They resolved to find a way to use the full power of their collaborative culture to address any issues that might prevent students from reaching that potential.

INTEGRATING DATA WISE INTO "THE WORK" OF THE SCHOOL

A few weeks after Anthony was hired as principal, he and the third-grade teaching team—Kristi Chenette, Tony Giacomazzi, Judy Pappas, and Shelby Van Doren—attended a week-long Data Wise Summer Institute at the Harvard Graduate School of Education. They hoped that the institute would provide them with a method for using the vast amount of data at their disposal to target the needs of individual students more effectively. West faculty were not new to the idea of examining data; they had been working with assessment data for years as part of the district's school reform initiative. But their work did not always feel productive. "I've been using data for the better part of seven years at this school," Shelby said. "But it has always been that we spent a great deal of time entering the data into the computer, and then no one ever looked at it again. We weren't really using it for anything."

As the institute unfolded, Anthony and the third-grade teachers discussed what they were learning. They agreed that the experience had helped them to appreciate both the importance of *narrowing* the focus of their improvement efforts and of *broadening* their definition of what kinds of data could be useful in addressing that focus. They decided to integrate these ideas from the institute into "The Work," their name for the multistep process they had developed several years earlier to guide their improvement efforts. "The Work" involved identifying student or classroom needs, defining a specific focus to address those needs, setting goals, designing a plan, putting that plan into action, analyzing the outcomes, and determining the next steps to be taken. By folding ideas from the Data Wise improvement process into the school's existing approach to school improvement, Anthony sought to avoid heaping one more initiative onto the backs of his hard-working teachers:

> "The Work" is the culture of the school. What we are doing with Data Wise is not a new program or initiative; it is all part of "The Work." Data Wise is the cohesive element that brings together all the disparate elements of what we were doing before. It's not an extra; it's central to the mission of our school.

Three "disparate elements" that the school already had in place, but which the team determined could be used more effectively, included analyzing interim assessment data; following the performance of a small number of individuals, known as "focal students"; and creating personalized education plans for all students. By working together to refine the way they used these three potentially valuable practices, the team hoped to help the school move past the surface "blues and greens" of their state assessment reports and really dig into understanding the educational needs of each student.

DIGGING INTO INTERIM ASSESSMENTS

Choosing a School-wide Focus

The institute gave the team a renewed appreciation of the importance of targeting their work toward a specific instructional area. "If your focus is on everything," Anthony said, "you are focusing on nothing." To choose the focus, that summer the faculty looked at school-wide performance on the state assessments from the previous spring. "We were looking at all the state test scores," said Kristi, "and we saw the dip in language arts score from the second to third grade, and

then from fourth to fifth grade. It dips in both grades. That's why we decided to make our school-wide focus language arts, because even though our average test scores are strong, we can identify an area where we can improve." After determining that language arts was the area in which their students could make the most improvement, the faculty agreed to have each grade-level team dig deeper into data and develop grade-specific goals that would support the school-wide focus. "It's really tempting to try to fix every single thing in the school," explained Shelby. "But what we've really tried to do is narrow it down using the data."

Choosing a Grade-level Focus

Each grade-level team began the school year by looking carefully at data. There was no shortage of information, since the district had invested in an interim assessment or "benchmark test" that provided detailed data on each child's performance four times a year. On each of the four tests, students read and answered questions about a set of literature passages. The test items were designed to measure students' mastery of twelve reading comprehension skills, such as "understanding the main idea," "making predictions," and "drawing inferences." Teachers entered the test results into a computer program from which they could generate reports showing individual students' performance in each skill on each testing occasion. The first assessment of the year provided baseline data, while the three subsequent assessments allowed teachers to track whether each student was "reaching benchmark" by attaining interim grade-level performance goals.

Kristi described how the third-grade

team selected the skills they would focus on that year:

> At the beginning of the year when we set our grade-level focus areas, we chose "figurative language" and "word meaning" because our kids were having a hard time with vocabulary and using the vocabulary in their writing. We look at all twelve of the strands in comprehension, but those are the two we are focusing on.

In addition to reviewing the performance of each of their new students on the third-grade baseline assessment, the team also looked at how their students had performed as second graders on the benchmark and state tests. They also considered the performance of their former third graders to get an idea of the concepts they had taught most and least effectively the previous year.

Digging into Interim Assessment Data

Analyzing data from the interim assessments was a relatively painless process because Judy Pappas, a third-grade teacher who also served as the school's data specialist, worked behind the scenes to create easy-to-interpret Excel charts. Judy took pleasure in her role as data specialist because she felt it was important to make working with data as easy on teachers as possible. "One of the things we've tried to do with the data is make it simple," said Judy. "Teachers need the data, but we don't want them spending all of their non-instructional time entering data; we want them to have that time for planning their instruction to address the problems that are indicated by the data." Judy's work ranged from creating straightforward charts of benchmark test score trends to developing more sophisticated templates that teachers

could use to create data reports for the school and district administration.

Judy noticed that it was not always the elaborate charts and templates that were most useful for teachers. For example, she found that by modifying a simple chart generated by the benchmark assessment software, she could produce "benchmark summary sheets" that helped teachers see at a glance how well their students performed on each of the twelve language arts skills. A sample benchmark summary sheet is shown in exhibit 4.1, where each row represents a single student, and the four columns under each skill heading represent the four testing occasions. An *x* in a cell indicates that the student "reached benchmark," or met the target score, for that particular skill.

The power of Judy's benchmark summary sheets lay in how teachers used them to identify common areas in which students were struggling. When the team met to discuss the summary sheets for each of their classes, they used crayons to create a visual display emphasizing the number of students who were having difficulty with each skill. Counting up from the bottom of the table, they shaded one box of each column for every student who did not make benchmark in that skill on that occasion. This practice gave teachers a simple way to review the sheets together, and it allowed them to instantly identify skills on which they needed to spend extra instructional time. By collectively examining the data in this way, they could easily talk to one another about patterns they were seeing. The opportunity to discuss patterns among classes also helped them decide on common areas of student weakness—in Data Wise parlance, *learner-centered*

EXHIBIT 4.1. *Benchmark Summary Sheet Indicating Which Students Met Benchmark on Six Reading Comprehension Skills*

	Main Idea				Sequence				Compare / Contrast				Making Predictions				Word Meaning				Conclusions and Inference			
	1	2	3	4	1	2	3	4	1	2	3	4	1	2	3	4	1	2	3	4	1	2	3	4
Andy	X	X	X		X	X	X			X	X		X	X	X		X	X	X			X	X	
Leon	X	X	X			X	X		X	X	X		X	X	X		X	X	X			X	X	
Katherina		X	X			X	X		X	X	X		X	X			X	X			X		X	
Sun-Ah		X	X		X										X									
Jeffery	X	X	X			X	X		X	X	X		X	X	X		X	X	X			X	X	
Nate	X	X	X		X	X	X		X	X	X		X	X			X	X	X		X	X	X	
Oliver	X	X	X		X	X	X			X	X		X	X	X		X	X	X		X	X	X	
Carly		X	X		X	X	X		X	X			X	X	X		X	X	X			X	X	
Becca	X	X	X			X	X		X	X	X		X	X	X		X	X	X			X	X	
Melanie	X	X	X		X	X	X		X	X	X		X	X	X			X			X	X	X	
Joey		X	X		X	X	X		X	X	X		X	X			X	X			X	X	X	
Di Won	X	X	X		X	X	X		X	X	X		X	X	X		X	X	X			X	X	
Meghan		X	X		X	X	X		X	X	X		X	X	X		X	X	X		X	X	X	
Allison		X	X			X	X			X			X	X			X	X	X		X	X	X	
Zoe		X	X		X	X				X	X		X	X				X	X		X	X		
Henry	X	X	X			X	X			X	X		X	X			X	X	X		X		X	
Jevon	X	X	X		X	X	X		X	X	X		X	X			X	X			X	X	X	
Jasmine	X	X	X		X	X	X			X	X		X				X	X	X		X	X	X	

Note: This table shows six of the twelve tested skill strands. The fourth column for each strand is blank because students had not yet taken the assessment that quarter. Teachers shaded the boxes in crayon so they could easily see the number of students not making benchmark for a particular skill in a given quarter.

problems—that seemed to warrant extra attention on everyone's part.

Examining data from the benchmark summary sheets allowed each teacher to tailor instruction to the unique needs of his or her students. "We can use the information from these sheets to pull small groups in our class," said Tony. "If my whole class is having trouble with a concept, then I'm *not* going to pull small groups—we will all work together on the skill. But if I have five kids who are struggling with 'Author's Purpose,' then I can put them in a group and work on that skill with that group."

Teachers also used information from the summary sheets to keep an eye on individual students. "We look at the kids who miss two or more questions on a specific skill and write their names down," Kristi explained. "We then keep track of those kids and the skills they are struggling with and give them individual attention when we are teaching that skill." Teachers then double-checked the students' understanding before moving on to more advanced concepts.

Using Data to Inspire Discussions about Practice

The grade-level teams found that the summary sheets also served as catalysts for thoughtful conversations about their teaching. Since data from each classroom were available to each team member, they could compare performance across classes. Moreover, the school's well-established norms for peer collaboration helped teachers trust one another as they compared students' strengths and weaknesses from one class to the next. "We have what we call 'positive intentionality' here at West," explained Anthony. "We

assume that everyone wants what is best for the students and that the students' interests are at the forefront of everyone's mind." Relying on this norm, teachers felt comfortable sharing their concerns about students' performance and soliciting one another's advice and feedback.

During one third-grade team meeting, for example, Kristi voiced frustration over her students' poor performance on the "making predictions" strand of the reading comprehension assessment. "It shocks me that we are struggling with making predictions, because it's a skill that we are covering every week in our curriculum," she said. "I mean, they are predicting what will happen in the story all the time, and they are great at it! They love to predict and they are naturals at predicting." As it happened, Kristi's comment made Judy think of something that had occurred in her class a few days prior, when her students had been discussing a biography of Dr. Seuss:

> You can take my example of Dr. Seuss. When the kids answered the question about why he wrote the books, they said that he did it for the money. But when I showed them that all through the passage it says that he did it so kids could enjoy reading, they said, "Yes, but people work for money—that's why he wrote the stories." I then spent class time explaining to them that their answers needed to be supported by the reading passage, not by what they think the answer is without using the reading.

The benchmark summary sheets from Kristi's class provided a jumping-off point for a conversation about a possible learner-centered problem underlying the data. Judy was able to offer a misconception she had identified among her own students as a possible explanation for Kristi's students' disappointing performance at making predictions. Judy's hypothesis—that students didn't always know when to rely on the text rather than on personal knowledge—gave Kristi and the other third-grade teachers fodder for future inquiry as they continued to explore areas in which students needed extra support.

Learning from Student Work

Although the interim assessments provided useful data, West teachers did not restrict their analyses to this type of information. They also took time to dig even deeper by looking carefully at the work that students were producing every day. In some cases, they discovered that students were not able to demonstrate true mastery of all the skills they were being taught. Shelby described why it was necessary to look beyond benchmark tests toward student work:

> We have realized that some assessments don't measure what we need to measure with our students. For instance, the benchmark assessments tell us a lot, but for some students not enough. Certain kids will score 11 out of 12 or 12 out of 12 on the multiple-choice assessment, but still cannot write a paragraph connecting the story to a real-life experience or compare and contrast the story with another story they've read.

Teachers knew that the stacks of essays, reports, and projects that their students produced over the course of a year comprised a veritable treasure trove of information about student learning—information that could shed light on problems not easily captured by standardized tests. However, the sheer volume of all this work made it cumbersome to talk about effectively with colleagues. How, they wondered, could they tap into this resource without getting buried alive?

REVAMPING THE "FOCAL STUDENTS" STRATEGY

One strategy for solving this conundrum involved revamping a practice called "focal students," which the school had used in the past, but with limited success. The practice, which West Hillsborough had adapted several years earlier through its involvement with a reform consortium, called for each teacher to pick a couple of students who would act as barometers for how well all students were learning the concepts presented in class. If focal students had difficulty with particular curricular objectives, the teacher could take a closer look at how well the class as a whole was mastering the material. For a variety of reasons, the focal student approach had never quite taken off at West in the past. However, Anthony and the third-grade team decided that, with some refinements, the strategy had the potential to be extremely useful in helping them dig into student data. A major advantage of the approach is that it would make the process of looking at student work more manageable. The team felt it would allow teachers to analyze samples of student work very closely without ceding all their planning time to data analysis. Motivated by the strategy's potential to help teachers identify and address students' learning challenges, they decided to engage the faculty as a whole in a conversation about how to revive and improve the practice.

CHOOSING FOCAL STUDENTS

The first step was deciding what the criteria for selecting focal students should be. The faculty agreed that students classified as having learning disabilities might not provide valid "dipstick" measurements of the overall needs of a class. However, they had some difficulty in deciding whether the focal students should be chosen among the low- or average-performing students in a classroom. The advantage of using the "average" students was that their needs might be more representative of the class as a whole. If the faculty were to select low-performing focal students, however, they would have the added benefit of looking deeply at the very students who were in most need of their attention. Fourth-grade teacher Sarah Lois explained why the faculty ultimately decided to use the low-performing students for their focus: "The focal students give an example of extreme needs, but they are still the needs of the whole class—the level of need is just more moderate for the class as a whole."

West faculty members were aware that, because focal students would be receiving "special attention" from the teachers and administration, parents might petition the school to have their children be focal students. Because this would undermine the whole purpose of the approach, the faculty decided not to inform either students or parents of who the focal students were. They came to a common understanding of the purpose of using focal students: to allow teachers to have in-depth conversations with one another and with the principal about how students were learning. If a teacher found that her focal students were struggling with a specific skill, she could look at a wide range of data sources to better understand the nature of those focal students' difficulties. She could then look at how well the class as a whole was performing on that skill. If the whole class was struggling with the concept, she could try new approaches to teaching the material, based in part on what she had learned by attending to her focal students' understanding.

Learning from Focal Students

The faculty agreed to make focal students a central component of their process for examining instruction. Anthony was pleased to find that this decision helped him carry out his role as the school's instructional leader. He knew who all the focal students were, so when he visited a classroom, he paid particular attention to observing how the teacher addressed the needs of those children. He talked with focal students about what they were learning and observed their approach to class assignments. Because his classroom visits had such a clear focus, he could then have very specific conversations with the teacher about what he saw.

Faculty also noticed that focal students often provided a starting point for discussions at whole-staff and grade-level meetings. Throughout the year, teachers reported on the progress of their focal students by sharing performance goals and providing examples of student work that showed evidence of progress toward those goals. Used in this way, the focal-student strategy provided a strong accountability component to the school's commitment to improvement. "The school can't just say we did our best and move on," explained Anthony. "These are real kids, *our kids*, who are being left behind." Sarah confirmed that the refined approach to focal students had a direct impact on practice: "When an assessment shows issues for the focal students, I know I need to go back and see what I can do differently. These students are not aware that they are focal students, but I am." Teachers were enthusiastic about the way that focusing on focal students helped them gain clarity on areas in which their students struggled most. Identifying common areas of struggle, or learner-centered problems, gave them insight on how to serve all students more effectively. For example, as they learned which concepts students grasped readily and which required extra teaching time or improved teaching strategies, they felt better prepared to allocate their teaching and planning time accordingly.

LETTING STUDENTS DIG INTO THEIR OWN DATA

Pleased with how their revamped focus on data was informing their teaching, teachers thought it was time to revamp how students used data to inform their own learning. To that end, they decided to refine their approach to students' Personal Education Plans (PEPs). These plans, which were collaboratively developed and revised in meetings between the student, parent, and classroom teacher, laid out each student's educational goals for the year. In order to enrich the quality of the PEP review meetings, the staff decided to have each student keep a portfolio of his or her work in what teachers decided to call an "evidentiary binder." The team that had attended the Data Wise Summer Institute was inspired to develop

these binders when they heard teachers from Boston's Murphy K–8 School describing how they collected exemplary student work in a "Mother Book" that provided evidence of each student's progress. "I thought that this was a great idea," Tony recalled, "but I thought we should have the *students* collect their own work and use it as part of the PEP process."

After returning from the summer institute, Tony and the others who had attended shared the idea of evidentiary binders with the full staff, who thought they would be a great way to make students more self-directed in their learning. Accordingly, in the fall teachers gave each student a binder, worked on setting goals, and asked each child to gather examples of work throughout the year that could be used to document whether the goals had been met. Teachers encouraged students to select work that showcased their successes as well as work that illustrated the difficulties they might be having in mastering a particular skill. Teachers soon found that the evidentiary binders allowed students to have candid conversations with their teacher and parents about which of their goals they had reached and which goals they were still working toward. The idea was to involve students in using concrete evidence as a basis for discussions about learning. In time, teachers found that involving students in the process of setting educational goals and documenting their own mastery made them much more likely to take those goals seriously. The experience of "Ricky," a bright but struggling fifth grader who had transferred to West that year, helps illustrate why.

Ricky had entered the school reading

at the first-grade level and was classified as both learning disabled and limited English proficient; his PEP was therefore also an Individualized Education Plan (IEP) involving the school's special-education faculty.

"Our need to constantly adjust and improve comes from the internal accountability that we have created among our staff and the district."

Ricky began his midyear meeting as most children would—head down, intently studying his nervously twitching feet. But when the special-education teachers brought out his evidentiary binder and list of educational goals and asked Ricky to explain them to his father, his affect was completely transformed. Ricky didn't just *tell* his father what his accomplishments were; he *showed* concrete evidence of his claims by sharing the work he had collected in his binder. Pointing to his reading fluency rates and other relevant performance statistics, Ricky explained how, in less than one school year, he had brought his reading performance up to the third-grade level. He then suggested what his new goals should be. Though he presented evidence of his progress, Ricky's evaluation of his own work was also quite balanced. He discussed his shortcomings and offered the opinion that he should continue to receive resource services in speech and language until he had progressed further toward his goals. Ricky's PEP meeting demonstrated that he was not just a passive recipient of instruction and specialized services but a child fully committed to raising his skills to the point where he

needed, and wanted, them to be.

Throughout the year, meetings to discuss PEPs took place for each student at West Hillsborough Elementary School. Although these meetings could be time-consuming and difficult to schedule, everyone involved seemed to feel that they were worthwhile. From the teachers' point of view, the fact that the meetings were grounded in the rich data of the evidentiary binders meant that they allowed West faculty to dig into data at the very deepest level—the level of individual student understanding.

SPREADING THE WORK

When Anthony brought the third-grade team to the Data Wise Summer Institute, he had hoped that the lessons learned would take firm hold within the third-grade team and then, as third-grade teachers interacted with their cross-grade teams and other school committees, spill into the other grade levels. He was pleased to see that, indeed, as the year wore on many other grade-level teams began incorporating more intensive use of data in their improvement efforts. Anthony was especially impressed with the way the first-grade team incorporated the Data Wise improvement process into their work: "This team has really taken up the challenge of using student data to target issues in instructional practice and student performance," he said. "Their ability to use interim assessments to identify potential issues in understanding for their students is as good, if not better, than the third-grade team who trained them." He was interested to see how teachers on the first-grade team became avid consumers of all types of student data, even seeking new sources so that their data would be "fresh" and informative about the educational needs of their students.

Although the increased emphasis on data was well received by most of the faculty at West Hillsborough Elementary, the kindergarten classes were somewhat slower to adopt the process of using data to identify areas of student difficulty. Anthony noticed that their hesitance was not grounded in an unwillingness to explore new approaches to instructional improvement. Instead, it came from a belief that certain types of data were less relevant to kindergarten, in which the learning objectives were more social than academic in nature. Anthony understood these teachers' reluctance to embrace data and felt that, as the instructional leader of the school, it was up to him to make the process relevant to the kindergarten team. "It's my job," he explained, "to show them how examining student data can help them understand why some students are better listeners than others, and why some of their students are acquiring appropriate social skills and others are not. They, like all the other teachers in this school, need to understand how this process will improve student performance or their own instruction. I need to help them make that connection."

As the year drew to a close, Anthony and the third-grade team reflected on the changes they had made since resolving the previous summer to sharpen the school's focus on data. Although they would not receive state assessment results for several months, they felt good about their progress. In fact, the faculty's enthusiasm for continuing the work was almost palpable. "The fact is that we no longer feel that we have accountability to the state," Kristi explained. "Our need to constantly adjust and improve comes from the internal accountability that we have created among our staff and the district. We know that students will meet expectations for state standards. What we strive to do is to get them ready for the following year. Our third-grade team feels that we are accountable to the fourth-grade team. We want to make sure that our students are set up with the higher-level skills they need to build upon the following year in order to be successful."

✳ LESSONS FROM THE CASE

Digging into data has the potential to be one of the most daunting steps of the Data Wise improvement process. When you take into account all the assessments, projects, and daily assignments that students produce, there are mounds of data at your disposal! Where should you plant your shovel? How vigorously should you dig? When will you know you've gone deep enough? West Hillsborough Elementary School's strategy for making the digging process manageable and productive may offer valuable lessons as you prepare to roll up your sleeves.

1. **Expand your definition of data.** As you become more sophisticated with using data to improve instruction, you'll be well served if you allow the term *data* to encompass much more than scores on a yearly state assessment. Results from such tests often wind up raising a lot

more questions than they answer: Why do our students struggle with number sense? What kind of supports would help our students write better? How come students leave so many open-response questions blank? To zero in on a learner-centered problem, you will need to bring to bear a wide range of data sources. West Hillsborough Elementary School's faculty approached this task with determination. They dug deep into interim assessment results, mining them for clues. They looked at student work. They investigated how the quality of that work correlated with assessment results. And, perhaps most important, they talked to the students themselves about what they were learning.

2. Make data manageable. This message, which was a central theme of the previous chapter on creating data overviews, is no less important during the "digging" stage of the game. If you and your colleagues want to make sense of data, it must be organized and contained. At West Hillsborough, Judy facilitated the process of digging deep into the data. In her role as data specialist, she spent many hours creating easy-to-read charts and templates that allowed her colleagues to get right to the heart of student learning needs. We have seen in school after school that having an on-site data manager makes implementing the Data Wise improvement process much easier for everyone. But what if you don't have a resident expert who is skilled at using spreadsheet software? Or what if you have folks with technical skills but just don't feel right burdening them with one more task?

In schools we have worked with, the data manager is usually not a technical wizard. In fact, as long as the person is reasonably comfortable with technology and eager to learn new things, the most important characteristic of the data manager seems to be that he or she has a strong connection to daily practice. The data manager needs to be able to present data in a way that sparks conversation. Quite often, a simple chart or table is all that is needed. At West, Judy found that one of the most effective ways to get teachers talking was to have them take out their crayons and analyze the table in exhibit 4.1.

Regarding the issue of how to make the data manager's task attractive to busy educators, we have seen several strategies work well. As described in chapter 7, the approach taken by Mason Elementary School was to have a teacher work half-time as data coordinator for one year while she established a system for using data. Once she had created data-collection templates and trained her colleagues to use them, her data responsibilities became more manageable, and she was able to carry them out while teaching full-time.

Depending on your district, you may find that the central office is able to provide some technology support. Turning to the district may be especially fruitful if your school is based in a small district where the central office serves only a few schools. For instance, as part of a three-school district, Pond Cove Elementary (which is profiled in chapter 1) was able to recruit the district's technology director to join the school's team of Data Enthusiasts.

In other schools, we have seen school leaders release the data manager from teaching a class, serving on committees, or taking lunch or bus duties in order to free them up to work with data. Sometimes, the principal has been able to provide additional compensation in recognition of the above-and-beyond nature of data work; at West, the district paid Judy a modest stipend to acknowledge the vital role she played. It is critical that data managers be recognized in some meaningful way for doing the work they do. In the end, however, you may find that your data manager is drawn to the work mostly because he or she senses that it is central to your school's mission. When people know that their hard work will be immediately pressed into use by their leaders and colleagues, it is amazing what they can do.

3. **Learn from the "many" as well as the "one."** At the Data Wise Summer Institute, the third-grade team from West Hillsborough was especially inspired by the comments of Harvard professor Steve Seidel during the session he led on examining student work. Steve framed the task of digging into data as one of striking a balance between finding the "one in the many" and the "many in the one." Looking for the "one in the many" means taking the time to appreciate that aggregated assessment results are nothing more than an accumulation of data about individual students, each of whom has a name and a face as well as unique talents and needs. This sensibility is evident at West Hillsborough Elementary in Anthony's determination to look deeply at state test results to identify and support the students who were barely scraping by. When they reduce students to numbers, schools sometimes find it all too easy to dismiss the lowest-scoring students as the ones that they are never going to reach. But when you put names to those numbers, as West Hillsborough did on its interim assessment tables, you can see the "one in the many" and deepen your commitment to reaching each one.

Looking for the "many in the one," on the other hand, involves finding ways to look deeply at an individual student's performance with the hope of gaining insight that will help you to teach *everyone* better. But it is simply not practical for teachers to collaborate on analyzing a whole classroom's worth of student work. What to do?

West's decision to track the performance of two "focal students" per class offers one solution to this problem. When teachers shared the performance of their focal students with Anthony or their colleagues, they were able to have concrete discussions about three kinds of questions. First, what was the nature of the content they were trying to teach? What would the students have needed to know to be able to complete a task successfully? Second, how did the focal students understand that content? What did they struggle with? What did they latch onto? Finally, what insight does looking at their work provide about how to teach the material more effectively? What needs to be taught again? How could they proactively address misconceptions the next time they teach this material? By reducing the *quantity* of student-level data that West teachers discussed with their colleagues, they were able to greatly increase the *quality* of those conversations.

Tracking focal students is one of many ways we have seen schools learn from diving deeply into the student data. More commonly, we have seen schools engage in "Looking at Student Work" protocols, in which teachers come together formally to analyze evidence of their students' learning. Sometimes it makes sense for a group of teachers to spend 40 minutes looking carefully at one child's assignment. At other times, it is helpful for teachers to bring a set of work samples representing a range of abilities and pass them around in an effort to get a "feel" for common strengths and weaknesses. The most important thing is not exactly how you structure the discussions but that you integrate this kind of very deep work into the fabric of your improvement efforts.

4. Dig into data with colleagues. While you can learn a great deal by digging into data alone— and good teachers do this all the time by reading papers, observing students, or analyzing test scores to decide whether to move on to the next topic—your learning is richer with a team of colleagues. You hear perspectives on the data that may be different from your own. You learn about a new approach to teaching a particular skill. You gain insight into the stumbling block that several of your students have in reading but that you weren't able to figure out yourself.

At West, years of investment in developing a collaborative culture and forging bonds of mutual respect and trust between teachers allowed them to speak openly about their data. This trust also made teachers feel comfortable opening their classroom doors and sharing their practice. The attitude of "positive intentionality" described by Anthony encouraged teachers to be receptive to new instructional practices. The school's determination to integrate data into their work meant that, as the year wore on, teachers became increasingly committed to confirming whether the effectiveness of their colleagues' instructional practices was indeed supported by empirical evidence.

You may be wondering whether a strong cultural foundation must be in place before your school attempts to implement the Data Wise improvement process. In this age of high-stakes accountability, most school leaders cannot afford to stage a cultural revolution unless they know the culture itself will have a direct impact on student achievement. But at West, a collaborative culture alone was not enough to take student performance to the next level.

The solution may lie in using the Data Wise improvement process itself to help establish a collaborative culture within your school. The sometimes uncomfortable conversations that can arise from the work of improvement can be mitigated when discussions follow structured protocols and are framed squarely in the context of the data. When decisions about what constitutes effective instructional practice are based not on individual preferences but on an objective assessment of student performance, the culture itself can begin to shift. The very act of focusing on data can be the genesis of a fundamental change in how teachers learn from, interact with, and collaborate with one another.

5. Think big but start small. Rome wasn't built in a day; neither was any school culture we've ever seen in which data are really used effectively. As an educator who believes that using data wisely can improve instruction, you may be tempted to sail in with the Data Wise improvement process and expect that teachers will climb instantly on board. Resist the temptation! Although it can be quite valuable to involve the whole faculty early on in learning about the process, in most schools, it will not be reasonable to expect that all teachers will flock to data from day one.

Even at a school like West, which had a track record of looking at student data, the process of revamping the school's approaches to data began with the third-grade team and the new principal. Together, they attended the Data Wise Summer Institute and then began to develop and roll out practices to the other grade-level teams. This team formed an excellent seedbed for innovation because team members already shared a solid working relationship and an openness to new instructional practices—and because Judy, who had experience in data analysis, was on the team. By investing in developing his own skills and the skills of a core group of teachers, Anthony planted seeds that could bear fruit throughout the year as the third-grade team shared their work with the rest of the school.

As you think about staging the work of improvement, it can be useful to consider whether there are particular groups of teachers who might be successful in leading the process of digging deeply into student data. Are there groups of teachers, skilled at looking at student work, who might appreciate having their efforts cultivated as part of a school-wide effort to use data wisely? Are there natural leaders who may not yet be experienced diggers but who could learn quickly and inspire others to follow their example? Eventually, the goal is indeed to have all teachers taking part in regular conversations with one another about evidence of student learning. But you've got to start somewhere.

✳ QUESTIONS FOR DISCUSSION

1. Beyond annual state test scores, what sources of data do teachers at your school examine systematically? How might you make even better use of the wealth of data that are available?

2. From your own context, give examples of how you could find the "one in the many" and the "many in the one." Which of these approaches to data feels most powerful to you? Why?

3. If you were to build the "digging" skills of a small group of your faculty, who would be in that group? What would be your strategy for allowing their work to spread?

4. Describe a success you have had with digging deeply into student work and coming to an understanding about students' learning needs. With whom did you work? What did you look at? What do you think made the experience successful?

Chapter 5

EXAMINING INSTRUCTION

Murphy K–8 School Unlocks the Classroom

Trent E. Kaufman

How do teachers get comfortable observing their colleagues' instruction and being observed by their peers? This is the question facing one educator when she is hired to teach at Murphy K–8 School in Boston, where peer observation is tightly woven into the fabric of the culture. Some teachers at "the Murphy" remember a time in the school's history when peer observation had yet to catch on, and even now, when the school is widely recognized for academic excellence, its staff must work to ensure that the collaborative culture does not unravel. This chapter demonstrates that sustaining a culture of peer observation means viewing all teachers as both learners and instructional leaders. It also means helping newly hired teachers acclimate to the culture by providing a clear process for sharing their practice with peers.

"When I came to the Murphy, I knew that meant I was going to have people in my classroom constantly. Did that make me nervous? Yes! I was scared to death to have my colleagues watch me teach." Such were the misgivings of second-grade teacher Tricia Lampron when she was hired three years earlier by Murphy K–8 School in Boston. Before joining "the Murphy," as it was known locally, Tricia had taught for ten years at an elementary school with a fairly traditional approach to classroom observations. At her previous school, observation meant that a busy administrator would visit once a year to make sure Tricia had a handle on things. Tricia acknowledged that she had not exactly begged for more observation at her old school. Though she had wanted to improve her teaching skills and learn from her peers, she hadn't been able to envision how a different approach to classroom observation would work. Over time, the closed-door culture had left her feeling "completely alone and isolated," and her isolation had resulted in uncertainty: "I attributed any successes, which were few, and failures, which were many, only to myself, because I didn't work closely with any other teachers, and I didn't have any other perspective. I didn't feel effective. I didn't feel like a professional."

Because faculty collaboration wasn't

Richard J. Murphy K–8 School
Boston, MA

Type: **Public**

Setting: **Urban**

Grades: **K–8**

Number of Students: **915**

Number of Teachers & Administrators: **67**

Students Qualifying for Free or Reduced-Price Lunch: **71%**

Students' Race/ Ethnicity Distribution

Asian **23%**

Black **37%**

Latino **7%**

Native American **1%**

White **32%**

part of her teaching experience, applying to teach at Murphy after taking time off for her family caused Tricia to confront the prospect of having colleagues analyze her teaching. She knew that working at a school known for its collaborative culture would amount to a quantum leap in her professional experience. On one hand, she was excited by the prospect, but on the other hand, as a person who already set high standards for herself, she was nervous about being the subject of scrutiny: "I work really hard and take my work seriously and personally. The last thing I needed was to have constant criticism. Teaching is hard enough without always being under the microscope."

Despite her hesitation, when Murphy K–8 School offered Tricia a teaching job, she accepted the challenge. She hoped that a collaborative environment would bring the instructional feedback and professional community that were missing from her previous job.

THE MURPHY

In downtown Boston, Richard J. Murphy K–8 School sits between a busy thoroughfare and a mostly residential part of downtown, where it serves roughly 900 students, 71 percent of whom qualify for free or reduced-price lunch. The school's ordinary brick façade and inner-city setting belie its status as a model of educational excellence. When Principal Mary Russo arrived to lead the school in 2000, more than half the students were failing the statewide accountability test. Seven years later, fewer than 15 percent were failing. Neither a charter school nor one of Boston's semi-autonomous pilot schools, Murphy had achieved this success as part of a large, urban school district, and its positive trends in student achievement had persisted across grades, ethnic minority groups, and socioeconomic categories.

Over time, Murphy's success at raising student achievement had attracted considerable local and state attention, and in 2004 Mary was named Massachusetts Principal of the Year. When asked regularly how she and her staff had achieved the results they did, Mary often spoke about the importance of using data to improve instruction. Data use was central to how teachers at Murphy thought about instructional improvement, and in their eyes, "data" went far beyond test scores; the term also encompassed student work as well as information that teachers gathered about pedagogy by watching their colleagues teach. In fact, Murphy's comprehensive approach to using data served as an important model for the Data Wise improvement process, and Mary and her after-school program administrator, Jonna Casey, became contributing *Data Wise* authors. Of course, teachers who had worked at Murphy School when Mary first arrived remembered a time when expectations were different. They recalled that Murphy's evidence-based culture, including teachers' collaborative process for examining instruction, had not taken shape overnight.

LAUNCHING PEER OBSERVATION

Seven years earlier, when Mary first came to the school and proposed the idea of examining instruction through regular peer observation, teachers were apprehensive. "I thought I would be constantly under the microscope," said Harry Gilliam, a middle school math teacher, when he thought back on that period. Others had a hard time differentiating between the kind of observation that Mary was proposing and the kind to which they were accustomed. One teacher said, "Before Mary arrived, the principal would come by a few times a year. I would be on my A-game for the visit, because I knew my evaluation depended on it. I thought my job was in jeopardy if I taught the way I did on normal days. Even my kids acted better when the principal was there."

Angel Petrie, a fifth-grade math teacher and instructional coach, agreed: "We were at a place where most teachers were scared to be watched, because they feared intense scrutiny and judgment." The teachers had difficulty envisioning something other than the "sit up straight" kind of formal observation that they were used to, where the purpose was for an authority figure to pass judgment. They found it difficult to imagine classroom observations performed by a group of peers for the purpose of discussing instruction. However, that collaborative scenario was exactly what Mary had in mind.

Having successfully developed a similar system at her previous school, Mary realized that a regular program of peer observation was crucial for improving teaching and learning. Yet experience also told her that reaping a culture of peer observation started with sowing the seeds. She and her administrative staff began devising a peer-observation process by trying to learn how teachers felt about examining instruction.

Angel remembered that the administration made every attempt to validate teachers' natural fears about being watched by their colleagues. Recalling why she took that approach, Mary said, "The first step in confronting fear is validating to the teachers that it is scary to put your practice out there and make it so public. Validating it is half the battle." Through a frank discussion with the faculty, Mary acknowledged that it would be challenging for them to open their "private practice" to the eyes of their colleagues.

"Once these highly respected teachers made mistakes, encouraged others to point them out, and showed a level of comfort doing that, everyone else fell in line. That was the key."

However, she pointed out that making teaching public presented an amazing opportunity for teachers to learn from one another's experience and insights.

When asked about their fears, several teachers expressed concern about what their colleagues would be looking for when they watched one another's lessons. Mary remembered schools she had seen where teachers or administrators walked into classrooms and "just took random notes about everything they thought wasn't perfect." Attempting to examine instruction using this "shotgun" approach was, in Mary's view, counterproductive. "Anyone can find fault," she explained. "Plus, it just doesn't help."

To help minimize teachers' uncertainty about what their peer observers would focus on, Mary again drew upon her prior experience. "I've learned that we all need structure," she explained. "You must balance uncertainty with structure. When things get rough, we need something to hold onto, something that makes us feel grounded." Building on a peer-observation model offered by the district, Mary worked with a group of teachers and administrators to develop a fixed peer-observation structure that would clarify expectations and minimize ambiguity. The group decided on a "model lesson" approach in which, at least once each academic quarter, a different teacher would deliver a lesson to his or her students while observed by a small group of colleagues. Typically, the observers would be teachers of the same grade level or (in the middle school grades) the same academic department. Prior to the lesson, the teacher doing the modeling would be able to specify aspects of the lesson on which he or she wanted feedback. Subsequently, the teacher and the peer-observers would discuss what had worked and what hadn't. The observers would also discuss ways of incorporating the most effective components of the lesson into their own practice.

After validating and responding to teachers' concerns, Mary and her administrative team encouraged a few highly respected teachers who were viewed as leaders by their peers to volunteer to be the first ones observed. "That's when the miracle happened," said Holly Concannon, a veteran teacher at Murphy. "These respected teachers gave real-life lessons, not perfect examples of pedagogy. They showed real weaknesses and made mistakes during their lessons." Their display of vulnerability and their sincere desire to improve was an example for other teachers in the school. Angel had a similar recollection: "Once these highly respected teachers made mistakes, encouraged others to point them out, and showed a level of comfort doing that, everyone else fell in line. That was the key." Holly said it was the first time many staff members realized that everyone around them wasn't perfect. She remembered the visible relief on her colleagues' faces.

After validating teachers' fears and minimizing ambiguity, Mary believed the next steps were to "set high expectations, establish a system—including periodic monitoring—and trust your teachers to be professionals." However, she knew that trusting teachers to be professionals also meant providing conditions that would allow them to flourish: "For every extra expectation we have of teachers, we need to provide extra support."

In part, providing support meant assuaging her staff's logistical concerns. Chief among these were teachers' concerns about leaving their students with substitutes while they observed their colleagues' lessons. "Sure, we are going to go and learn through the professional development," said Katie Grassa, one of Murphy's newest teachers, "but if I thought my kids were going to sit with just any substitute and lose valuable instructional time, then anything I learn wouldn't be worth it." Understanding the legitimacy of this concern, Mary addressed it directly by training a cadre of substitutes

to fill in for teachers on peer-observation days. The substitutes covered for one team of peer observers in the morning and another team in the afternoon. They were trained to take over a lesson at exactly the point where a teacher left off so that instructional time would not be wasted.

Teachers were grateful that they could take part in professional development without worrying constantly about what was happening in their classrooms. "Logistical issues like time and coverage can get in the way of valuable observation," said Angel. "We feel well supported when Mary takes care of those seemingly small things so we can focus on the business of improving teaching and learning."

By listening to teachers' concerns and taking steps to minimize them, Mary and her staff created a culture in which conversations about instruction were grounded in concrete data gathered from classroom observations. As faculty became more comfortable watching and discussing their colleagues' lessons, they came to see peer observation as an essential data source for guiding instructional decisions. They also knew that their commitment to examining instruction represented a break from the traditional, closed-door culture of many schools. Thus, they understood that sustaining the culture over time would mean not just maintaining their own dedication to the process but helping new staff members thrive in that environment as well.

ONE TEACHER'S INTRODUCTION TO PEER OBSERVATION

Tricia Lampron joined the Murphy faculty in 2004, four years into Mary's tenure, by which time the process of using data to inform instruction was already deeply ingrained in the school's culture. This included the aspect of data use that Tricia found most intimidating—examining instruction through routine peer observations. Tricia understood that the purpose of examining instruction was to share and refine effective teaching strategies, and this was a goal she believed in. Also, she was happy to discover that she could leave her students in the hands of well-trained substitutes while she observed her colleagues. Still, she had a nagging concern that the criteria her peers would use to critique her practice would be subjective and unhelpful. Tricia regarded her colleagues as excellent instructors, but she still wondered whether they were qualified to make off-the-cuff judgments about her teaching. "Besides," she wondered, "what will they be looking for? Is there really any one way to define high-quality instruction?"

She also wondered how they would be able to draw inferences from watching only one lesson at a time. "What if the one day I teach, I happen not to use cooperative learning? For all they know, I never let kids talk to each other. Is it realistic to think that colleagues can help each other by watching each other for a few hours a month?"

The fixed structure of Murphy's peer-observation process proved vital in helping Tricia understand what her colleagues would expect to see:

> If there were no steps or pre-designed process, I wouldn't have known how to prepare or what my peers would be watching. But the structured process provided an opportunity to focus the observation. In other words, the first time my colleagues watched me teach, they knew exactly what I was trying to

accomplish. More importantly, I knew what they were going to look for. That made all the difference.

In addition, the school used a common set of classroom expectations that teachers and administrators had developed collaboratively. These lists, an example of which is shown in exhibit 5.1, provided added structure to the observation process and helped clarify for Tricia—and for everyone—how a Murphy classroom should function. That being said, the classroom expectations were general enough that Tricia did not feel they stifled her creativity or pedagogical style. They simply made the school-wide expectations more transparent.

Finally, Tricia began to feel more at ease with the process of examining instruction after sitting through several of her grade-level teammates' lessons, which were followed by debriefing conversations about what students did or did not seem to be learning. "Once I saw how the process made the observation very focused and more about the learning than the teaching," she said, "I was ready to volunteer."

By observing her peers' lessons, Tricia had become familiar with the six steps of Murphy's process of examining instruction:

1. Focus the observation as a team and prepare the model lesson.

2. Introduce the lesson immediately prior to the observation.

3. Conduct and observe the lesson.

4. Debrief the lesson.

5. Plan the next steps for all members of the team.

6. Debrief the team-wide implementation.

EXHIBIT 5.1. *Classroom Expectations Document from Richard J. Murphy School (abridged)*

Expectations for Classrooms: Mathematics

- All classrooms should prominently post the times designated for Reading Workshop, Writing Workshop, and Mathematics.

- All classrooms should have an area set aside for books and reading

- All students should demonstrate awareness of workshop learning routines, such as when to transition from whole groups to small groups, or from group work to individual work.

Time	Practices and Content	EVIDENCE: What should we see?
15 minutes daily	Warm-up / Do Now	• Teachers facilitating Warm-up/Do Now. • Students engaged in Warm-up/Do Now on current content or skill review.
1 hour daily 80 minutes daily	Elementary Math - or - Middle School Math	**CLASSROOM** • Seating arrangements that facilitate collaborative learning • Classroom math materials ready for student use • Overhead projector for whole-group learning • Math Notebooks in desks or organized in central location • Display of math vocabulary on wall or in Math Notebooks • Larger manipulatives for classes of special-needs learners **STUDENTS** • Students learning from one another and through classroom discourse • Students spending most of their time working and discussing • Students working in pairs or groups under teacher direction • Students explaining their answers and choice of strategies • Students attempting to use the most efficient and accurate strategies • Students using math vocabulary in their oral and written answers • Students thinking about other ways to solve problems • Students thinking about the most efficient ways to solve problems • Students taking notes on current content **TEACHER** • Lesson introductions by teachers are kept to a minimum • Teacher asking questions that stimulate student thinking • Teacher facilitating students learning from one another • Teacher modeling efficient and accurate strategies • Teacher explaining and using math vocabulary • Teacher calling attention to different ways students have solved problems • Teachers using assessment data to plan instruction in math • Teacher providing students with opportunities to master basic facts • Teacher differentiating instruction for all learners as needed

EXHIBIT 5.1. *(continued)*

Time	Practices and Content	EVIDENCE: What should we see?
1 hour daily - or - 80 minutes daily	Elementary Math - or - Middle School Math	**STUDENT WORK** • Math Notebooks with warm-ups, math vocabulary, and reflections • Math work displayed explaining how students have solved problems • Math portfolios containing all assessments in all grade levels • Data displays reflect students' analysis of information
At least once every other week	Math Reflections	• Teachers posing questions related to current skills and/or concepts • Students utilizing math vocabulary in written reflections • Teachers providing brief responses to student reflections • Students maintaining reflections in Math Notebooks

Still, it wasn't until she began planning to teach her own model lesson to her peers that she fully understood the value of each step. Step one, *focusing the observation and preparing the lesson*, first meant choosing the skill that the lesson would cover. "Within the grade-level teams," said Angel Petrie, "we first use data to find common areas of needed improvement." Similarly, Holly noted that the skills taught in the model lessons were always "based on a need we found in the data." In terms of the Data Wise process, this meant that model lessons always targeted a predefined *learner-centered problem*.

Each grade-level team in Murphy's elementary school and each academic department in the middle school defined its own learner-centered problem. Earlier in the school year, teachers and administrators had realized that their students were performing poorly on nearly all the state test questions that required high levels of reading comprehension. After further discussions of the data, Tricia's second-grade team responded by focusing on vocabulary-building, a component of effective reading comprehension

that seemed to give their students particular trouble. They concluded that the learner-centered problem was that many students lacked strong strategies for learning new vocabulary words, and they set about focusing on this skill in the next few peer-observation sessions. Given this grade-level focus, Tricia chose to model a vocabulary-building lesson that she had taught successfully in her previous school on several occasions. The lesson she selected was designed to help struggling readers adopt the strategies stronger readers used when they confronted unfamiliar words in a passage.

At 8:30 in the morning on Tricia's observation day, several substitutes from the trained cadre arrived at the school and dispersed to their preassigned classrooms. Their arrival allowed Tricia to meet with her grade-level team for 45 minutes to carry out step two: *introducing the model lesson*. During the meeting, Tricia explained the lesson she was about to give, the materials she had prepared, and the goals she hoped to accomplish. She also described how she would gauge her own success in meeting those goals—namely, through informal questioning at the end of class. The team listened carefully to Tricia's goals and asked her what kind of observing and note-taking she would find most helpful. Tricia asked for suggestions, and one team member suggested that they take notes on what the students were actually doing and saying. Tricia liked this suggestion, and after thinking for a minute, she made it more specific by asking her colleagues to watch a few students in particular—one from each reading level represented in her class. She suggested that they even sit next to those students and observe their reactions during each part of the lesson. By asking her colleagues to focus on students with a range of reading skill levels, she hoped the observers would be able to discuss whether the transfer of reading strategies from strong to struggling readers was happening in the way she had planned.

At 10:00, it was time for step three: *conducting and observing the lesson*. Tricia returned to her classroom to take over for the substitute, while her grade-level team filed in and found seats near the students on whom they'd been asked to focus. The strategy of taking notes about focal students was one that Murphy teachers had used before, but it was just one of many in their repertoire. For example, when they observed lessons that focused on whole-class discussions, they often transcribed students' conversations word-for-word. Alternatively, if a lesson focused on asking higher-order questions, observers would transcribe the teacher's questions and later discuss each question's level of cognitive demand. The teachers had learned these careful analysis strategies by working

with Lauren Grace, a literacy coach who had facilitated their professional-development sessions the previous year and whom teachers regarded as a real expert.

As she began to teach, Tricia felt her heart beating wildly, but as the lesson got underway, she quickly relaxed and eased into business as usual. Tricia first introduced her second graders to the topic of figuring out unfamiliar words in a text. She distributed a short biography of Helen Keller, which contained some words that students were unlikely to recognize. Then she called on a few students to read the first parts of the story aloud. At the end of the read-alouds, she asked the class to name words they had just seen and heard but didn't know. Each time a student named a challenging word, she elicited his or her best guess as to what it might mean, and she asked how the student had arrived at that guess. Then she wrote their words and guessing strategies on the board. Finally, she gave students the actual definitions of the words, a few of which the students had surmised correctly. In wrapping up this mini-lesson, she summarized the different thought processes students had used to arrive at the correct definitions.

Next, it was time for the students to read independently. Tricia gave the students ten minutes to finish reading the book silently and to take note of unfamiliar words they encountered. As the students read quietly, the observers took their own notes on what the students were doing, recording whether they were staying on task, writing things down, rereading difficult sentences, and so forth. Next, Tricia directed the students to pair up with each other to show their words and talk about how they figured out the meanings. At the end of the lesson, Tricia gathered the whole class together to discuss the strategies they had used when they reached a tough word. The observers watched and documented all the strategies that students volunteered. For instance, one student mentioned how he had used a word's prefix to narrow down its meaning. Another student talked about figuring out the meaning of a word from the context of the story. To conclude, Tricia asked the students to try out someone else's strategy on a few other words she herself picked out from passages in the book.

As the lesson progressed, Tricia found herself looking forward to hearing her colleagues' observations. When teaching, she often wished that she had more than one pair of eyes so she could keep track of what several students were doing at once. Today, her colleagues were providing those extra pairs of eyes.

When Tricia wrapped up the lesson at 11:00, she and the observers met to carry out step four: *debriefing the lesson*. During the first part of their 45-minute meeting, the teachers gave Tricia feedback. Adhering to their goals from the pre-observation meeting, teachers first described what they had noticed about how students tackled difficult vocabulary. As their observation protocol suggested, teachers focused initially not on passing judgment or interpreting what they had witnessed, but on simply describing behavior they had seen with phrases like "I observed," "I heard," and "I wondered why." Tricia later remembered the tone of this conversation as helpful, supportive, and nonjudgmental.

The debriefing yielded two general findings. First, teachers were impressed by some of the students' sophisticated strategies for understanding unfamiliar words, such as

their attention to prefixes and context clues. Teachers realized that these students could be important resources for other readers in the class who, when they encountered tough vocabulary words, appeared just to shrug or move on. Second, the teachers realized that having students talk about their effective strategies with the other students did not necessarily ensure that the struggling students would adopt those strategies as their own. Tricia had ended the lesson with a review, in which some struggling readers had recounted their classmates' vocabulary-building strategies and tried out new ones. Nevertheless, it was impossible to tell from this lesson alone whether those students would begin to use the strategies in their own reading.

As the team talked about this limitation, they discussed ways that future lessons might help struggling students start to rely on their peers' vocabulary-building strategies. Buoyed by her colleagues' support and interest, Tricia felt her anxiety about hearing critical feedback swiftly dissipate. In fact, she was pleased to have this many educators thinking alongside her about ways to improve the lesson. Though she had taught the lesson many times before, she had never been able to stand outside the process and observe how each component played out. Now, as a result of her colleagues' observation, she had an opportunity to refine her tactics, eliminate weak or ineffective aspects, and focus on elements to which students had responded well. This, she felt, was the essence of examining instruction with one's colleagues. It was what she had missed in her years of teaching elsewhere.

The second part of the post-observation meeting was devoted to step five: *planning next steps for the team*, in which the second-grade team considered ways to improve their own practice by incorporating elements from the lessons they had just seen. For this part of the discussion, Tricia was a valuable resource. She had devised and planned the lesson and was now in a position to advise her team. The teachers unanimously decided they would try to build on Tricia's model lesson in their classrooms, and they discussed a variety of ways in which they might do so. For instance, one suggestion was that they could teach mini-lessons around student-generated strategies, perhaps using the student experts as lesson helpers. Then they could assess (through readers' notebooks or similar work) the extent to which students were using the strategies to interpret new words.

When the post-observation meeting adjourned, each team member planned to deliver a lesson to their students that would use aspects of Tricia's model lesson. However, they also planned to generate and try new ways to encourage students to adopt one another's vocabulary-building strategies.

One week after Tricia taught her model lesson, the second-grade teachers met to recount what happened when they implemented aspects of her lesson and tried to help students use one another's word-analysis strategies. In Murphy's process of examining instruction, this follow-up meeting was step six: *debriefing team-wide implementation*. Their meeting followed a standard format in which each teacher was given a few minutes to reflect on his or her teaching experi-

ences. After each person described his or her instructional approach and what happened in the classroom, the rest of the group asked questions and offered suggestions to address the speaker's needs. The meeting concluded with a few remarks by each teacher about any valuable lessons they learned during the process. As Tricia later recalled, "The sense of accountability was real, and the friendships were only strengthened by the high expectations we held for each other." The debriefing meeting concluded with the team making initial plans for the next round of peer observations, when a different teacher would choose a different vocabulary-based instructional strategy to model for the rest of the team.

After Tricia experienced this six-step process, she was no longer worried about teachers making snap judgments about her every move. Instead, she realized that the teacher leading the model lesson could focus the observation on areas in which he or she most wanted instructional feedback. She also understood that part of the value of being observed lay in having other sets of eyes to watch the dynamic processes of the classroom and gauge students' learning. Finally, she realized that each round was a learning experience for both the demonstrating teacher and the peer observers. Looking back, she regarded her first experience modeling a lesson as a kind of welcoming initiation, after which she felt more effective as an observer as well.

LEARNING FROM ONE ANOTHER

Tricia learned that even as a teacher new to Murphy, she possessed expertise that could benefit her colleagues, including those more senior and experienced than she. Modeling a lesson and receiving feedback was a two-way street of professional development: she was teaching her colleagues a new strategy, and they were helping her think about how to make it better so they all could add it to their teaching repertoires. "That is a huge part of being a professional," said Holly, "feeling like even the newest team member has something to contribute to the effectiveness of the whole team. It is great to model vulnerability and use positive feedback to improve your teaching."

Of course, the process of examining instruction also gave newer teachers a chance to benefit from their more senior colleagues' experience. Tricia, for instance, described an important, somewhat counterintuitive insight she gained from watching Holly's lessons:

> When I observe Holly, I realize that it is okay and even advisable to leave kids wondering about something. Before, I would always tell kids why things are the way they are. Now, when they are stuck, sometimes I'll say, "maybe you ought to sleep on that tonight and tell me what you think tomorrow." It's harder to let the learning emerge like Holly does—it takes more time and a lot more patience—but it is worth it.

After recognizing Holly's talent at encouraging students to generate their own conclusions, Tricia began to incorporate that pedagogical patience into her own lessons. The results, she said, were exciting:

> We were building patterns recently with cubes, in a lesson where I was trying to teach both patterns and odd/even numbers. I asked the students to make a pattern with two colors. Kids would all do red, blue, red, blue, red, blue. Then I asked them to draw a picture of it and number the cubes and mention anything they noticed. Immediately kids were saying: "Do you know what? When I number the pattern, all the red cubes are odd numbers and all the blue cubes are even." They developed a deep understanding of the concept of odd and even numbers. Before the peer-observation experience with Holly, I would have just told them what odd and even numbers were.

The second-grade teachers' peer-observation team provided powerful learning experiences for all its members. Holly, for instance, was enthusiastic about what she had learned by watching Tricia:

> I have learned from the way Tricia celebrates every student. It is a big deal when students explain things in her class. And the way she celebrates her students makes it so motivating. They all want to participate. If you walked into her room and asked to see their math notebooks, every kid would volunteer. She has this way of fostering a very positive environment.

In fact, Holly noted that observing Tricia's classroom had influenced her own practice and enhanced students' class participation:

> I have improved my teaching by watching Tricia, because while I used to celebrate only right answers, now I celebrate all students who are brave enough to take risks and answer questions. I get a lot more participation now, and I know that kids are learning more since they are willing to take risks even when they are not positive about something.

Tricia's initial experience with peer observation at Murphy was not unique. Teachers of various grade levels and academic subjects said they were pleased with the school's process of examining instruction. For example, Harry, the middle school math teacher, recalled an experience that had helped him better assess his students' mathematical knowledge and misconceptions:

> One of the teachers I worked with a few years ago was really good at pulling information out of children, teasing out what they knew and didn't know, and learning what misconceptions they had. She volunteered to do a model lesson that included a lot of questioning. This was very meaningful for me. It wouldn't have been as powerful had it come from a textbook or another type of professional development. Until you see someone engage real kids with high-order questions, you can't learn it.

Harry said he went on from that experience to "practice some of the techniques and talk about my efforts with colleagues. In my opinion, that is how you improve as a teacher." Harry's experience also reinforced his sense of professional community: "If you work in isolation in any profession, you stagnate. You can only become as good as your own internal resources and prior experience. Sometimes just a fresh set of eyes is all it takes for me to improve my teaching."

At Murphy, teams of teachers typically examined instruction at least four times per year, though some teams went through the process much more frequently. Examining instruction in this way not only helped teachers improve, but it also increased their sense of team responsibility. "It really does give every member of the teaching staff the sense of ownership and accountability to one another," said Holly. "When you decide as a team to try a new approach to a lesson, and

you know others are going to ask you how it went, you are more inclined not only to try it but to give it your best effort."

ROOM FOR IMPROVEMENT

While Murphy School had received recognition for its process of examining instruction, its overall use of data, and its students' outstanding success, the staff members still found room for improvement in two important areas: leadership and mindset. First, faculty agreed to keep finding ways to develop all teachers' leadership capacities. "There are still some teachers who have a lot to share but who don't feel comfortable taking leadership roles," said Angel. She explained that while the vast majority of teachers at Murphy regularly and fully participated in the peer-observation process, not all felt comfortable taking leadership roles or frequently modeling lessons. "I'm worried that some of our strongest teachers feel intimidated to step up and lead," Holly added. "I'd like to see a school full of teacher-leaders, though I'm not sure exactly what that would look like."

Second, teachers at Murphy agreed that it was sometimes difficult to prioritize peer observation because of the effort it required. They noticed that as the process of examining instruction lost its novelty, some teachers seemed to lose momentum, particularly those who had been sustaining the process for a while. "It is an easy trap for a veteran to fall into," said Holly, "to start thinking that peer observation is intended for the less-experienced teachers, and to resist the personal vulnerability necessary to learn from others." The consequence was that staff members had to be vigilant about maintaining their collaborative culture. Being vigilant meant not only bringing new Murphy teachers like Tricia into the fold but also sustaining enthusiasm among those who had helped build the culture from the ground up.

Teachers at Murphy felt confident that they were on an upward trajectory. As testimony to their continued growth, they cited two pieces of evidence: student learning and teacher satisfaction. First, staff members believed that the steady increase in student performance over the last few years was largely attributable to their sincere efforts to help one another become better teachers through peer observation. Second, despite teachers' initial hesitation to open their personal teaching practice to public view, staff members agreed that teachers' morale and effectiveness had improved markedly since Murphy had begun making practice public. Both trends indicated that the school was still moving in the right direction.

Tricia was grateful for her students' achievement growth, her own professional growth, and the sense of community she felt among her colleagues. She realized that coming to Murphy had definitely been the right move. "I realized shortly after arriving," she said, "that when you feel important to your team and supported by your team, you get better as a teacher, and your kids learn more. This improves the culture of the school and makes your career that much more fulfilling."

✳ LESSONS FROM THE CASE

Inherent in developing a peer-observation process like Murphy's is a dilemma familiar to many educators. On one hand, experienced educators recognize the truth behind Harry's statement about the risk of stagnation when professionals work in isolation. On the other hand, meaningful peer observation remains elusive for many schools, in part because of the closed-door culture to which many educators have become accustomed, and in part because of the logistical complexity of implementing regular, school-wide observations. Still, the success of Murphy—a large, urban school serving both elementary and middle grades—suggests that both obstacles can be surmounted. It also suggests that efforts to overcome these obstacles may be handsomely rewarded by increased teacher morale and improved student achievement. For any school ready to take a closer look at instruction, Murphy School's story of building and sustaining a collaborative peer-observation process offers several important lessons.

1. **Frame peer observations as nonthreatening.** Tricia's initial fear of "constant criticism" made her nervous about having peers observe her teaching. When teachers associate classroom observations with negative feedback and even career jeopardy, as some Murphy teachers did initially, it is not surprising that they are reluctant to share their teaching practice with others. The challenge is to develop an atmosphere of support, in which peer observation is seen not as threatening but as a natural, healthy part of professional growth. Educators can facilitate this mindset by being clear about the purpose of the observations and by modeling the process.

   Clarifying the purpose is the first step in creating a nonthreatening atmosphere. It is important to convey to teachers that peer observations are designed not as evaluations but as collective faculty learning experiences in which observers record what they see, avoid passing judgment, and debrief their observations with the teacher of the model lesson. At Murphy, when Tricia asked her observers to take verbatim notes on what individual children were and were not saying during the lesson, she not only prompted them to collect data that she needed, but she also helped focus their task of taking objective notes.

As Holly suggested, it can also be helpful for highly respected teachers to deliver the first few model lessons. By placing themselves in a vulnerable situation, these instructors highlight the fact that everyone makes mistakes and that mistakes should not impede growth. An alternative possibility is for a principal or another administrator to model a lesson. Seeing an administrator teach a lesson and consider feedback can be very meaningful to teachers. Many administrators entered their roles with the desire to be instructional leaders; the experience of modeling lessons may be both professionally rewarding to administrators and helpful to their staff. Admittedly, this approach can be a bit more challenging in a high school setting, since an administrator's knowledge of Latin or physics, for instance, may not be extensive enough for teaching a lesson. In this situation, administrators can model a lesson in a subject with which they feel comfortable or even study an unfamiliar unit until they feel prepared to teach it.

2. **Provide a clear structure for the peer-observation process.** Along with framing the peer-observation process as nonthreatening, Mary attributed a large part of her school's success with peer observations to the structure the staff created. By initiating a transparent, step-by-step process for focused observation, Mary and her staff helped minimize the threat of ambiguous expectations. Teachers like Tricia were especially reassured knowing they would have both the ability to choose a focus area and the opportunity to debrief the lesson with their peers immediately afterward.

   Having used a range of data to define a learner-centered problem—the essence of step four of the Data Wise improvement process—grade-level teams at Murphy School used that learner-centered problem to choose a focus for their peer observations. When teachers agree that there is ample evidence that the designated focus area is indeed an area of weakness for their students, they develop a shared sense of urgency for finding effective instructional strategies.

   The process of debriefing the lesson and deciding on next steps is important for at least two reasons. First, the debriefing discussion can generate answers to questions the teacher initially posed. Focusing the discussion on these initial questions and on predefined instructional goals ensures a meaningful experience for the whole group, including the teacher who just put his or her practice on display. Second, when the debriefing ends with teachers agreeing to implement an aspect of the lesson with their own students, staff members feel a level of accountability to one another to innovate, reflect, and improve. As Angel pointed out, knowing they have to report on their experiences motivates teachers to give it their all. Also, as Tricia noted, implementing successful techniques usually boosts teachers' satisfaction as well as students' learning. Everyone wants to be successful at what they do; examining instruction simply gives teachers a support structure that fosters their classroom success.

3. **Collaboratively define effective practice.** An essential part of effectively examining instruction is developing a shared understanding of high-quality instruction. *Data Wise* explains that without a common language that defines effective teaching and learning, peer observation can often lack focus and organization. However, teachers are sometimes hesitant to engage in conversations that would help them develop a shared understanding about effective practice. Their hesitation can stem from negative prior experiences and/or misunderstandings about what such a shared definition would require of individual teachers and the school as a whole. Studying Murphy's approach to developing a collaborative definition of effective practice can offer a solution to many teachers' concerns.

"Consistency not conformity," a phrase often repeated by teachers and administrators at the school, embodies Murphy's approach to developing a shared understanding of effective instruction. As Angel explained, "Consistency means uniformity of things that we all agree improve student learning, like limiting teacher talk time and having students work cooperatively. We also decide on consistency in certain classroom routines and time spent on various subjects. You can have a lot of freedom within these constraints." These shared beliefs about effective teaching were the foundation for Murphy School's "Classroom Expectations" documents, which the teachers and administrators developed collaboratively (one of which is displayed in exhibit 5.1). Murphy administration encouraged teachers to follow these guidelines for the sake of instructional consistency but left them free to work within that structure, recognizing the important role teachers' individual creativity plays in the student experience. Every school deals differently with the tension between consistency of practice and teacher autonomy. Both Murphy's story and our experiences with other schools suggest that extremes rarely work very well. In other words, principals who attempt to micromanage every detail of their teachers' pedagogy typically find themselves frustrated and their teachers disillusioned. On the other hand, principals who think that teachers perform best when left completely alone are often faced with wide variation in rigor among classrooms and a lack of mechanisms for sharing successful practices across the school.

It is important to note that discussions about effective practice that are not grounded in real classroom-observation data typically go nowhere. Murphy's story illustrates that educators can open effective discussions about pedagogy when they have classroom-observation data readily available. It also shows that the potential benefits of a collaborative approach are significant. Schools can begin by building a shared pedagogical vocabulary to ensure that staff can communicate clearly about teaching and learning. This sounds obvious but is often overlooked, and well-meaning educators can end up talking right past each other. Teachers can start building a common vocabulary by collaboratively defining and describing such terms as *scaffolding*, *child-centered*, and *differentiated instruction*. Sharing a common language and set of assumptions about good teaching makes it much easier for teachers to work collaboratively to improve instruction.

4. **Explore various styles of peer observation.** Murphy School used a "model lesson" approach to peer observation. This method requires a volunteer to teach a lesson that addresses a learner-centered problem, while observers record what they see and offer constructive feedback. However, there are other ways of designing a peer-observation process. Examining alternative approaches may be particularly helpful for large middle or high schools, where it can be difficult to find time for a team of teachers to observe a mutually relevant class and debrief afterward.

    Aside from the model lesson approach, another promising way to organize peer observations is to pair up teachers from the same academic department or grade level. If these teachers have common planning time, they may be available for debriefing after the lesson, although substitute coverage would be required during the observation. If they have different allotted planning times, they could observe each other during their planning times, but debriefing might have to take place after school. With such a buddy system, teachers often find it useful to plan a lesson together, watch each other teach the same lesson, and then debrief with an eye toward improvement of their lesson planning and delivery.

    Yet another approach to peer observations is more informal and may be a good starting place for schools that are new to the idea of examining instruction. Many principals encourage teachers to include one or more peer observations in their annual goals. If most or all of the staff members make peer observation a formal goal, then the practice may eventually become common enough that teachers see it as more helpful than threatening. The school's leadership team might promote this objective by leading discussions of teachers' peer-observation experiences during staff meeting time.

5. **Peer observation can also help schools define a problem of practice.** There remains one purpose for examining instruction that doesn't emerge specifically in Murphy's story but which is important to the Data Wise improvement process. Peer observation can be a valuable tool for helping staff members define a common *problem of practice*, or a statement of what teachers might do differently to address the learner-centered problem. The Data Wise improvement process suggests that schools identify a way in which teachers can modify their teaching to address the learner-centered problem across the school. To do this, they need to examine instruction in a variety of ways. In this context, examining school-wide instruction includes but is not limited to peer observation. It also includes surveys, focus groups, and informal conversations with teachers and students.

    In one high school we have worked with, students were struggling with math concepts that required critical thinking, and the staff had identified this as an important learner-centered problem. Test data showed that students were skilled in number sense and solving equations but that they had a hard time applying these skills to word problems or transferring them to new contexts. The leadership team, which included teachers and administrators, decided to observe each ninth-grade math class for ten or fifteen minutes. With the learner-centered problem in mind, the team noticed that during their visits, they didn't see even one instance of students being given the opportunity to do the kind of critical thinking relevant to the learner-centered problem. Instead, teachers presented the material for the day, and the students completed practice problems similar to the ones the teacher had worked out in front of the class.

In numerous observations on other days and in other classrooms, the team found the same lack of explicit demand for critical thinking skills. Hence, through their observations, team members had uncovered a problem of practice: teachers were not providing sufficient opportunities for students to apply their knowledge in various contexts or to think critically about the concepts they had learned. When shared nonjudgmentally, with concrete-but-anonymous examples, this finding actually galvanized the faculty. In a way, it affirmed that what they had been doing was very effective—they had been teaching students to solve decontextualized problems, and standardized test results showed that their students did that very well. However, the finding also highlighted a clear instructional need, and thus it prepared the staff for the next phase of the Data Wise improvement process, in which they would take action to improve teaching and learning.

✳ QUESTIONS FOR DISCUSSION

1. To what extent do teachers at your school engage in substantive conversations about instruction and share a common definition of effective instruction? How might you foster those conversations and help teachers develop a shared definition of effective practice?

2. How might teachers at your school respond to the idea of a peer-observation process like Murphy's? What might be their concerns? What features might you include in the process to assuage those concerns?

3. Think of a learner-centered problem that your school currently faces. How might a process of examining instruction help your staff members figure out a problem of practice underlying student learning difficulties? What would you focus on during peer observations? How could you use other strategies for examining instruction, such as surveys, focus groups, or interviews, to gain insight on ways to improve instruction across the school?

4. Think of a time you have had success with peer observation, and describe the situation. Explain what made it challenging and what you think made it ultimately successful.

Phase III: **ACT**

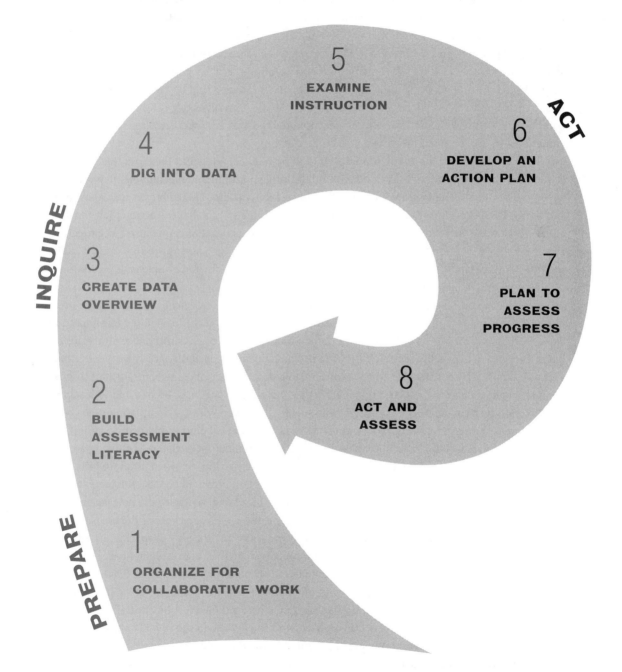

INQUIRE

PREPARE

ACT

5
EXAMINE
INSTRUCTION

4
DIG INTO DATA

6
DEVELOP AN
ACTION PLAN

3
CREATE DATA
OVERVIEW

7
PLAN TO
ASSESS
PROGRESS

2
BUILD
ASSESSMENT
LITERACY

8
ACT AND
ASSESS

1
ORGANIZE FOR
COLLABORATIVE WORK

Once teachers in your school have examined a broad range of data, identified an important area of student learning that needs improvement, and identified a problem of practice, it is time to take action. The *Act* phase of the Data Wise improvement process is the phase in which the rubber meets the road. This is the point at which your examination of data in the *Inquire* phase actually begins to drive instructional improvement across the school.

The act phase begins with step six, *Develop an Action Plan*, in which teachers craft an instructional plan to which they feel committed and accountable. This step involves choosing an instructional solution to the learner-centered problem—a process that began when you examined instruction in step five. Developing an action plan also involves deciding how broadly the solution will be implemented, how it can be implemented and adapted across grade levels and content areas, and on what timeline it will be carried out.

To help ensure that the action plan doesn't fall by the wayside amid the daily hustle of school life, any instructional improvement undertaking should include a concrete plan for measuring how well the changes are working. For this reason, *Plan to Assess Progress* is the seventh step in the Data Wise improvement process. The idea of this step is that the action plan must include measurable short-term, medium-term, and long-term goals that can be used to gauge the plan's success and guide revisions and improvements. Planning to assess progress means taking the time to agree upon and record those goals as a faculty, then devising a schedule to take stock of how well the plan is working to improve student learning.

The eighth and final step of the Data Wise improvement process, *Act and Assess*, is the point at which your school finally carries out the action plan. This step includes not just implementing new instructional strategies but also using data to measure how consistently those strategies are being carried out across the school. If they are not being used consistently, it is possible that the plan is too narrowly constructed to be applicable to a broad range of classrooms, or that teachers feel skeptical about new instructional strategies included in the plan. Ideally, many teachers helped craft the plan and feel committed to its success, but even when action planning has been collaborative, your school needs to examine how well the plan is being implemented and, if implementation is lackluster, to understand why. Acting and assessing also means using a range of student achievement data to determine whether students are indeed learning more from the new instructional approaches. If the approaches are being implemented consistently and student work is not improving, it is possible that teachers are still learning to master the new strategies, but it is also possible that the strategies themselves need to be refined or reconsidered.

In practice, the three phases of the Data Wise improvement process—preparing, inquiring, and acting—are less discrete than they seem on paper. As they are implemented, phases often blend and overlap. *Action*, for instance, is never completely divorced from *Inquiry:* schools continue to ask questions of data as they implement and assess their action plans. Similarly, teachers continue to build assessment literacy as they create a data overview and dig into data. Individual steps may also overlap within a phase, and thus you will see diverse approaches to action planning, implementation, and assessment in the three chapters that follow. These stories remind us that a school's approach to action planning is invariably tailored to the unique circumstances it faces.

Chapter 6

DEVELOPING
AN ACTION PLAN

Two Rivers Public Charter School
Focuses on Instruction

Michelle L. Forman

What is the ideal scope of an action plan to improve instruction? How much direction and discretion should school leaders offer their faculty in deciding how big of a bite to take? This case describes how Two Rivers Public Charter School comes to terms with these questions. After opening a new school that is committed to teachers' professional growth, the Two Rivers leadership team develops a collaborative process to help teachers use data to improve their practice. In doing so, the team realizes that half the battle is developing a shared, school-wide understanding of what makes an effective action plan. Over time—drawing on insights gleaned from the Data Wise improvement process—the team learns to help staff members choose, implement, and evaluate action plans that support real improvements in teaching.

In the fall of 2004, Two Rivers Public Charter School opened its doors to 152 students in grades preschool through three. Designed to grow in the next five years to serve students through grade eight, Two Rivers was founded in the District of Columbia by a group of local parents including Principal Jessica Wodatch, Instructional Guide Jeff Heyck-Williams, and Assistant Principal Jim May. The three administrators had been colleagues at their previous school before banding together to found Two Rivers. As longtime educators, Jessica, Jeff, and Jim had encountered a wide range of schools—both public and private—and they were determined to take the best of what they had seen and discard the worst. Their goal was to create a vibrant community of both staff and student learners. They each knew of schools where instructional initiatives were handed down from administrators like decrees from on high, and they firmly agreed that this was not going to be the Two Rivers model. They also believed that if they were to create a true learning organization, then ongoing, collaborative professional development would have to become the school's number-one priority. Not only did they personally want to be part of such a community, but they also had a clear mandate from the group of parent founders to ensure that Two Rivers teachers were

> **Two Rivers Public Charter School**
> *Washington, DC*
>
> Type: **Public, Charter**
>
> Setting: **Urban**
>
> Grades: **Preschool–5**
>
> Number of Students: **256**
>
> Number of Teachers & Administrators: **38**
>
> Students Qualifying for Free or Reduced-Price Lunch: **36%**
>
> **Students' Race/ Ethnicity Distribution**
>
> Asian   **2%**
>
> Black   **48%**
>
> Latino   **5%**
>
> Native American   **0%**
>
> White   **36%**
>
> Other   **9%**

comfortable in their role as learners.

Jessica, Jeff, and Jim understood that creating a collaborative culture from scratch would demand commitment, and commitment was a trait they had in spades. Also working in their favor was their crackerjack team of teachers, who brought both insight and passion to their work. Still, the effort needed to get a new school off the ground was enormous—there were no precedents to fall back on, so every policy and procedure had to be newly invented. Feeling that they were often being pulled in twenty directions at once, the leadership team found that their desire to create sophisticated professional development opportunities was periodically buried by more immediate demands.

In fact, it was not until the end of the school's first year of operation that the leadership team fully saw how essential it would be to ground the *staff's learning* in data about *student learning*. This insight had emerged piecemeal over the year. For instance, Jim recalled that the staff had "wanted to work on differentiating instruction, but our teachers were having a hard time. We realized we hadn't given them the tools to determine the ability levels of different students." Jessica, too, realized that the leadership team had not taken enough time with the staff to formulate a clear instructional vision. "We had teachers ask us how they were doing that first year," she recalled, "and we had no formal means of answering their question." It wasn't that teachers weren't talking to one another about instruction; rather, these conversations were not as systematic or rich as they might have been with a more structured, data-driven process.

Jessica, Jeff, and Jim now paused to acknowledge that the passion for the work which had carried them so far would not be enough to transform the plucky startup into an oasis of collaborative learning. They realized they would need to ground professional development in the collection and analysis of student assessment data. What was not yet clear was how they would bring that idea to life.

ACTION PLANNING TRIALS, ERRORS, AND INSIGHTS

That summer Jim and Jessica investigated various ways of working with data in schools. Guided by their research, they designed a three-step process to help teachers use data to examine and improve their own instruction. This initial process would involve grouping teachers into grade-level teams and having each team answer three questions: *Where do I want to go? Where am I now? And how will I get there?* As part of the approach, the members of a grade-level team would work together to identify something they wanted to do differently in their classrooms. Then they would make an action plan to try that strategy within the next week, and each teacher would collect data about how the strategy worked in his or her own classroom. The following week, the teams would reconvene during staff-meeting

time to share the data they had collected. By examining that data, they would determine how well their actions had paid off, and they would jointly decide whether to modify and extend the action plan or try something new. The school leaders designed the process as a "loop" or cycle in which data analysis from one teaching strategy would inform the development of a new or improved strategy.

Knowing that the teaching staff was already interested in data use, the leadership team was excited for the new data work to get underway in the fall. However, the three-step process, which was new and untested, got off to a rocky start. Jessica, Jim, and Jeff soon realized that in their enthusiasm to roll out the new approach, they had not anticipated all the possible pitfalls. "We launched the process," Jeff said, "but we didn't do it well. We went through a couple of cycles, and teachers were confused, and we were confused. Teachers would say, 'Here's my data, I tried this strategy . . .'" but the data did not necessarily show growth in student learning. While Jeff acknowledged that "the process *did* serve to get the faculty to start seeing itself as a learning community," he conceded that "we did not see it lead to much change in the classroom."

The first challenge the leadership team faced was helping teachers prioritize particular content-area goals. "Unfortunately," said Jeff, "identifying those goals proved more challenging than we originally thought." In keeping with the District of Columbia's academic content standards and their own high expectations, Two Rivers teachers had *many* goals for their students, including mastery of a wide range of academic content. Still, the leadership team felt it was important to base these goals on data from the school's twice-yearly mathematics and reading assessment. They asked teachers to set learning targets that addressed skills or concepts with which students clearly struggled.

The second challenge the leadership team faced was helping faculty arrive at a common understanding of *what kind* of changes each grade-level team should be implementing in its action plan. Several unforeseen problems with the size or focus of the grade-level teams' instructional action plans emerged at this stage. One problem was that some of the goals the grade-level teams generated were too narrow and imme-diate. Others goals were more ambitious but were not tied to specific student outcomes, and still others were mainly procedural and could be achieved with minimal instructional change.

An instance of narrow action plan-ning occurred when one team focused on a problem that emerged from the fall test results. "Our first-grade class identified their goal as: 'Students will associate the *th* sound with the *th* blend,'" Jeff remembered. "So the teacher taught a series of three lessons and brought back data showing that her students for the most part had mastered the *th* blend." Though the plan had been suc-cessful in helping students learn a concept they had not previously mastered, it tackled a fairly straightforward, isolated skill. Ac-cording to the process the leadership team had envisioned, the first-grade team's next move should have been to identify new strategies to attack the problem or to tweak the prior strategy. However, Jeff noted that

the follow-up step proved unnecessary in this case: "When the teachers looked at the data, no one had a suggestion about where she should go next other than 'continue what you are doing with other blends.'"

Realizing that they hadn't offered clear enough guidance about the scope or focus of the action plans, the leadership team now asked teachers to place their action plans within the context of instructional planning that was already underway. For example, the preschool and pre-K teachers were preparing a thematic unit on heroes, and the kindergar-ten and second-grade teachers were in the midst of refining how they used instructional centers in their classrooms. Jessica, Jim, and Jeff suggested to each group that they embed their respective action plans within these comprehensive planning efforts.

This approach did, in fact, lead teachers to choose goals that were more expansive. However, the leadership team again real-ized they hadn't clarified their expectations when they found that some of the resulting action plans lacked clear goals for improved student achievement. For instance, Jeff said the early-childhood team had decided that their students would "develop content knowledge within the context of a study on heroes," a goal that held vague promise but lacked specificity about the type of content knowledge that students would acquire. Each teacher had identified specific he-roes on which his or her class would focus (including mail carriers, guide dogs, and emergency medical technicians), but when it was time to collect data for the staff meeting, the team members' amorphous goal threw them off track. "They weren't clear about what data they should be bringing back to the group to analyze," Jeff said. "Connecting their plans to specific learning goals for early childhood was difficult, particularly when they had only defined their target as teaching content." He realized that he, Jessica, and Jim still hadn't clarified their vision for the faculty and that this could be because they, as a leadership team, were still working out the kinks in their own minds.

A third result of the unclear expectations was that some teachers set goals that were relevant to classroom procedures but peripheral to instructional improvement. For example, one teacher crafted a goal stating, "I will use running records to place students in guided reading groups." While the teacher was clearly thinking about how data could inform her decisions, her plan was more organizational than pedagogical. In other words, it had clear implications for the grouping of students but not necessarily for the instruction they would receive.

"The focus of our professional development is on kids, but it was hard to get clear on that," Jim said. "Teachers think, 'Is it about my own actions?' What it needs to be about is student data that reflects our actions." The leadership team realized that if teachers' work with data was to result in improved instruction, then they themselves—Jessica, Jeff, and Jim—would need to clarify that using data to guide instruction meant focusing on student-centered outcomes as measured by tests, class work, homework, and other evidence of student learning.

Even amid the trial and error, there were pockets of true success, and these helped to sustain the school's faith in a data-driven process. A turning point occurred when second-grade teacher Elaine Hou developed

an action plan to change the way she used literacy centers—areas of her classroom where students worked independently or in teams on such skills as spelling, word study, independent reading, or guided reading. The center that Elaine found most vexing was independent reading because the work of that center did not generate a written product. Elaine had tried to introduce accountability by having students complete character maps, summary pictures, or cause-and-effect descriptions of the books they were reading, but she did not find the resulting products to be very illuminating:

> Before I engaged in this data work, the literacy centers in my classroom were diverse and lively. Students were engaged in many forms of reading and writing in independent crews. However, we did not have a formal system to capture their learning beyond general tasks and anecdotal notes, which made it difficult to use what students were doing in literacy centers to drive instruction.

As part of the team focusing on literacy centers, Elaine knew that her independent-reading center was the one she most wanted to improve. She identified just one concept—cause and effect—and decided that in her action plan, she would teach a series of mini-lessons helping students describe cause-and-effect relationships in books they read independently. Then she decided to ask students working in the independent-reading center to focus *only* on the cause-and-effect description assignment. Finally, she used students' work on the assignment to guide what she taught in the next mini-lesson. After several mini-lessons informed by students' work, Elaine brought recent cause-

and-effect assignments to the data team to analyze. The team felt that the assignments showed marked improvement over what students had previously produced in the center. It appeared that the series of data-informed mini-lessons had improved students' ability to describe cause-and-effect relationships in books.

Looking at the work with her peers also gave Elaine ideas about how to extend students' learning: "I realized I could use this process for *any* literacy center or for any other learning structure in the classroom," she said. Jessica also remembered Elaine's elation: "When she brought back data after making her instructional changes, Elaine was able to see an increase in the caliber of her students' work. After that, Elaine became convinced that looking at data was an amazingly helpful strategy. She became a data convert."

As the school year drew to a close, stories like Elaine's reinforced the leadership team's conviction that a strong learning organization depended on the systematic use of data. Still, the team was not satisfied with the overall outcomes of the data process. They knew they were still on the steep part of the learning curve. Not enough teachers had been able to translate what they had learned from analyzing their data into concrete instructional improvements. Jeff, Jessica, and Jim were determined to figure out how to better support their teachers not only in finding an appropriate focus for their action plans but also in crafting the kind of lessons that would yield student data appropriate for in-depth examination. Otherwise, the team feared, their data work would never result in meaningful changes to practice or improved student learning.

TURNING INWARD, THEN LOOKING OUTWARD

At the close of the school year, Jim, Jeff and Jessica sat down to discuss how to modify their approach. First, they talked about how to clarify their action-planning expectations so that teachers focused on instruction and measurable learning outcomes. However, in examining their own tacit expectations about what good action plans should entail, they realized that they needed to learn about how other schools had used data effectively. They also wanted to expand their own and their faculty members' understanding of children's cognitive development. As Jessica explained, that would mean seeking outside sources of expertise:

> We realized that we as a staff lacked expertise in such key areas as: How do children learn to read, and how does one reading skill build on the next one? Or, how do you diagnose a problem in basic math comprehension that might be causing other problems? Basically, how do the skills our kids learn in preschool and pre-K affect the issues they're going to have in third and fourth grade? We needed to know these things. We needed more education.

Cognizant of the gaps in their own knowledge, the team used the summer months to seek external expertise on a number of topics, including the use of data to guide instructional improvement. Hoping for insight on how to refine their data-use process, Jim and Jessica headed to Harvard for a week at the Data Wise Summer Institute. As they learned about the Data Wise improvement process, they were pleased to note several ways in which it was consistent with what they had already been doing. Not only did Two Rivers already emphasize staff collaboration and professional development, but they also had been using test data to identify areas of student weakness, developing instructional plans to address those areas, setting improvement goals, and

> ## "When she brought back data after making her instructional changes, Elaine was able to see an increase in the caliber of her students' work."

collecting data on how well their plans had worked. Still, the points of divergence were what gave Jim and Jessica food for thought. Their first "aha" moment at the institute concerned the very challenge they had been grappling with all year: the scope of the task they would set for their teachers. Institute presentations about developing an action plan convinced them that their data process needed a *specific focus* grounded not in a very narrow skill (like the *th* blend) but in the details of effective pedagogy.

"'You have to get specific.' We heard it over and over again at the institute," Jessica remembered. She also knew that getting specific would be a painful process: "We had so much to focus on in those first years—implementing Balanced Literacy, Everyday Math, the Science and Social Studies Learning Expeditions. We had all new programs, new kids, and a new staff. We knew that we were most concerned about our reading scores, but focusing on reading meant we would

not be focusing on math or science or social studies." Despite this tension, a presentation by Harvard professor Richard Elmore, an expert on school reform, had a strong effect on them. "Richard said 'if it's not specific, it doesn't matter.' A focus on reading was too broad, a focus on comprehension was too broad . . ." Getting specific, Jessica recalled, was take-away number one.

Take-away number two came later in the week. At the institute's final presentation, three Boston-area principals well advanced in their data work came to discuss how the Data Wise improvement process was being implemented in their schools. Jim remembered Mary Russo, principal of Boston's Murphy School, handing out a list of classroom expectations that the teachers had developed, which she referred to as "The Murphy Way." Jim recalled Mary explaining that the classroom expectations listed on the sheet were valued across the school and used consistently across grades (see exhibit 5.1 in chapter 5).

Seeing Mary's presentation reignited an interest that the Two Rivers leadership team had been pondering—namely, how to support their students' long-term intellectual development by establishing continuity across grades. "We had started to see certain practices evolve across the grades," Jessica reflected. "And we saw that kids who had been with us longer were able to fall in with those practices more quickly and get more learning done." Hearing from Mary Russo at the institute confirmed Two Rivers' commitment to becoming more directive and intentional in the strategies their teachers used and helped them recognize that they could use their data work as a means to do so. Jim and Jessica began to discuss the idea of creating a set of shared classroom expectations called "The Two Rivers Way." They also talked about asking all teachers to focus on a single, school-wide learning objective in their data work for the coming year. In short, takeaway number two was getting everyone on the same page with regard to instruction.

Back in Washington, Jim, Jessica, and Jeff began to plan for the summer orientation and a new, improved process for data-driven professional development. "We spent twelve or fourteen hours on conversation, and then three full days of planning. It was a huge time commitment and an exhausting process, but we loved it," said Jessica. Jim agreed, saying, "We can't overstate the planning that goes into professional development at Two Rivers. We know that our staff is everything, and our job is all about keeping the staff learning." During these planning sessions the three filled an entire wall with adhesive notes detailing everything they hoped to cover in the coming year's professional development. Then they began to get specific themselves and to zero in on data work.

GETTING ON THE SAME PAGE

When school resumed that fall, the data process at Two Rivers looked quite different from the previous year's approach. The biggest difference was that action-plan implementation would occur at the school level instead of at individual grade levels. As Jeff explained, "We tightened the process into a cycle during which the entire school would study a single strategy in depth."

Also, each professional-development cycle now focused on a particular student learning objective that emerged from an area of student weakness in the data—what the Data Wise process calls a *learner-centered problem*. While individual grade-level teams had previously used test scores to identify areas where their own students were struggling, the leadership team was now heeding Richard Elmore's exhortation to "get specific" about which particular skills the whole school should focus upon. Results from the newly implemented District of Columbia accountability test and their own internal assessments demonstrated that Two Rivers students struggled with reading comprehension and mathematical problem solving. The team saw that information as a useful starting point, but they realized that these content areas were too broad, by themselves, to determine targeted instructional goals. They would need to identify a more specific learner-centered problem and then tie it to what Data Wise calls a *problem of practice*—a particular teaching challenge that was contributing to the learner-centered problem across the school.

In thinking about problems of practice the faculty could work on to improve students' reading comprehension and mathematical problem solving, the leadership team turned to each other, to the staff members, and to the literature. They sought rich, multifaceted issues that could be taught with different levels of sophistication at different grade levels. "We wanted something grades preschool through five could understand," said Jessica, and they wanted to emphasize that what students learned in early grades made a major difference in later grades. Jeff bounced ideas off the other leadership team members and talked with teachers about what skills they felt the school needed to emphasize. After much thought, conversation, and reading, the team defined two problems of practice on which they would focus in the next two data cycles: teaching students to *make connections to text*, and teaching them to *use data tables to solve mathematical problems.*

As they prepared to share with faculty the new approach to data, the leadership team acknowledged to one another that choosing school-wide learning objectives felt tricky. From its inception, Two Rivers had used an instructional model that advocated teachers' flexibility and autonomy. Also, the school had a philosophy of "active pedagogy," which meant that lesson plans were generated on an ongoing basis rather than reused from year to year. While this practice kept teachers' instructional methods fresh, it also resulted in considerable variation from one classroom to the next. Still, the team had no intention of asking teachers to implement a scripted or inflexible curriculum—far from it. Instead, because the instructional action plan would be implemented in classrooms from preschool to fifth grade, the plan was that each grade-level team would devise a way to teach the school-wide learning objective in a manner appropriate to its students' age group. The teachers who weighed in early on this new approach said they expected the common area of instructional focus to bring clarity and consistency to the data process.

Another feature of the data process that had changed from the prior year was the structure of the cycle itself. This year, in an effort to build up the staff's shared pedagogical knowledge base, Jeff and the leadership team had allocated time for reading and discussing professional literature about the school-wide learning objective. The purpose of this step was to allow faculty to explore, debate, and understand the pedagogical rationales underlying their action plans. The new data process also placed increased emphasis on model lessons and peer observation, and it incorporated a number of discussion and reflection templates (professionally designed by a Two Rivers parent) for such tasks as responding to professional literature, observing model lessons, planning future lessons, looking at student work, and reflecting on action plan results. The core steps of the data process were as follows:

1. During a staff meeting, teachers read a professional article describing the new school-wide learning objective (e.g., making connections to text). Then, Jeff taught a model lesson that informed teachers about the new objective while demonstrating how they might teach it. Next, teachers discussed the model lesson and the professional reading. In grade-level teams, they then devised a lesson plan with measurable objectives that each would teach before the next staff meeting, and they planned how they would assess the lesson's effectiveness.

2. Teachers delivered to their students the lesson they had jointly planned. They also collected students' work so they could assess how well the lesson had met its objectives.

3. At the next staff meeting, in grade-level teams, teachers used protocols to share and analyze the student work they had collected. Based on their findings, they developed a follow-up lesson and planned how they would collect data to assess its effectiveness.

4. Teachers taught the new lesson to their students and observed another member of their respective grade-level teams delivering the lesson. They also collected data from their own students' work in response to the lesson.

5. At the next staff meeting, teachers discussed what they had learned from the peer observations, and they again shared and analyzed student work in grade-level teams. Finally, they wrote and shared reflections about their learning from the whole action-planning cycle.

In practice, this approach to planning, evaluating, and revising an action plan using student data led to provocative conversations about how to develop students' sophisticated cognitive skills. For example, at the first staff meeting devoted to making connections to text, Jeff asked the faculty to read an article on reading comprehension. This literature explained that skilled readers comprehend and retain information they read by automatically making mental connections to their personal experiences, knowledge of the world, and recollection of other texts they have read. Teaching students to make connections meant making this cognitive strategy explicit so novice readers could consciously incorporate it into their reading habits. Jeff facilitated a discussion in which

teachers defined what it meant to make connections, explained why good readers make connections when they read, and described how good readers use those connections to deepen their understanding. Teachers were also asked to review the District of Columbia learning standards to determine how and where the target strategy fit in. After this discussion, the faculty broke into grade-level teams to decide what this skill would look like for their students and what teaching strategies their lessons should entail.

Still, it was only *after* all teachers had taught their initial lessons and had brought students' work back to their grade-level teams that teachers really understood the power of using student work to assess and revise an action plan. For instance, Elaine and the second-grade team had taught students to make text-to-self connections (in which students attend to similarities between their own lives and the lives of characters in a book) and had asked students to write each of their text-to-self connections on adhesive notes as they read. The next week, Elaine brought all of her students' adhesive notes to the staff meeting on a pad of poster paper. The other teachers analyzed the students' connections using a discussion protocol in which Elaine herself could listen but could not respond or explain. By listening to her colleagues' feedback, Elaine realized that students had made many kinds of connections. Some of these connections were quite insightful, but many others, such as "Arthur has a red sweater, and so do I," did not seem likely to enhance their understanding of the books they were reading.

Connections of this nature prompted a staff-wide debate as to whether superficial connections were a necessary starting point, especially for students in the early grades. Everyone agreed that older students should be able to make more sophisticated text-to-world and text-to-text connections, eventually developing the skill of identifying subtle thematic similarities across texts or situations. However, teachers of older students who *had* taught their students to make text-to-world or text-to-text connections pointed out that they had also observed some superficial connections. One teacher, at this point feeling skeptical, said to Jeff, "Help us understand how this helps kids." Jeff explained that making connections among similar situations or themes is a skill that lies at the heart of critical thinking. It is central, he reminded them, to the use of precedents in legal arguments and to the use of tropes and genres in literature. It is why action films and romantic comedies seem novel to adolescents but hackneyed to veteran filmgoers. In fact, he noted, the ability to make connections between situations is what allows each of us to learn from experience and to apply past insights to new circumstances.

Hearing Jeff's justification of the making-connections strategy, third-grade teacher Sarah Garb thought of a way to modify her next lesson on making connections. She began teaching students to respond to three prompts about their reading: *I read ——, which reminds me of ——, and from this I conclude ——.* The final prompt marked her attempt to teach students *why* they were making connections. When she brought the results of the revised lesson to the next staff meeting, she and her colleagues noticed that prompting students for their conclusions had improved the sophistication of the connec-

tions they made. Jessica said that "having really on-top-of-it teachers giving each other very honest, critical feedback" seemed to catalyze this kind of teacher innovation.

Though data use was off to a great start that year with the "making connections" action plan, the school-wide focus of the second action plan—using a data table in mathematical problem solving—proved trickier than the first, particularly for the early-childhood teachers. "What would creating mathematical tables look like at the pre-K level?" Jim remembered the teaching team asking. "What authentic experiences exist in which we could ask our students to think in this way?"

At first, the pre-K team considered having students use a data table to record how many animals of each type they saw at the zoo or how many cars passed by the school, but they came to the conclusion that this was just information gathering. "Using a table in that way would entail no thinking from their students; no problem solving or depth," said Jim. So the pre-K team shifted their thinking to consider their students' current needs and realized they were already working on different ways to add to ten. "They ultimately decided to physically create a table in the classroom by taping squares on the rug," Jim explained. "Then they used it for students to record different ways they could create the number ten by putting a different number of blocks in each column." In this three-by-two table, which is shown in exhibit 6.1, teachers asked students to place exactly ten wooden blocks in each row. In row 1, the students put five blocks in column A and five blocks in column B—a 50-50 split. In row 2, they put nine blocks in column A and one block in column B. In row 3, they placed six blocks in column A and four in column B. By doing this, the students found three different combinations that equal ten and also began learning some basic terminology for data tables, such as "rows" and "columns."

EXHIBIT 6.1. *Pre-K Team's Table for Recording Ways to Make the Number Ten*

	A	B
1	☐☐☐ ☐☐	☐☐☐ ☐☐
2	☐☐☐ ☐☐☐ ☐☐☐	☐
3	☐☐☐ ☐☐☐	☐☐ ☐☐

To collect data on whether students understood the concept or were just moving blocks, the pre-K teaching team created a replica of the taped grid on a table top where individual students could try the exercise on their own. In planning how they would assess progress, they developed a set of expected responses to the challenge that would serve as criteria for success. Students would be considered to have mastered the task if they could create a different configuration from the whole-group model on the rug and if they completed the task using exactly ten objects. Teachers would take photographs of the finished products and bring them to the staff meeting for discussion.

In the first round of data collection, they asked their students to come to the table in groups but quickly realized that this method was problematic: "The team noticed that the more able students took on the task immediately, and the other students in the group would attempt to copy the first kid's work," Jeff recalled. The second time around, the team altered their data collection process by having students come to the table individually. This modification allowed them to bring photographs to the staff meeting that best represented the achievement of each student.

Like the pre-K teachers, teachers of special subjects (including drama, Spanish, and physical education) also had to get creative when integrating the school-wide learning objectives into their curricula. The leadership team believed that professional development should strive to include everyone, so they worked with the special-subject teachers to find a way to make the action plans relevant to their work. "Our major goal is to help kids become effective people with strong skills in literacy, math, social studies, et cetera," said Jessica, "and that mission needs to be tied throughout the school. Our teachers need to realize that literacy skills don't just get developed when it's time for language arts."

The school's commitment to include everyone in the action-planning process meant that the special-subject teachers formed the equivalent of a grade-level team during the staff meetings, and they worked together to adapt the school-wide learning target to their classes and their own instructional goals. During the action plan devoted to making connections, P.E. teacher Craig Peppers found a way to maintain his goal of keeping students active for forty-five minutes while simultaneously teaching them to make text-to-self connections. "The goal of this assignment," he said, "was for third-grade students to gain a deeper understanding of the skeletal system by making authentic connections to self." The lesson was part of the P.E. curriculum that called for students to learn about the 206 bones in the human body. "When I introduced the specific bones, I asked students to touch and move the [corresponding] bones in their body. . . . We also discussed what action each bone allowed them to perform during any physical activity."

To measure how well students had learned the material, Craig handed out an illustration of the skeletal system and asked students to label the illustration from memory. He designed the lesson to take only 30 minutes, leaving 15 for an outdoor game that would give students some exercise. Craig's lesson stayed true to the underlying principle embodied in the school-wide objective—deepening students' learning by helping them connect the curriculum to their own lives. By creatively adapting the specific details of the school-wide learning objective, Craig was able to help implement the action plan without sacrificing his goals for students' physical education.

The special-education teachers were also integrated into the data process, although in a somewhat different fashion. They were not asked to collect data on their own but to help other teachers implement their chosen strategies and collect achievement data in a manner appropriate for special-education students. Despite the challenges inherent to the school-wide approach, Jim, Jeff, and Jessica were gratified that focusing on a common strategy seemed to have increased teachers' feelings of professional community across the school.

First-grade teacher Laura Marsh appreciated that the data process had prompted

faculty to think in terms of common, school-wide strategies. Even though she had initially struggled to figure out a way to make the mathematics problem-solving strategy applicable to her young students, she found that connecting her work to a school-wide action plan gave her a clearer understanding of the big picture: "Our work with data helped me to fit myself and my program into the school-wide goal. It gave me a better understanding of what we're all trying to accomplish. Because we're doing this as a faculty, we get presented with the span of what we all need to cover, so we can always figure out where we want to place our next focus." As an added dimension of the common focus, Laura found that the shared expectation that all teachers would work on a specific skill enhanced her commitment to implementing the changes in her classroom. "When you're working on a strategy by yourself, you can fudge it," she admitted, "but when you're working on a strategy as a whole faculty, you have the social accountability."

CELEBRATING SUCCESS WHILE ANTICIPATING FUTURE CHALLENGES

As the school's second year of data work drew to a close, the staff felt they had made progress worthy of celebration. First, the leadership team had led the entire faculty to focus on two concrete instructional practices that responded to students' demonstrated learning needs. Second, the team had refined their professional-development sessions to support teachers in devising action plans, implementing instructional changes, gathering student achievement data, and changing their instruction in light of the results. By focusing on broadly defined strategies that would become more sophisticated as students grew, the staff had begun to define a "Two Rivers Way" in which faculty shared an instructional repertoire and an underlying knowledge base. Jeff was pleased that the administrators "were able to help teachers develop a lesson with reasonable learning targets defined narrowly enough" to provide a clear focus for data collection.

Jessica was also enthusiastic about the progress Two Rivers had made that year. "We have no regrets," she said. "We couldn't have done it any better. We needed to engage in the process, and we're not going to set our expectations too high. You can't just say, 'We're going to become a data-driven school.' You need to spend the time to do it right."

Despite having built a healthy community focused on professional development, the leadership team knew they still faced challenges in perfecting their efforts to use data to drive instructional improvement. As the school "grew up" by adding middle school grades over the next three years, maintaining a single, school-wide focus would become an even greater challenge. "Educating three-year olds and ten-year olds and twelve-year olds are very different propositions," Jim pointed out. "And identifying strategies broad enough to be applicable to all grade levels but specific enough to ground conversations in concrete classroom practices will be quite difficult." Nevertheless, Jim and the rest of the team were still committed to maintaining the sense of connection and continuity that they had begun and fostering a version of the "Two Rivers Way" appropriate for both elementary and middle schools. "As we bring in new students and faculty and grow into a middle school," said Jim, "we hope to carry over some of the culture we've created but to make the experience different too." Specifically, they hoped to keep the strategy and culture of the data work consistent across grade levels, even as the process itself evolved to meet the needs of an expanding learning organization.

✳ LESSONS FROM THE CASE

The Two Rivers leadership team's early ups and downs illustrate the inherent difficulty of designing a powerful action plan even when you have a collaborative and motivated staff. Perhaps especially in a new school, where there is no institutional memory to fall back on, selecting the size, scope, subject, and focus of an instructional plan requires making a number of tough choices and then carefully monitoring their payoff. Still, the school's eventual success in choosing, implementing, and assessing two instructional action plans highlights the importance of creativity and persistence in this process. Amid the daunting work of creating and running a new charter school, Jessica, Jim, and Jeff grappled with how to provide the balance of structure and supports that would guide teachers toward instructional improvement. It is a testament to the value of "revising as you go" that even as they worked to find a suitable action-planning process for their faculty, the leadership team was implementing, assessing, and revising their own metaplan for school-wide professional development. Thus, on multiple levels, the experience of the Two Rivers leadership team illustrates several noteworthy aspects of a school-wide improvement process.

1. **Action plans should emerge in response to data about student learning.** The overarching goal of the Data Wise improvement process is to help educators sharpen their instructional practice in the service of improved student learning. Action plans should therefore directly respond to problems of understanding or skill that are common to many students and which, if solved, would contribute to the larger goals of the school. A broad array of data sources can provide insight into these problems. Two Rivers' leadership identified areas of their students' weakness through a focus on internal assessments and, later, through a district-wide accountability test. To identify learner-centered problems, schools can also gather student such data as in-class and independent work, classroom observations, and direct reporting from students in focus groups or surveys. Regardless of the type of data schools utilize in the improvement cycle, an identified area of student difficulty should be the problem that drives the action plan.

   A brief caution is nevertheless in order. In Two Rivers' first year of data use, some grade-level teams interpreted students' diagnostic test results to mean that they should focus on very narrow skills, such as weak knowledge of the *th* blend. We have seen entire schools adopt strategies akin to the *th*-blend approach in a well-meaning but misguided attempt to let students' performance on single test items or clusters of items drive their curricula. As chapter 2 notes, single test items are not only narrow but unreliable. Moreover, even if there are many test items showing weakness on the same very narrow skill (such as using commas with quotation marks or factoring polynomials with the quadratic equation), devoting grade-level or school-wide action plans to these skills may not be the best use of time and resources. Such skills are certainly worth mastering (as are consonant blends!), but they are fairly straightforward to teach, and taken alone, they lack far-reaching implications for a student's general academic achievement. A more proactive approach is to look, as Two Rivers did, at high-leverage skills with which students are struggling (such as understanding prose passages or tabular data) and to develop and refine ways of teaching those skills more effectively.

2. **Action plans should focus on how to improve instruction.** This lesson is less intuitive than it seems. When they were still becoming familiar with the process of action planning, some grade-level teams at Two Rivers developed plans that did not directly change their instructional practice. That they did so is both commonplace and completely understandable. In the absence of clear parameters about what the action plan should entail, thoughtful educators often gravitate toward peripheral changes that they value but have not had time to prioritize. Topics like classroom discipline and organization, school supplies management, and data management are common choices. Nor is there anything especially wrong with these choices, except that focusing on these issues rather than on pedagogical change does not further the goal of instructional improvement, which is central to the Data Wise process. While these issues may have an indirect effect on some students' learning, they are unlikely to result in a systematic improvement in student achievement.

In Two Rivers' second year of data work, the leadership team directly addressed this problem by determining that all action plans would require teachers to implement a specific instructional strategy that addressed a measurable learner-centered problem. The leadership team also took other steps to ensure that instructional improvement remained front and center. For instance, they asked teachers to discuss professional literature that pertained to a learner-centered problem, to develop and teach a lesson that might mitigate that problem, and to share data with their peers about the success of that lesson. While the most appropriate strategies for keeping the process focused on instruction will vary from school to school, the centrality of instructional change is nonnegotiable for an action plan focused on raising student achievement.

3. **Action plans should include measurable goals for improved student learning.** An essential part of designing a strong action plan is deciding how to measure progress toward the stated goals. One problem that the Two Rivers leadership team encountered in the early stages of their data work was that some teachers developed action plans that lacked measurable achievement goals. For instance, the early-childhood team defined their goal as "students will learn content in the context of a study on heroes," but when the time came to collect data, they realized that they had not determined how they would know whether students had met this goal. Thus, in the school's second year of data work, Jeff used a series of planning templates to encourage faculty to plan ahead for how they would measure student learning. He asked teachers not only to outline the instructional strategies they would employ but also to state concrete and reasonable objectives for student learning. In particular, he prompted teachers to ask themselves, "How will I collect data on student achievement of the learning target?" and "How will I measure success?" One group that responded creatively to such prompting was the early-childhood team. They established criteria for what students' successful use of data tables would look like, and they took photographs to determine whether students had met the target.

Too often, educators begin implementing the strategies outlined in their action plans without considering how they will assess student achievement, and as a result, they are unlikely to know whether they are making progress. In fact, this is a challenge facing the Mason School at the beginning of the next chapter, which focuses on planning to assess progress. We suggest that action plans include ways of measuring student learning throughout the year rather than relying only on annual state test results. In our experience, schools benefit from setting clear goals for student growth and proficiency and deciding in advance how and when they will measure progress toward those goals.

4. **Action plans are collective endeavors.** Whenever possible, developing an action plan should be a collective undertaking. At Two Rivers, when teachers came together with a shared focus on making connections to texts, they began to push one another's thinking and pedagogy, and they challenged each other to look carefully at student work. In other words, they catalyzed and supported collective learning across the entire school.

We stress that action planning should be a collective endeavor for two reasons. The first is that, in our experience, the more teachers are involved in choosing the instructional strategies for the action plan, the more committed they are to the challenging work of implementing them. The second is that the Data Wise process is intended to provide a structure for the amorphous task of turning schools into organizations capable of instructional learning. The act of coming together to develop instructional solutions to students' learning needs can foster professional community among faculty. In order to design an action plan, teachers must come to some agreement about expectations for student learning and ways to help students meet those expectations. Furthermore, the debates that precede an agreement may sharpen the whole community's thinking about pedagogy. As described in chapter 5, the Murphy School saw marked improvement in student achievement as teachers established common instructional expectations, values, and repertoires across the school. If school leaders allow teachers to develop action plans in isolation, they forgo the opportunity to build cohesion and collaborative learning among their staff—qualities consistently associated with improving schools.

That being said, asking every teacher in the school to implement a variation of the same instructional strategy, as the leadership team did at Two Rivers, may not be appropriate in every context. High schools, schools with very large student populations, or schools with many skeptical staff members may approach action planning in a variety of ways. For instance, a high school principal might ask teachers to develop departmental action plans to cultivate vertical alignment from grade to grade within the school's science, math, social studies, and English curricula. Alternatively, a school with many reluctant staff members might choose to pilot the Data Wise process with a particular grade level or group of teachers who are interested in the work, in the hope that their success might serve to encourage others in the future. Of course, the Two Rivers story suggests that even schools that adopt schoolwide learning targets can leave room for flexible adaptation of those targets. Jessica, Jim, and Jeff found that in terms of collegiality, depth of faculty discussions, and academic consistency, the benefits of getting everyone "on the same page" were worth the challenges.

Another aspect highlighted in the Two Rivers case was the leadership team's conscientious inclusion of *all* faculty members into their action planning. In the second year of data work, the team insisted that special-subject teachers integrate the work of the plan into their classrooms and that special-education teachers take on a consulting role to ensure that action planning addressed the needs of special-education students. As Jessica said, if the school was going to achieve its mission of turning all students into skilled practitioners of literacy, critical thinking, and mathematics, then the work of the faculty needed to go beyond the limits of English or mathematics lessons. In general, schools should work to ensure that action planning and data-driven professional development do not exclude faculty who teach nontested subjects, for if any task calls for all hands on deck, it is the task of improving student learning and achievement.

5. Action plans should be grounded in collective understanding. At Two Rivers, the leadership team made a concerted effort to ensure that teachers understood the school-wide learning objective inside and out. Jeff set out to equip the whole staff with a common body of pedagogical knowledge, and he encouraged discussion and debate about the rationale for each skill. The result was that teachers were intellectually engaged with the strategies they were working to implement. The cost of such a strategy is that it is unquestionably time-consuming. However, by leading their staff on this kind of collective investigation, the Two Rivers administrators reaped numerous benefits. First, both they and the faculty gained new knowledge about how students learn, and this knowledge improved their ability to make instructional decisions. By its very nature, action planning asks teachers to choose instructional solutions for identified areas of student need. As the Two Rivers team acknowledged, faculty needed to be armed with rigorous information in order to make wise choices. Taking care to nuture a collective understanding of effective instructional practice is a critical step in action planning. We have seen schools forgo the benefits of collective learning as they choose the first handy "solution" as the focus of their plan. In contrast, the Two Rivers leadership team increased the faculty's knowledge base, gave teachers an understanding of "the big picture," and fostered teachers' commitment to successful action-plan implementation.

✳ QUESTIONS FOR DISCUSSION

1. How would you go about choosing the instructional focus for the action plan at your school? What data would you draw upon? For what level of specificity would you aim?

2. What would be the most appropriate unit of analysis for developing an action plan in your school—a grade level, a subject area, or the whole school? What benefits or difficulties might result from each choice?

3. How might you build instructional expertise among faculty at your school? Would teachers at your school be more receptive to learning from outside experts or from one another? Why?

4. Describe a success you have had in designing an instructional plan or initiative. What was the plan, and who else was involved in either its design or implementation? What do you think made the process work well?

Chapter 7

PLANNING TO ASSESS PROGRESS

Mason Elementary School Refines an Instructional Strategy

Sarah E. Fiarman

After creating an action plan, how will you plan to assess its effectiveness? How will everyone agree on what success looks like? When working to change practice, it's important to articulate your goals for improving teaching and learning and to determine how you'll know whether you've met them. This chapter describes the process of planning to assess progress used by teachers at the Mason Elementary School in Boston. Working together on a focused action plan designed to help students write critically about their reading, teachers agree on when and how they will assess progress and then use the evidence they collect to inform their evolving action plan. Their story, which tracks the eight steps of the Data Wise improvement process quite closely, shows teachers working together frequently to interpret and act upon their data.

ORGANIZING FOR COLLABORATIVE WORK

Samuel Mason Elementary School in Boston had spent many years cultivating a small and dedicated faculty known for their initiative, leadership, and commitment to collaboration. Each week, Principal Janet Palmer-Owens released teachers for 90 minutes to meet in cross-grade teams to discuss curriculum, divide planning duties, and share ideas. Faculty at "the Mason," as it is known, set their own agendas for these meetings and highly valued this opportunity to work closely with colleagues. "We're conditioned to collaborate here," said one teacher. However, over the years, a few teachers worried that they were sometimes spinning their wheels in these meetings. One teacher said, "We talked about problems a lot, but we didn't talk about what was *working*. We needed to know what was working in order to replicate it."

Samuel Mason Elementary School
Boston, MA
Type: **Public**
Setting: **Urban**
Grades: **K–5**
Number of Students: **216**
Number of Teachers & Administrators: **23**
Students Qualifying for Free or Reduced-Price Lunch: **77%**
Students' Race/ Ethnicity Distribution
Asian   **0%**
Black   **65%**
Latino **25%**
Native American **2%**
White   **8%**

BUILDING ASSESSMENT LITERACY

In the fall of 2004, Janet enrolled in a graduate course on using data to improve instruction and invited Hilary Shea, a master's student in education serving as a principal intern at Mason, to join her in taking the class. Both Hilary and Janet were enthusiastic about the ideas from the course, and they became determined to infuse them through-

out the work of the school. One of these ideas was the importance of implementing an instructional action plan, collecting data to assess whether students were learning more under the plan, and determining next steps based on what the data showed. This process appealed to Janet because it pushed teachers to evaluate their own work in terms of student learning:

We're trying to develop a real sense of collective responsibility for student achievement here. All of our professional development, our teaching, our planning—it all has to be based on the students in front of us and what the data say they need. Did we meet our learning goals? What do they still have to learn? We keep coming back to the data to measure our progress.

During Hilary's internship year, Janet gave Hilary responsibility for assembling and analyzing data and engaging teachers in the improvement process. The following year, she hired Hilary to work part-time as a fourth-grade teacher and part-time as the school's data coordinator, a job that required her to establish a system for collecting and analyzing data. In this capacity, Hilary shared key assessment literacy concepts with her colleagues and helped them become comfortable using data to measure student learning. The following year, Hilary assumed a full-time position as a fifth-grade teacher and continued to maintain the data systems she had put in place. Hilary enjoyed sharing her passion for data with her third- to fifth-grade colleagues:

> I had seen in my own teaching how the consistent use of data can lead to instructional improvement and how much more powerful that improvement can be when you work as a team. You can look at results together and have discussions about them, and you have evidence to back up whether something works.

Team members appreciated Hilary's support as both fellow teacher and data coordinator. Fourth-grade teacher Karolyn said, "People listen to Hilary. She always has a lot of data to back up what she's saying." Aadina Balti, who taught across the hall from Hilary, said:

> Hilary came onto the team with a lot of knowledge and teaching experience. She really pushed this whole idea of using data, and everyone is seeing the positive results from that. She pushes us to push our kids even further. It isn't that whatever Hilary says goes—everyone has their different ideas. But she encourages us to think about different things.

CREATING A DATA OVERVIEW

In her role as data coordinator, Hilary continued to create data presentations for the staff, known in the Data Wise improvement process as *data overviews*. It was while putting together one of these overviews that Hilary noticed a weakness in students' literacy skills. Although students' reading performance on the statewide accountability test was higher at Mason than at most other schools in the city, her charts revealed a specific area in which there was room

for improvement. According to Hilary's analysis, students' difficulty lay in demonstrating their comprehension of literature passages on open-response test questions. Even among students scoring in the *proficient* category overall on the state language arts test, students' scores on open-response literature questions had averaged only 2.3 out of 4 points over the past two years. Given that their school had posted strong literacy performance since adopting a new, reading-intensive literacy curriculum several years earlier, Hilary said that she and her colleagues were flummoxed by the finding:

> We shouldn't struggle with that part of the test. Kids read real literature all the time at the Mason, and they respond in writing. It's part of our curriculum, and yet they're bombing the open-response questions. Our kids should do really well on this part—they do that kind of writing all the time.

DIGGING INTO DATA

When teachers looked at other assessments that required writing, they began to see a pattern. On formative literacy assessments administered in each class, students also scored lower on the written open-response questions than on the oral questions. And, when they thought about it, the writing that students were producing in a key component of their literacy curriculum was not always stellar either.

In addition to reading assigned books in small groups under the guidance of the teacher, the Mason School's literacy curriculum required that students choose books to read independently. In grades three to five, teachers monitored students' independent reading by holding one-on-one conferences with students and by reviewing letters students wrote in their readers' notebooks. The purpose of the letters, which students typically addressed to the teacher, was to let the teacher know that the student was comprehending the text and making connections while reading.

On one hand, the letters could offer what third-grade teacher Amelia Gorman described as "a window into kids' understanding of what they're reading." On the other hand, however, the letters could be dull and tedious, even when students were excited about what they were reading. Exhibit 7.1 displays an example of a letter that, in the teacher's view, did not do justice to the student's understanding of the text. This discrepancy between students' reading comprehension and the sophistication of their letters was prevalent among a wide range of students: "The kids were able to analyze books and have great literature discussions, but that wasn't apparent in their writing,"

EXHIBIT 7.1. *Letter Written by "Kiara" before Teachers Implemented the Action Plan to Improve Reading Response Letters*

> I just read a fantastic book called The Golden Cadillac by Mildred D. Taylor. This story is simalar to black history because a girl named Louies and her family are going south. But it was her dads idea he wanted to go south to see his parents in the golden cadillac he bought. Louies' mom hated the car and was mad at dad for a long time. But if he was going south she was. She did not want her husband to get hurt.
>
> While they were driveing on the road dad got arested by the police. They clamed the cadillac was stolen! 2 hours later he came out. Every thing was fine. They got to see their grand parents too. Dad enden up selling the car.
>
> I remember when my dad rented a car and it was addorible. I addored that car so much! I wanted to keep it so badly. But he had to bring it back. I felt so sad.

Aadina explained. "The quality of the letters didn't match what I knew the kids were capable of."

Teachers also noticed that the quality of student letters did not seem to change much during a year; indeed, in many cases the quality did not really improve from one grade to the next! One teacher admitted, "I didn't see much use in these letters. I would start doing them at the beginning of the year and then peter out because I couldn't see the purpose in doing them." Others experimented on their own with various ways of improving the letters, such as giving students checklists of what to include or specific writing prompts. In general, the letters remained solidly mediocre. Student performance on the open-response portion of the state assessment caused teachers to look at the reading response letter assignment in a new light. "We needed to collect data to figure out what was going on and to establish expectations of where we were going," said Hilary. "We needed a shared sense of what the purpose was for these letters. We realized kids didn't know what information should go into the letters, and there was not enough scaffolding or instruction around the writing skills involved. Most importantly, we didn't have shared expectations for letter quality."

One Monday morning, after spending hours reading and responding to readers' notebooks over the weekend, Amelia sat down with Hilary and discussed the poor quality of many of the reading response letters. They realized that they had to do something. When they raised the topic at a team meeting, their colleagues readily agreed. The combination of test-score data and teachers' knowledge of their students' writing helped the teachers zero in on what Data Wise calls a *learner-centered problem.* Across classrooms and grade levels, many students were having difficulty writing effectively about what they read. Mason teachers were ready to put their heads together and address that problem.

EXAMINING INSTRUCTION

The third- to fifth-grade team believed that if they improved the way they taught reading response letters, students would improve their ability to write critically about what they read. Accordingly, they decided to spend the next four team meetings analyzing how they each had been using the letters up to that point and planning how they could use them more effectively in the future.

The team decided to begin each meeting by first observing one team member's class and then discussing what they'd seen. During the discussion that followed their first observation, teachers quickly realized that they all had different ideas about what should be included in a reading response letter and how the letter should be written. Each teacher also had different requirements for how regularly students had to write one of the letters; some required a letter every week, others required one each time a child finished a book. In addition, they found variation in their standards for quality work. Some teachers felt the assignment was specifically content-based, so spelling and writing mechanics shouldn't count. Other teachers felt that standards for writing conventions should be part of the assignment. They realized that this lack of agreement about how to teach students to write strong letters could be defined in Data Wise terms as their *problem of practice.*

DEVELOPING AN ACTION PLAN

After much negotiation, by the end of that first meeting the team had agreed on the beginning steps of an action plan. They decided they would teach specific literary terms and writing conventions—they called these "components" of the letters—and expect each student to include a minimum number of these components in each letter. But how would they determine which components to include? Would the components be the same for each grade or different? In making one decision, the team realized they had raised a host of new questions.

Setting Common Goals and Expectations

In the next team meeting, Hilary encouraged the third- to fifth- grade team to decide collaboratively on a set of common goals and expectations for each grade level. Up to this point, each teacher had decided independently what should be included in the letters. For example, when she arrived at Mason as a new teacher, Karolyn hadn't known quite what to expect from the letters. "I talked to the students about what I liked about their letters, but I didn't have a structure," she said. "The resource texts that we shared weren't really clear about what to look for, so it was up to each of us individually to decide what a good letter looked like."

Aadina explained that the wide variation in teachers' expectations was a central challenge facing the team. "In reading the kids' letters, you could see there were differences in the way the previous teachers were having kids write the letters. The components of the letter were different depending on what teacher the students came from. There was

a lack of consistency in what we expected in the letters." The teachers agreed that, within their grade-level teams, they needed to be more consistent about what they taught. Because there was no set teachers' manual for literacy, teachers had substantial leeway in what they decided to teach. This resulted in some third graders learning about the use of metaphor in depth throughout the year while others spent only a week on the same topic.

Hilary encouraged the team to work on what she called "vertical alignment"—ensuring that each grade built on the skills learned in the previous grade rather than repeating the same lessons and skills without deepening students' understanding. She argued that vertical alignment was central to their enterprise as a team:

> If we don't have vertical alignment, I have serious questions about whether there will be a point of doing this at all. Suppose that I met with my fourth-grade colleague, and only the two of us chose a new approach to the letters. If we didn't have vertical alignment, kids coming up to us from third grade would have no knowledge of what we were expecting, and once they moved on, it would all be lost. The biggest advantage that elementary schools have is that we have kids for so many years. Building the scope and sequence from one grade to the next is a strategy that should work in our favor.

Although the teachers valued their individual creativity, when they discussed what they believed students should learn from the letters and what a quality letter should look like, they saw the need for compromise. "We agreed that no one wanted just a book report," Aadina explained. "We wanted more—lessons that dealt with making connections and that tapped into kids' thinking and deeper understanding. But everyone had their ideas of what was important for the letters."

To supplement this discussion, Hilary printed out a glossary of literary concepts—terms such as plot, character, figurative language, and metaphor—from the state's language arts standards. She felt that focusing on the state standards would help move teachers toward a consensus about the scope and sequencing of curriculum:

> We want to be sure that we don't just teach the material we're particularly good at or overemphasize the material that we happen to enjoy teaching. If we all just pick and choose what we think kids need to know and teach that, they're not going to get where they need to be by the end of high school. We teach a standards-based curriculum, which means we rely on the standards to provide guidance about where we need to go. No one can get to a finish line if they don't know where it is.

The standards themselves were broadly stated, and the glossary didn't specify which terms should be taught to what extent in each grade. While Mason faculty had historically used state standards to inform their reading and writing curricula, they hadn't collectively applied particular standards to the reading response assignment itself. After much discussion, the team produced a list of components that they wanted their students to include in the letters. Exhibit 7.2 shows the expected components of fifth-grade letters; the teachers created similar documents for the third and fourth grades.

Putting the Plan on Paper

After determining the components that students should master at each grade level, the team addressed ways in which teachers of prior and subsequent grades could support the components that they were not asked to teach directly. The teachers called this process "ramping up and ramping down." For example, the team decided that third-grade teachers would introduce figurative language and that other teachers would review and deepen students' understanding of this concept. Fifth graders would be expected to include quotations in their letters, so teachers in earlier grades could introduce this skill without expecting mastery.

The team was eager to begin teaching the components right away, and those who did so found that the approach made sense. For instance, Aadina found that the cross-grade scope and sequence helped to focus her instructional goals:

> The "components" helped me organize my teaching and my use of time. I was able to home in on the ones that were my responsibility, because I would know that other teachers were taking responsibility for teaching the other components. For example, in third grade, they focus on summarizing. I don't need to spend a whole unit on summarizing because I know they've already learned that, so I don't have to teach that from scratch. It helps me push the kids further in other areas.

Nevertheless, as they worked, the teachers realized that if their approach to reading response letters was really to take root, they would need to spend time that spring planning how they would formally launch the new approach in the fall. Consequently, they spent part of their fourth meeting working

EXHIBIT 7.2. *Components of Reading Response Letters for Fifth Grade*

Paragraph 1: *Introduction*	
Should include:	
Book information	**Book summary**
• Heading	• Topic sentence (What is your letter going to be about?)
• Title	• A brief book summary (2–3 sentences)
• Author	
• Genre	

Paragraph 2: *Connection—What is your connection to the book?*	
Could include:	
Text-to-self connection (What does the book make you think about?)	**Text-to-text connection**
• Author's message—has this book taught you any lessons?	• Make a connection between this book and another book by the same author (author's style)
• Make a connection to a character	• Make a connection to another book that this book reminds you of

Paragraph 3: *Book Noticings—What do you notice in the book?*	
Could include:	
• Predictions (this is for people who just started a new book)	• Author's use of foreshadowing
• Author's use of symbolism	• Identification of the theme of the book
• Author's use of imagery	• Author's use of humor

Paragraph 4: *Conclusion*	**REMEMBER . . .**
Should include:	High-quality response letters **always** include:
• Reader's review or recommendation	• Actual quotes from the text
• Closing question or comment	• Specific details from the text
• Signature	• Lots of evidence and examples
© Hilary Shea 2006	

in grade-level groups to choose the sequence of lessons they would use and to decide how that sequence would fit within their over-arching literacy curriculum. "At that point," said Hilary, "it was pretty straightforward. We knew that each component would be a mini-lesson, and we knew which components were ours to cover for our grade level."

Teachers worked together to determine just what these mini-lessons would look like. For example, one of the early fifth-grade lessons would be a group activity in which students would collaboratively write an introduction to a reading response letter reflecting on *The Miraculous Journey of Edward Tulane*, the book they would be reading aloud together. This group-writing activity would be followed by a discussion of what makes a good introductory paragraph to a reader's response letter and an opportunity for students to begin their own letters in response to the book. Each grade-level team created a document specifying both the content they would teach for each component and the specific instructional strategy—such as modeling, group writing, or peer editing—that they would use to help students master each component.

PLANNING TO ASSESS PROGRESS

At the fourth team meeting that spring, Hilary said people were "feeling good about all the decisions we'd made, but we didn't feel finished. We still didn't have a way of measuring progress." So the team agreed to devise indicators of progress, to set aside four meetings in the fall to revisit the topic of the reading response letters, and to review evidence of improved student learning during those meetings. "It's important to remember that when you make change, you have to assess it and have to keep updating it," Aadina explained. "Just because we made a change doesn't mean it's going to stay like that forever. You have to keep checking in and keep communicating with colleagues to make sure you're staying on top of what is best for the kids."

To assess implementation of the action plan, they planned to look closely at their own practice. They identified three sources of data that would help them evaluate whether their own instruction was changing. One approach involved looking carefully at student work with an eye toward how it might reflect what students were being taught. A second strategy was to observe each other teaching the letter-writing components to look for changes in teaching practices and students' responses. Finally, the team planned to check in with both Janet and the school's literacy coach—both of whom would be visiting classrooms as part of their regular practice—to see if they too were seeing changes in instruction.

The team also decided to measure student progress in several ways. First, each teacher agreed to monitor the letter writing closely in her class to see if there were changes in students' approaches to the letters. Second, the team planned to start their first fall meeting by having each teacher bring sample letters that they all could collectively evaluate for signs of improvement from the previous year. This plan helped ensure that their focus would remain on the instructional strategy they were working so hard to improve. "This also established accountability," said Hilary. "People knew that they would be asked to bring letters to those first meetings, so they were more likely to implement the steps we'd agreed to." Teachers agreed that another way of measuring student learning would be to examine scores on the school-wide benchmark literacy tests and the state accountability test given in the spring. Teachers hoped that their focus on literary terms—and how to identify and write about them in the letters—would translate into an improvement in students' responses to literature passages on the tests.

As their final meeting about reading response letters drew to a close, teachers on the team felt pleased with how much they had accomplished. Still, while they hoped to see positive results in the months to come, they were not sure whether their hard work would pay off. Would they as teachers be consistent about putting the new expectations into practice? And, more importantly, would students begin writing more effective letters?

ACTING AND ASSESSING

Teachers who were already using the components were alert to early signs of improvement. During the final months of the school year, teachers shared informally that students' writing in response to literature was getting better. They were encouraged to see that students were structuring their letters more effectively and making interesting connections.

The following fall, teachers learned that students' performance on the reading comprehension section of the state test that spring had improved. On the open-response questions, they saw that substantially more of the school's fourth graders had scored at least 3 out of 4 points compared to previous years. In addition, for the first time since the test was given, no Mason fourth grader scored in the failing category. Hilary acknowledged that comparing two years of data meant comparing two different cohorts of students. However, the teachers' knowledge of the different cohorts, combined with the fact that the gain was substantial, led

them to believe that these data might indeed reflect real improvement. Further corroborating this conclusion was the fact that student performance had also improved on the writing portion of the fall benchmark literacy test.

At a meeting before school started in the fall, Hilary shared these data as part of a larger presentation to the whole faculty on student assessment results. As the third- to fifth-grade teachers discussed the results, they were pleased to see some confirmation of what they'd sensed at the end of the previous year. Their work on the letters seemed to be making a difference in student learning. They were eager to learn more about whether the progress was consistent across classrooms and whether students were meeting the specific expectations for the letters that the team had established the previous spring.

In early October, with the school year well underway, the team began their second in-depth examination of the letters. For the next four weeks, they engaged in a process similar to one they had used in the spring: each team meeting began with a classroom observation, followed by a discussion of what they'd seen and how they would improve their use of the letters. From the first classroom observation, teachers felt that they could see a difference in instruction. "We saw how much information the kids had retained from the previous year," Hilary said. "It was the power of using consistent language. I thought, 'Man, if we did this with everything, we could go so much further in depth; we wouldn't have to spend time on the same basic skills each year.'"

Individual teachers also perceived growth in their teaching as a result of the team's work. For instance, Aadina said, "Before, in my own teaching, I wasn't as explicit when I was teaching a specific component. I was teaching lots of different things, but they weren't as direct or focused." Hilary said that the observations helped confirm the usefulness of the work they'd begun in the spring: "People left Aadina's classroom saying, 'Look at the way kids are talking about the letter, and look at the letter that she's using on the overhead. We would never have had that last year.'"

"We saw tremendous growth," Hilary said. "The tone was basically, 'Wow! These kids are writing much better letters, and their stamina has improved.'"

Immediately after leaving the observation classroom, the third- to fifth-grade team met together to begin the next phase of assessing their progress. They swapped the sample letters they had each brought, reading through them with an eye toward finding evidence of progress. Teachers could see right away that the letters were markedly different from the letters students had been writing a year earlier. Children were making connections between the books they were reading and their own lives. They were discussing the literary strategies they saw authors employ. Exhibit 7.3 illustrates how one student's skills had improved since spring. In the first letter by Kiara (a pseudonym), which is shown in exhibit 7.1, her text-to-self connection was superficial, as was her treatment of the book's theme of racial injustice. In the second letter, her text-to-self connec-

tion concerned the protagonist's smart, creative personality (which reminded Kiara of her own), and she used an extended quotation to illustrate the author's use of imagery. Although Kiara's writing still had room for improvement, her teacher was pleased that she was beginning to demonstrate a deeper understanding of what she was reading.

Happily, Kiara's case was not unusual; it appeared that students of all skill levels were showing similar improvement. Hilary and her colleagues were delighted by the clear evidence of student learning. "We saw tremendous growth," Hilary said. "The tone was basically, 'Wow! These kids are writing much better letters, and their stamina has improved. Kids I never thought could do it are doing it.' It was really encouraging."

An interesting set of circumstances allowed Mason teachers to see the influence of their collaborative work from the previous spring. Karolyn, the fourth-grade teacher, had been on maternity leave the year before and had consequently missed the team's initial work on the letters. When she returned in the fall, teammates updated her on new developments, including the list of letter components and their plan for launching the fall literacy curriculum. Without having experienced the model lessons or witnessed the improvements her colleagues had seen, however, Karolyn had little reason to expect anything different from her fourth graders' work on the assignment. Therefore, she taught the letters in the way she and her colleagues always had. She knew the letters were not stellar, but she simply remembered that this was what everyone had been

EXHIBIT 7.3. *Letter Written by "Kiara" after Teachers Implemented the Action Plan to Improve Reading Response Letters*

I'm reading a very emotional book called <u>A Summer to Die</u> by <u>Lovis Lowry</u>. This book is fiction, but yet it seems so real. When I say "emotional book", I mean the words in the book can bring emotions to the reader. Meg, (the main character) and her family has moved to a new house, were Meg has to share a room with her older sister. Who draws a line separating eachother having their own sides of the room. Then one day Meg and Molly – her older sister – are arguing and they go to bed mad at each other. When Meg wakes up she finds Molly's pillow + face + hands drenched in blood. Molly gets rushed to the hospital and Meg feels it's her/fault. Molly gets sick and has many blood transplanted! That's the day Megs world changes forever.

Meg reminds me of me. Meg is smart, she's very creative, and she thinks of others. I find myself pretty much like all of that. Meg is 13 years old. She isn't so thrilled when she finds out she has to share a room with Molly. and I wasn't when I moved and found out I had to share my room. I have to accept a lot in my life and so does Meg. We have plenty similaritys.

What I notice in the book is how the author uses such details that you can get a picture of what's going on in your head. Such as: "Meg", said Molly, as if she was captured and couldn't move. "Call Mom and Dad quick". Meg ran from the room through the shadows in the hall and woke her parents. "Somethings wrong", said Meg, "Somethings wrong with Molly. When their father turned on the light everything was there, so much was there so bright and horrible Meg turned her face to the wall. Her eyes closed tight and tears coming out.

> Molly was covered with blood. Her pillow, her hair, her face all wet with it. Her eyes were open, frightened, and her hands were at her face trying to stop it and hold it back. But it was still coming pouring from her nose, on to her sheet and blanket in moving streams, and splattering on the wall behind her bed. Could you see that in your mind?
>
> I love this emotional book and I'm sure many people would. Which makes me want to recommend this book to all third graders and up, and teachers at the Maron School. Again, I love this book and I can't wait to see the ending. Or do I want to see it?

complaining about when she had gone on maternity leave the previous year.

Thus, at the first meeting in October, she was surprised at her colleagues' reaction to her students' letters. After reading the letters, teachers who had taught her students the year before looked puzzled. One said, "I know these aren't their best letters. I know they can do much better." Other teachers at the table suggested that Karolyn put the letter components on an overhead and remind the students of what they'd learned the previous year. The students would recognize the components, they assured her. Karolyn followed the advice of her colleagues, and when the letters came back, she was glad to see that they were much stronger. "Students," she explained, "weren't rising to the expectations I had until I put a structure in place. This process helped me put that structure in place for my kids."

To Hilary, Karolyn's initial situation was just a reminder of how important it was to have all teachers on the same page: "We talked about this as a team. We agreed that we can change the components along the

way, but we're all going to teach this and are really going to share the same expectations for student work. This is a really important and really hard part."

The team had collected enough evidence to infer that their new expectations for letters were paying off. They decided to spend the rest of their October team meetings further improving how they taught reading response letters. In particular, they hoped to find ways of keeping track of student's learning so they could continually push students to improve.

Updating the Action Plan Collaboratively

After looking at the letters that Hilary's students had written, Karolyn was impressed. "I want my kids to write like that," she remarked. "How did you get them to that level?" Hilary shared a rubric with which she had been experimenting, and the team decided to investigate the use of a rubric as a possible teaching strategy to further improve student achievement. Together, they decided to focus each of their upcoming classroom visits on the different ways teachers used rubrics to teach and evaluate reading response letters.

At the same time, one teacher from each grade volunteered to design a first draft of a rubric for that grade level. Subsequently, they began each team meeting with a brief classroom observation, followed by a discussion of what they'd seen, and then a refinement of the rubrics that students and teachers could use to guide their work. "Prior to that cycle of observations," said Aadina, "we all had different ways of assessing letters." In fact, some teachers had questioned whether letters should be assessed at all, wondering if they should remain an informal way of monitoring students' reading comprehension.

The teachers who were being observed used the rubric in a variety of ways. During one observation, after reading a short story to the class, the teacher engaged students in writing a whole-class letter about the story using the rubric as a guide. Another teacher reviewed the rubric with her class and then had students use it to assess their own letters. During another observation, the teacher made an overhead transparency of one student's letter and involved the whole class in assessing the letter by using the rubric. After each observation, the teaching team met to discuss what worked and what didn't about the rubric itself, how it was used, and how it seemed to affect students' understanding. Through the course of these observations, teachers adjusted their rubrics until the instrument captured what they'd learned and what they hoped would solidify students' learning. According to Karolyn, the rubrics "raised the bar for everyone."

Hilary agreed. "We realized that the expectations needed to be different from grade to grade. So we came up with separate rubrics for each grade, using similar language and all scored on the same basis." Exhibit 7.4 shows the fifth-grade rubric. At that point teachers agreed that students would write letters once each week. They also set guidelines for whether the assignment would be completed at school or at home, depending on the grade level.

Before moving on to their November team meetings, which would focus on math, the teachers once again discussed what their goals would be for student learning and how they would know if they were making progress toward those goals. They agreed that teachers would score each letter and that students would be required to receive at least three out of four points on their letters. A student receiving anything lower would have to rewrite his or her letter. Hilary explained how they agreed to this standard:

> Developing rubrics was a means of developing expectations for what kids would achieve. We teach in a full-inclusion school. We'll always have kids who are struggling, kids who are meeting and who are exceeding expectations. We wanted to take the bell curve on the state test [where the neediest students fall in the failing category] and shift it over so that more kids are in the advanced level and so that no kids are in the "needs improvement" category. That's what we're working on now.

Hilary suggested that the team plan to assess the letters again to see if the rubrics were working, if teachers shared similar expectations, and if student writing continued to progress. The team agreed to revisit the letters in January. Rather than commit to another month-long cycle, however, they decided to spend just one meeting looking

EXHIBIT 7.4. *Sample Reading Response Letter Rubric for Fifth Grade*

Fiction Letter Rubric

	4	3	2	1
Introduction	Your introduction includes: • Heading • Title • Genre • Author • Brief and accurate summary *You have a creative and insightful beginning.*	Your introduction includes: • Heading • Title • Genre • Author • Brief and accurate summary	Your introduction includes: • Heading • Title • Genre • Author • Brief summary	Your introduction includes some of the following: • Heading • Title • Genre • Author
Connection (text-to-text or text-to-self)	*You make a clear, accurate, insightful and thoughtful connection and include specific details from the book.*	*You make a clear, accurate and thoughtful connection and include some specific details from the book.*	*You make a connection but do not include enough details or your connection is inaccurate.*	*You make a connection that is not clear, accurate and does not include enough information.*
Book Noticing	*Your book noticing is on a well-chosen and difficult topic and includes quotes from the text.*	*Your book noticing is on a well-chosen topic and includes a quote from the text.*	*Your book noticing either does not fit with your book or you do not provide evidence to support your noticing.*	*Your book noticing does not have enough detail and is not on a well-chosen topic.*
Conclusion	*Your conclusion is well written and includes questions and a review or recommendation.*	*Your conclusion includes questions and a review or recommendation.*	*Your conclusion includes questions or a review or recommendation.*	*Your conclusion is not well written and does not include questions, a review or recommendation.*
Conventions	*Your letter is well edited and includes few or no spelling or grammar mistakes.*	*Your letter is well edited and includes few spelling or grammar mistakes.*	*Your letter is not well edited and includes spelling and grammar mistakes.*	*Your letter is not well edited and shows little effort on spelling or grammar.*

Mason School, 2007

at student work. They decided that each teacher would bring copies of letters, but this time they would each bring letters that represented the range of needs of each class—that is, letters from the high, medium, and low performers within each class, as well as from English-language learners and children identified as having special needs. Meanwhile, teachers began the work of incorporating rubrics into their instruction.

Adapting the Plan to Meet Classroom-level Needs

Although the team stopped formally discussing rubrics, Mason teachers continued to adapt and experiment with them to better meet students' needs. Aadina explained that these adaptations were part of an ongoing improvement process:

> The standards can change, and you want to continue to up the ante and push kids even further. If we're making changes and improvements each year, the next year they're even further, so you have to keep your standards high. And just because you've made lots of improvement here, it doesn't mean you stop. You have to keep figuring out where you're going to push them next.

Third-grade teacher Amelia continued to revise the rubric and her use of it. She said that one of the things she liked about the team's process was that she felt enabled, rather than constrained, by the rubrics they'd developed collaboratively. "We agreed that there needed to be a rubric—something in place to hold kids accountable for their writing," she said. "But there's room for slight differences in how we each use it. The rubric isn't something that's set in stone—if I notice something that one student is doing that's

EXHIBIT 7.5. *Writing Conventions for Reading Response Letters*

Capitals
(beginning of sentences, names and titles, I)

Understanding
(Does every sentence make sense? Are my sentences smooth?)

Punctuation
(periods, exclamation marks, question marks, commas, indent)

Spelling
(circle your words, then use your quick-word dictionary)

Mason School, 2007

spectacular and that could become one of the components, I'll add it."

In fact, immediately after Amelia began using the rubric with her students, she found the need to make a slight revision. Each rubric included the expectation that students would attend to the writing conventions that Mason teachers referred to as "CUPS," which were defined on a large poster in Amelia's room and are displayed in exhibit 7.5.

However, Amelia found that the conventions section of the rubric didn't support her students in an area where they were struggling. The issue was one of language. Many of her students spoke Cape Verdean Creole at home, and they told her that in Creole, nouns and verbs had the same endings whether they were plural or singular. For this reason, Amelia's students often forgot to put noun and verb endings on the English words in their writing. She and her students realized that they needed another expectation in the "CUPS" acronym, so they made it "CUPES" to include an *E* for "Endings."

Amelia and other teachers explicitly taught students to use the rubric to assess their own work. Aadina explained that her students all had copies of the rubric next to them when they wrote their letters. "They see that the rubrics are fairly consistent from year to year, so they understand what's expected of them, and they can build on what they've learned before," she said. "They know what they need to do to get a three or a four."

Before turning in their letters, students assessed their work and checked off each number that corresponded to the achievement level they felt they had met on the rubric. Hilary explained that the rubrics were teaching tools that guided students as they wrote, reminding them what to include and how to organize their letters:

> We want kids to be reflective thinkers, and this is another way for them to reflect upon their learning. "Did I include all the elements? Did I make a relevant connection to the text? Is my introduction creative? Did I summarize accurately?" These are the questions the rubric prompts them to ask themselves.

Despite their overall enthusiasm, after several months of using rubrics, a few teachers began to notice a potential pitfall. Some students turned to the rubric as a formula rather than as a guide. As a consequence, some letters began to sound wooden and formulaic. Candace, a fourth-grade teacher, said: "I do think there's always the potential for a kid who has a checklist in front of him to go through it and say, 'I did all that,' and for the letter still to be lifeless and dull. I don't think that's a reason to never to use a rubric, though." Hilary explained why she had pushed so hard for the team to adopt

rubrics and how she thought the rote letters could be addressed:

> You can have all the ideas and voice that you want in your writing, but if your writing is disorganized and lacks structure and focus, the rest doesn't matter because no one is going to understand what you write. Some kids spend the whole time mastering the components. For other kids, like Joanna (a pseudonym), after five or six letters, they're going to be ready for more. I don't abandon the rubric with her, I just push her further. She couldn't have arrived there if she hadn't had the scaffolding. The rubric is the scaffolding that allows students to achieve and reach high expectations.

During a discussion of this pitfall at one team meeting, Amelia described how she pushed students to go beyond the rubric. Each week, she shared an exemplary letter with her class to emphasize the importance of voice in writing and the importance of making personal connections while reading. "Your mini-lessons can teach kids to work outside the rubric," she said.

Interestingly, at a conference on literacy, Amelia heard a speaker say that reading response letters should exclusively focus on students' reactions to text, with no requirements about writing conventions or otherwise structured letter components. "Part of me does agree with that," she reflected, "but then there are some learners who aren't going to learn the conventions or any sense of structure if we aren't explicit about them and if we don't expect them consistently. Especially considering our population—a large number of English-language learners and children with special needs—the structure really helps them write a letter successfully."

Mason teachers weighed the opposing

EXHIBIT 7.6. *Template for Collecting Student Achievement Data from the Reading Response Letter Rubric*

	Introduction	Connection	Book Noticing	Conclusion	Conventions
Erica	2	2	2	2	1
Bradley	2	2	3	2	4
Kiara	3	3	3	3	2
Jayla	1	2	1	2	2
Beatriz	2	3	3	3	3
Joelle	3	3	2	3	2
Antwi	3	3	3	3	4

Mason School, 2007.

arguments about writing conventions at multiple meetings. They decided to include the conventions in the rubric, but because of the strong and differing opinions on the team, this was a conversation that they continued to revisit.

Amelia also designed a method for using the rubric data to decide what her next lessons should be. She created a chart to record students' scores on each aspect of the rubric, and then she analyzed the resulting data in aggregate; exhibit 7.6 shows the table she used to record her data. She explained that the chart allowed her to look at the data across the class. "If there are common traits that the kids don't perform as well on, that tells me what kind of mini-lessons I need to be teaching the whole class. Whereas if only a pocket of kids need this skill, that's more of a guided writing lesson. If only one or two kids are doing poorly, I work with them one-on-one. It allows me to keep track of what the kids are learning."

Amelia also frequently invited her students to analyze the aggregate classroom data in order to reflect on their performance as a group. Hilary said, "It's amazing what she teaches these kids—little kids!—to do. They're making inferences and reflecting on the data and talking about why the class overall might struggle with a particular topic." Amelia shared her data collection and analysis strategies with colleagues at a team meeting, where she received an enthusiastic response.

SUSTAINING THE WORK

When January came, almost a year had gone by since the teachers had begun their focus on reading response letters. While the team hadn't formally met about the letters since October, individual teachers had continued to work on refining their teaching around the assignment. Hilary started a binder of "anchor" letters that would exemplify each score level on the rubric. "The anchor letters will help us maintain consistent expectations across classrooms," she said. "Teachers can use them when they want to know, 'So just what does a '3' look like for a third-grade letter?'" A few teachers contributed to the binder, which remained "a work in progress" during the fall.

Hilary noted that even when they moved into their next language arts topic, expository writing, members of the team continued to refer to what they'd learned from their previous focus on the reading response letters. "Everyone agreed from the beginning that we would work on scaffolding the skills kids needed to learn while moving up the grades," Hilary said. "After our work on the letters, that was almost a given." Still, Hilary acknowledged that it would be a challenge over the long term to maintain stamina and focus on the letters when the team wasn't devoting professional-development time to them. She thought she might create a survey to ask her teammates whether they felt they had received quality letters from students at the end of the year, and if so, what they thought the contributing factors were. "We'll need to bring this up again next fall just to remind ourselves of what we agreed to," she said. "I might ask, 'Does anyone need a copy of the components? How are people planning to use rubrics during the launch?'" .

In this way, Hilary planned to keep the team's learning about reading response letters front and center. As she saw it, the big lesson from her team's process resulted from choosing a manageably sized action plan and then assessing progress until it seemed they'd gotten it right:

> Everyone wants a quick fix and they want it in a big area. This focus on reading response letters is so nitty-gritty, and look how many hours it took! But if you want improvement, this is what you have to do. If you say, "I want improvement on reading comprehension," you can't tackle everything at once. Getting people to choose small topics is so important. Particularly for the first time, but really always.

✳ LESSONS FROM THE CASE

Coming up with an action plan for improving instruction involves considerable work and compromise. Once a group has set its course, the inclination is often to launch right in to the work. This would skip an important step of the process, though—one that is key to the long-term success of a team's collaborative work. Because of its indispensability, planning to assess progress is the seventh step in the Data Wise improvement process. The teachers at Mason undertook this step by agreeing on clear goals for their own practice and their students' learning, then determining how they would know whether they had reached those goals. As a result, they clarified expectations, established consistency across grades, and fostered a sense of accountability to one another that spurred them to continue to revisit and improve their practice. Their process reveals several important lessons on how to plan to assess progress.

1. **Keep the scope of the action plan manageable.** Don't worry if the plan for improving instruction that results from your Data Wise inquiry is much more humble than the tome-length improvement plan that your district central office or state education department may require. As Hilary explained, the "nitty gritty" strategy of improving reading response letters was only one of many strategies Mason teachers used to teach reading comprehension and

writing skills. Yet it is precisely because teachers were willing to keep a sustained focus on just this strategy that students seemed to make such headway in their ability to think critically and write effectively about what they read.

The Mason School's plan didn't overwhelm teachers. After establishing consistency in the spring by agreeing on a list of components they wanted to see in the letters, the team allowed themselves several months to adjust their teaching to incorporate lessons on those components. An action plan that calls for small-but-concrete changes in practice implemented one step at a time may be less intimidating (and thus more effective) for teachers than a plan that calls for sudden, sweeping change. A teacher who is skeptical about some aspects of a plan, like the Mason teacher who was concerned about rubrics stifling students' creativity, might find the proposed changes more palatable if he or she knows that there will be time to assess and readjust them along the way.

Allowing some breathing room between steps of the plan also allows individual teachers to go beyond the plan's outline if they choose. At Mason, some teachers who were comfortable teaching the components went on to experiment with rubrics and other means of assessing student learning. These individual experiments then seeded later discussions about the next level of work. By fall, teachers felt ready to take the next step toward establishing shared expectations for student work and supporting all students in producing high-quality letters.

2. **Set teaching goals collaboratively.** The first thing Mason teachers did was articulate their purpose for using reading response letters. Some might argue this was an unnecessary step since the strategy itself was outlined in their curriculum resources. The benefit of the conversation, however, was that it allowed teachers to share their various interpretations of the question, "Why do *we* think this instructional strategy is useful for *our* students?" and then work together to develop a common vision for what they were trying to do instructionally. Working together to articulate clear teaching goals helps teachers feel a sense of ownership of their decisions and builds each teacher's sense of responsibility to both colleagues and the curriculum.

As a fourth-grade teacher, Aadina was willing to adjust the way she taught because she had heard the third-grade teachers make a commitment to teach summarizing. At the same time, she knew she had to introduce the skill of quoting from the text because her fifth-grade colleagues were designing lessons that depended upon it. By assigning and claiming responsibilities publicly, teachers feel a greater sense of ownership and accountability for reaching their shared goals.

3. **Agree on how to assess whether practice has changed.** Once you have a shared vision of how you hope to improve instruction, it is important to think about how you will keep track of what changes are actually occurring in classroom practice. Mason teachers agreed that they would monitor their implementation of the plan in three ways: by watching each other teach, by having the principal and literacy coach visit classrooms regularly, and by engaging

in structured conversations about practice. Because they had decided on the types of instruction they were expecting to see, these observations and discussions could focus on concrete evidence of whether that instruction was actually occurring.

4. **Set student learning goals collaboratively.** After establishing shared goals for curriculum scope and sequence, the Mason teaching team created rubrics to define their goals for the quality of student work they were hoping to see. By doing this as a group, they ensured that "good work" would look the same from classroom to classroom. In order to establish shared expectations, it's useful to work together to envision the final product and then to describe it in specific, detailed terms. This process ensures that everyone is describing the same outcome.

    At Mason, creating rubrics and eventually identifying "anchor letters" to go with each rubric score gave teachers a clear picture of what they were looking for. Like sculptors who turn frequently to models to inform their work, teachers need to know their end goal as they craft assignments, provide feedback, and determine the pace and depth of their lessons. As an added benefit, this practice allows students to focus on refining a consistent set of skills rather than constantly recalibrating their efforts to a new teacher's standards.

    In addition to calling upon their own expertise, the Mason team also looked to an outside reference, the state standards, to inform their learning goals for the letters. This step is valuable because it prevents standards from slowly and unnoticeably sagging over the years. By turning to the state standards, the teachers at Mason avoided unintentionally diluting the curriculum and ensured that their writing goals for students in grades three through five were at least on par with those facing students across the state.

5. **Use multiple measures to assess whether student achievement is improving.** Just as it is important to consider a range of data sources when determining how to focus your action plan, it is also important to consider multiple measures when evaluating that plan's effectiveness in improving student learning. At Mason, teachers agreed to monitor students' progress by tracking short-, medium-, and long-term data sources. Taken together, these three kinds of data allowed them to "triangulate" their conclusions about student performance—that is, to check for consistencies and inconsistencies among the data sources—in order to understand whether students' writing about literature was improving.

    Short-term data include information that can be collected daily or weekly from students' work and classroom interactions. At Mason, teachers agreed to track three primary sources of short-term data for evaluating the action plan: the reading letters themselves, classroom observations about how students were approaching their writing, and conferences with students about their work. Amelia's careful attention to how her Cape Verdean students were performing on the conventions portion of their letters led her to adjust the rubric—and her teaching—to ensure that she placed appropriate emphasis on helping students think about the endings of words. By assessing student performance every week, Amelia and her colleagues kept close watch on how students were responding to their instruction.

Medium-term data include both internal and external data on student performance that is gathered systematically and at wider intervals throughout the year. At Mason, the benchmark literacy tests that teachers gave students in the fall, winter (as needed), and spring provided a valuable source of data about students' critical reading and writing skills that was independent of the reading response letters themselves.

Finally, long-term data include information collected on an annual basis, such as state assessments. Mason teachers were interested to learn whether, at the end of the year, student performance on the language arts portion of the state test had improved over the previous year. In Massachusetts, as in many states, these assessments are not "vertically equatable" in the sense of allowing for measurement of changes in the performance of an individual child as that student progresses from one grade to the next. Instead, schools must compare the performance of this year's fourth graders to the performance of the children who were in fourth grade last year. Although not ideal, this long-term data can sometimes provide valuable information about trends in student performance, especially if the populations comprising one cohort of students and the next are similar. At Mason, the fact that average open-response scores improved over time provided some additional evidence that the team's focus on reading response letters may indeed have improved students' ability to write critically about what they read.

6. **Support teachers in leading instructional change.** For an action plan to be effective, it is essential that teachers feel empowered to implement it well. As principal, Janet had worked for years to foster a culture of inquiry and collaboration at Mason. By tapping Hilary as the school's data coordinator, she demonstrated a willingness to delegate responsibility and distribute leadership. By having a school schedule that provided for 90 minutes a week of common planning time, she ensured that teachers would have regular opportunities to reflect deeply on their practice. By trusting teachers to lead their own inquiry into their practice, she unleashed their creativity. It is doubtful that Mason teachers would have brought as much enthusiasm, ownership, and commitment to the process if the principal had handed down her own plan and required them to implement and assess it.

Although creating, implementing, and assessing an action plan are all steps intended to increase student learning, they are also vehicles for teaching people how to work together for continual improvement. Too often, dedicated teachers feel stuck in well-intentioned meetings that lack a clear sense of progress or direction. Sometimes this happens after years of engaging in initiative after initiative without ever taking the time to assess whether any of them "works."

Assessing progress in meeting a set of commonly established goals can enhance teachers' sense of effectiveness. Collecting concrete evidence of improvement in student learning can help reinforce teachers' core belief that improving how well they teach will lead to improving how well their students learn. Once teachers have learned to set new goals collaboratively and keep track of progress, they can apply this understanding to everything they do. At Mason, teachers found that creating action plans and setting goals in other content areas was much easier after they had already done these things for reading, since they were familiar with the steps of the process and had developed confidence that their work would make a difference.

✳ QUESTIONS FOR DISCUSSION

1. What would have been lost if the Mason team had skipped the step of planning to assess progress and gone directly to implementing their plan?

2. What kinds of short-, medium-, and long-term data would you want to include in a realistic plan to assess student progress at your school? How might you and your colleagues decide on appropriate student achievement goals?

3. To what extent does your school foster a culture of collaboration that supports teachers in implementing and regularly assessing changes to their practice? Are there steps your school could take to assess progress more readily? If so, what would they be?

4. Think of a time you have had success using student achievement results to evaluate an instructional program or approach. Describe the circumstances, the kinds of data you used, and the results. What do you think made the experience successful?

Chapter 8

ACTING
AND
ASSESSING

Community Academy
Gets Serious about Homework

Jennifer L. Steele

How do you lift an action plan off the paper and make it come to life in your school? And how do you then determine how well it's achieving the results you intended? In this chapter, the instructional leadership team at Community Academy, an alternative high school in Boston, works with faculty to implement and assesses an action plan for making homework more central to the school's culture. By seeking teachers' input, the team generates agreement about the plan's importance but finds that external circumstances can complicate even the best-laid plans. This school's story shows that sustaining an action plan over time requires not only a strong commitment but also the flexibility to take stock of what is and isn't working and refine the action plan accordingly.

A NEW SCHOOL WITH A LONG PAST

When Lindsa McIntyre was hired as headmaster of Community Academy, she brought years of experience in urban high school reform, having worked as a charter high school principal, a special-education teacher, and an administrator for students with behavioral problems. She was eager to steer this small high school in Boston, which catered largely to students who had been expelled from other public schools in the district, but she knew that running an alternative high school would pose a new kind of professional challenge.

A few months before Lindsa's appointment, the district had designated Community Academy as an official "school" with diploma-granting authority. This was a major event in the organization's history, because since its founding in 1994, Community Academy's status had been that of a "program," operating on the margins of the district by taking in students who had run into trouble, doing what it could to help them, and, in the successful cases, returning them to traditional schools where they could finish their diplomas. Prior to landing five years earlier in the location where Lindsa was to work—a cramped building on a treeless, asphalt lot—the program had been shuffled from one school to the next, in perpetual search of a building with classrooms to spare. Malcolm Bryant, a longtime English teacher at Community Academy, recalled that local business leaders had opposed a permanent location for the school by saying, "I don't want all of these thugs in the neighborhood." He also remembered the frustration he and his colleagues had felt at not having a long-term home. "For six years," he said, "we were intellectual vagabonds."

The faculty and previous headmaster had lobbied for official "school" status in order to burnish Community Academy's public and private image, and obtaining that status was cause for celebration. However, Lindsa quickly saw that attaining official high school status was only a first step toward changing the way people—including students—thought about the school. Thus, as the new headmaster, her challenge would be to make the school's internal culture keep pace with its newfound authority. In order to ensure that a Community Academy diploma was worth every bit as much as one from a traditional high school, she believed that she and her staff would have to raise their achievement expectations and focus on holding all students to high academic standards. In a setting with 69 percent daily student attendance (compared to 91 percent in the district) and an annual student dropout rate of 32 percent (compared to 8 percent for all district high schools), Lindsa knew she had her work cut out for her.

Community Academy
Boston, MA

Type: **Public, Alternative**

Setting: **Urban**

Grades: **9–12**

Number of Students: **144**

Number of Teachers & Administrators: **12**

Students Qualifying for Free or Reduced-Price Lunch: **60%**

Students' Race/ Ethnicity Distribution

Asian   **1%**

Black   **73%**

Latino **23%**

Native American **0%**

White   **3%**

HATCHING AN ACTION PLAN

Lindsa took the helm of Community Academy at a time of staff transition. She brought with her Kennedy Omolo, an accomplished mathematics teacher and colleague from her previous school, and she hired an instructional administrator, Jennifer Levine, to join her in supporting high-quality teaching and learning. Ryan Casey, another mathematics teacher, was also new that year, having been hired by Lindsa's predecessor just prior to his departure.

Including Lindsa, the four new staff members comprised a third of the school's professional staff. A few of the remaining staff members had been hired in recent years, but several others, like Malcolm, had worked at the school since its inception. Malcolm described his commitment to Community Academy as a matter of conscience. Concerned about the many injustices his students—most of them students of color—faced every day, he had fashioned his classroom into an engaging learning environment that immersed students in literature. "We need to have these students become the superstars," he said. Malcolm felt that examining great writing, especially by authors of color, could spark students' intellectual passion and motivation.

Although many veteran faculty members were trying to do the right thing, Lindsa knew that students needed to be performing much better academically. Results on the state test were bleak. Of the seventeen students with scores on record for the previous spring, 68 percent had failed the language arts sections of the statewide accountability test (compared to 25 percent in the district),

while only 6 percent—one student—had scored at the *proficient* level (versus 29 percent in the district).

Lindsa's new staff members were eager to get started on the process of school change. She wanted to harness their energy to drive the change, but she knew that putting all the responsibility on their shoulders could easily drive a schism between new hires and seasoned teachers. The potential for conflict was real. As a newcomer to the school herself, she wondered how she could best establish trust among *all* staff in the interest of school-wide improvement.

As a first step, Lindsa and Jennifer assembled an instructional leadership team that comprised both veteran and new faculty. In addition to themselves, the team included Kennedy and Ryan—both math teachers new to the school—and Malcolm, who represented veteran staff members as well as the English department. The work of the leadership team, they decided, would be to ratchet up the academic expectations across the school.

Several team members were already partial to the idea that instructional reforms at the school should be based on data. Lindsa and Kennedy had recently left a charter school that used data, and Jennifer and Ryan had just completed graduate programs that emphasized the importance of grounding action in evidence. Still, the team did not have a clear strategy for how to go about using data to improve instruction. Therefore, when Lindsa's district supervisor asked her if she wanted to enroll in a Data Wise course at the Harvard Graduate School of Education, she jumped at the opportunity and asked Jennifer to enroll with her. Their plan was to use what they learned in the course to help guide the work of the instructional leadership team.

In their Data Wise class, Lindsa and Jennifer realized that by forming a leadership team (which, given the school's small size, would also serve as the data team), they had already tackled the first step of the improvement process—organizing for collaborative work. Through the class, Lindsa and Jennifer sharpened their understanding of how assessment results are reported and how they can be used. By later sharing what they learned with the leadership team, they also made progress on step two—building assessment literacy.

To engage in the third step of the process, they created a data overview and discussed it with the instructional leadership team. Their overview highlighted the sharp discrepancy between Community Academy students' report card grades, which were respectable, and their pass rates on the state tests, which were far less so. Some teachers pointed out that the discrepancy was not too surprising because, in addition to academic skills, grades reflect ongoing attitudes and industry. Arguing that these qualities were essential to real-world success, some team members questioned the grade-to-test score comparison. However, the team ultimately agreed that the school should do a better job of holding students accountable for learning the material that would enable them to pass the state test, which under state law was a requirement for receiving a diploma. Students' academic futures were very much at stake.

As the fall semester progressed, the leadership team began to "dig deeper" into data by looking at students' class work, quiz-zes, and tests. When they looked at student work, the team saw evidence that students were successfully completing class work on new content but were not remembering that content on quizzes and tests. Thus, the team identified as a *learner-centered problem* the fact that students were not retaining the content that was being taught in class.

The team then set out to examine instruction to see what might be happening instructionally that could explain this problem. One fact that emerged in conversations with colleagues and students was, as Ryan put it, that "there was not much expectation of doing homework throughout the school." The result was that students were not doing independent work outside of class to internalize skills that were taught during the school day. The leadership team identified this as a major constraint on student learning. "Homework weans students off the dependency on a teacher. It tries to push them a little bit," explained Ryan. The pattern of not assigning homework created a self-perpetuating cycle in which students did not see homework as part of the school's expectations, so when it was assigned, they failed to complete it. Their shirking, in turn, made teachers increasingly reluctant to assign it. The team began to feel quite strongly that the *problem of practice* they needed to tackle was low and inconsistent expectations toward homework. To really address this problem, which cut across subject areas and grade levels, they would need to involve every teacher in the building.

The leadership team was eager to develop and implement an action plan focused on increasing homework expectations. The team knew, however, that a school-wide homework policy might be a tough sell, since not everyone shared their conviction that an increased emphasis on homework was best for students. Teachers had many reasons for not assigning homework. Not only was it the path of least resistance in light of students' reluctance, but a greater emphasis on homework might unfairly favor students with more stable home lives. In addition, some teachers were reluctant to allow students to take their textbooks home because students sometimes lost them or forgot to bring them back.

Though the leadership team understood these perspectives, they felt that developing an action plan around homework was a critical step in creating a more rigorous school culture. They decided to solicit teachers' input by broaching the idea at the next whole-faculty meeting.

THE QUEST FOR CONSENSUS

When the leadership team discussed the possibility of doing something about homework with the full faculty, in some ways the reaction was more subdued than team members had anticipated. Kennedy recalled that "the teachers took the idea positively, that homework is important." He also noted that he and the other math teachers "took it a bit more seriously, because the students need to practice. Many of them are struggling with math, and they need practice so they really become comfortable with it." Similarly, Ryan remembered that, although "there was little disagreement during the meeting," there was "no great excitement" either. After the meeting, however, both Malcolm and Ryan noted that voices of concern began to crop up dur-

ing informal conversations among teachers. Malcolm recounted some of their concerns:

> A major argument was that teachers didn't want to punish students for lack of a series of completed assignments. Some students simply don't have a personal space at home in which to think independently. . . . To punish them for that, even though they may struggle to try to make it happen, is a double blow to their ego, to their intelligence, to a lot of different things. Some of these students have a lot of problems that they have to wade through. It's like, we may expect clear water, and they're wading through sewage everyday.

Chris McLaughlin, a math teacher who had joined the staff a year earlier, echoed these concerns. He felt sympathetic to the team's goals but skeptical about their focus on homework per se: "When I heard about the initiative, my initial thought was that it wouldn't work. . . . Some of my students work after school, care for siblings or children of their own, or even just hang out with friends everyday." Given students' diverse personal circumstances, Chris worried that "daily homework assignments would have a negative effect on most of the students' overall grades."

As well intended as all of these concerns might have been, the team felt it was urgent to help teachers move past them. The point, Malcolm explained, "is that they have to do it, regardless of their home circumstances. They can stay here for a little while longer; they can go to the library. They can make hope where there is hopelessness. . . . We have to trap them into success." He suggested, for instance, creating a study hall at the end of the school day in which students could find a quiet work space and a teacher willing to provide homework support.

Lindsa listened carefully to these ideas. She wanted to be sure that the school did whatever it took to ensure that students would succeed under a homework-focused action plan: "The biggest struggle is creating the expectation that kids will do homework. This meant removing all the obstacles, leaving the building open for them before and after school, whatever we had to do."

The instructional leadership team continued the conversation with teachers about homework. At some faculty meetings, Lindsa and Jennifer asked teachers to bring examples of homework assignments they had created. This allowed the group to ground in real evidence their discussions about what would constitute meaningful, intellectually rich homework assignments. For example, when Ryan presented handouts he developed for his math classes, he sparked conversations about the kind of work students needed to be doing to internalize the course content. Having people share assignments also helped develop a sense of shared responsibility for thinking through the issues. "People had to come in and present something to the group," recalled Ryan. "It was about really holding people accountable."

By mid-spring, Community Academy staff members had devoted considerable attention to examining instructional practice around homework, but they had not yet worked out the details of a formal plan. To ensure that the whole staff could participate in crafting the official action plan, Lindsa and Jennifer planned a weekend staff retreat to a rural conference center in early May. Jennifer wrote at the time that a central goal of the

retreat was "to have teachers refine the action plan and give their own input as to initiatives/ideas that we may not have thought of." Questions on the agenda included how many times a week teachers should assign homework, what percentage of a student's grade homework should constitute, whether students would be permitted to take their textbooks home, and how implementation and student achievement growth would be assessed.

Amid the conference center's bucolic surroundings, the faculty laid aside the daily pressures of the classroom and concentrated on a longer-term vision for the school, including what role homework should play in students' learning. They talked concretely about what a homework-focused action plan should entail and finally decided on a plan in which homework would make up at least 15 percent of a student's grade in each course. The teachers decided that they should *aim* to assign meaningful homework every day, but in an acknowledgment of their different content areas, teaching styles, and assignment scope, they left the precise number of weekly homework assignments to teachers' discretion. Though some teachers said they rarely used textbooks to generate their assignments, they collectively decided that students should be permitted to take their textbooks home as needed to complete their assignments. To support teachers in their work, Lindsa and Jennifer offered to provide resources and support, such as furnishing students with notebooks for recording homework assignments and asking the literacy coach to work with teachers on developing meaningful homework assignments.

Lindsa and Jennifer knew from the Data Wise course that the time to plan how they would assess implementation and progress was while they were hammering out the action plan. Thus, part of their work on the retreat was to identify strategies for assessing how well the plan was being implemented and whether it was leading to increased student learning. For implementation, they agreed to assess progress in four ways. First, Lindsa or Jennifer would visit classrooms at least weekly to look for evidence of the plan in action, including homework assignment prompts written on the board under the daily agenda, collection of students' assignments at the beginning of class, and a stack of completed homework assignments on hand. Second, they would continue their habit of chatting with students at the end of the school day, using that opportunity to ask whether they were taking work home with them. Third, they would survey faculty during the fall semester to learn about how they were implementing the action plan and how students were responding. Finally, if resources permitted, the school would purchase an online gradebook program that would easily allow teachers to share their grade distributions with administrators.

Teachers, in turn, agreed to monitor the action plan's apparent impact on student learning by tracking students' homework completion rates, homework quality, and performance on classroom tests and quizzes. In addition, the school would use students' performance on the annual state accountability test to determine whether the homework initiative and other efforts to improve student achievement seemed to be making a difference.

By the end of the May retreat, two im-portant hurdles had been cleared in the effort to increase student achievement across the school. First, the faculty had come together to craft the details of an action plan that would affect each of their classrooms. And perhaps just as important, they had dedicated time away from their school site for talking meaningfully about practice and building camaraderie and trust. They decided to begin implementing the plan at the start of the next school year, so now they had not only an action plan but a timeline.

THE WINDS OF CHANGE

By the time Lindsa embarked on her second year at Community Academy, two key changes had occurred at the school. One was that Jennifer had taken an extended maternity leave. Given her leadership role in creating the action plan, the team would need to adjust to the fact of her long-term absence. The other was that district leadership had just implemented a homework policy similar to the plan the Community Academy faculty had generated in May. Lindsa was both surprised and pleased at how prescient the school's work had turned out to be. She hoped that the district policy might add credence to the school's policy in the eyes of some of the more reluctant staff. In terms of implementing the action plan, she said, "it probably helped that the district moved in a direction we were already going."

During a faculty meeting in early September, Lindsa took the opportunity to review the homework action plan that the teachers had agreed upon the previous spring. She reminded them of their commitment to assign meaningful homework regularly and to make it at least 15 percent of the course grade. She also noted that, as they had discussed in May, she would be assessing implementation by visiting classrooms, and she asked them to monitor the policy's success in raising their students' performance.

The teachers on the instructional leadership team were particularly eager to monitor whether the action plan was enhancing student learning in their own classes. They kept

> ## "They no longer say, 'I don't know how to do the homework.' Now their questions are very specific. They say, 'Can you help me with a question I have about number two?'"

careful track of students' homework completion rates as well as their test and quiz results. From the very beginning of the school year, some teachers began noticing a change for the better. "The previous school year, the students didn't want to do much," said Kennedy. But when he started his second year at the school with clear expectations for both class work and homework, "it worked very well. . . . What this did for my students is it made them very mathematically literate." Kennedy explained that from the first day of school, he was able to create the expectation that students would work independently. Thus, within a short period of time, he found that "they no longer say, 'I don't know how to do the homework.' Now their questions are very specific. They say, 'Can you help me with a question I have about number two?'"

Kennedy's enthusiasm for the homework initiative allowed him to carry it well beyond the directives of the school's

homework policy. Not only did he count homework as a full 25 percent (rather than 15 percent) of students' grades, but he also implemented a complementary portfolio requirement. For the latter, he gave each student a three-inch, three-ring binder and taught them to use the binder to organize all their homework, class work, and class notes throughout the year. He stored the binders in a file cabinet in the classroom, and he set up a grading policy in which 25 percent of the grade was based on class work, 25 percent on tests, 25 percent on homework, 15 percent on participation, and 10 percent on regular use and maintenance of the portfolio itself.

Kennedy found that his geometry class latched onto the portfolio idea enthusiastically. "After the first quarter grading period," he said, "students were committed to the system because they wanted to maintain the grades they had earned in the first marking period." Since then, students' homework completion rates in that class had continued to hover around 100 percent, despite the fact that he assigned homework five nights a week. He noted that completion rates were less spectacular, but still improved, in his Algebra I class.

Besides noticing the impact of the homework initiative on his students' homework completion, he also took careful note of how it affected their overall academic achievement. For some students, the effect was dramatic. Kennedy recounted the story of a senior who had never been successful in mathematics until he began doing homework in Kennedy's geometry class that year. In the past, Kennedy explained, this young man "didn't know he could do math on his own." However, once he was essentially forced to work on his math assignments outside of class, he realized he had a knack for them, and then he "went back and did more" until he had worked through Algebra II and embarked upon a precalculus independent-study project.

While Kennedy acknowledged that cases like this were unusual in any school, he was quick to point out the ripple effects of such success. Because of the boy's popularity, "his friends were buying in now" to the idea of math achievement. Kennedy's recounting of this story was illustrated by his collection of carefully maintained student portfolios and by the students who approached him during its retelling to attest that "Mr. Omolo is the best teacher around."

Though Kennedy was an experienced math teacher before he arrived at Community Academy, he pointed to the school's homework initiative as transformative in terms of his success at the school. He said that the leadership team's commitment to the action plan "made me realize I could start something like this and be supported. If it was not for the team, I would not have started something like this, with the organization, and the portfolios, and students keeping track of their own work. They made me see that this can be done."

Ryan noticed less dramatic, but still noteworthy, improvements when he began implementing the action plan that year. Once he began assigning homework four times a week, he found that up to 90 percent of students completed it at least once a week. "They come in apologetic if they don't have

it," he said. "I never saw that last year."

Malcolm, who had been assigning homework at Community Academy for years, continued to give extended assignments twice a week so students would have two nights to complete the work. However, he began weighting homework more heavily than he had in the past, at 34 percent of the grade. Also, when the homework initiative got underway that year, he created a homework chart and posted it on the wall, so he could display students' homework completion rates. He said that students took the chart very seriously and, immediately upon turning in assignments, would insist that their work be recorded on the chart. "If you didn't put it up there right away," Malcolm remembered, "they would say, 'Let's put it up there, because I did mine.'"

It was not only members of the leadership team who took the homework initiative and ran with it. When Lindsa conducted her weekly classroom visits in September and October, she was pleased to find that most teachers were writing their homework assignments on the board and collecting assignments at the beginning of class, and that several, like Malcolm, had posted charts showing students' homework completion rates. "Our teachers," she said proudly, "have done an outstanding job."

For example, Chris's initial concerns about the action plan had led him to think carefully about how best to implement it. To encourage transparency and to recognize students' hard work, he designated part of his dry-erase board as "The Homework Board." On it, he displayed the name of each student in his classes and the share of total homework assignments each student had completed. He also color-coded their names according to their completion rates. Those with the lowest homework completion rates were coded red for "danger"; the next level up were green for "on the money"; the third level were blue for "flying high," and students in the top level were coded black for "homework heaven." Chris found that this system encouraged both the low and high flyers, because it gave them motivation to attain a goal and encouraged friendly competition by allowing them to see how well their peers were doing. When students attained "homework heaven" for the first time, Chris bought them a sandwich for lunch.

Lindsa was happy with the evidence of implementation she saw in classrooms. Still, she knew from having studied the Data Wise improvement process that no single source of evidence, such as her classroom visits, could tell the whole story of how well faculty were following through on the action plan. Of course, when they decided on the action plan in May, teachers had agreed to be surveyed in the fall about their implementation of the homework policy. Thus, in October, with the school year in full swing, Lindsa wrote and disseminated a staff survey to measure teachers' implementation of the action plan, including the frequency with which they were assigning and receiving homework. While Lindsa acknowledged that the self-reported survey data were only as honest as the teachers would permit themselves to be, she knew Community Academy's teachers to be an outspoken and forthright group. She felt that the survey would help her capture a range of attitudes about the initiative and its effects on the school.

The eight-question survey, which is displayed in exhibit 8.1, was disseminated both on paper and via e-mail. Eight of the school's ten teachers completed the survey, and the results were compiled anonymously by Wendy Hernandez, a member of the administrative staff. Survey results indicated that most teachers were assigning homework and that, on average, teachers had seen notable improvement in students' homework completion rates. Key findings included the following:

1. Teachers reported giving an average of 3.9 homework assignments per week.

2. When asked what percentage of their students' grades were attributable to homework, teachers' answers ranged from 10 percent to 40 percent, with an average of 23 percent.

3. Out of eight respondents, six said their assignments often asked students to apply or evaluate prior learning, and four said their assignments often summarized prior lessons.

4. Seven out of eight teachers said their homework assignments were always or usually posted on the board.

5. Six out of eight teachers said they typically reviewed homework assignments with students during class, including one teacher who reported using a question from the previous night's homework as a warm-up at the beginning of class.

6. Teachers reported that the average homework completion rate during the prior year was 48 percent, versus 64 percent during the current year, for an average increase of 16 percentage points.

EXHIBIT 8.1. *Community Academy's Homework Initiative Teacher Survey*

---

1. How often do you assign homework?

2. What percentage of a student's grade does homework account for in your classes?

3. Which of the following best describes the way in which you use homework assignments? (Select all that apply and describe as needed.)
   a. Summarizing a prior lesson
   b. Introducing new learning
   c. Applying or evaluating prior learning

4. Are your homework assignments listed on the board daily?

5. How is homework incorporated into your daily class lesson or agenda?

6. What percentage of homework assignments did students complete in your classes last school year?

7. What percentage of homework assignments do students complete in your classes this school year?

8. Is there anything more you would like to share about homework as it relates to your classes?

Thank you for taking the time to complete this survey!

When the survey asked teachers whether there was anything else they would like to share about homework, two teachers recommended additional ways to increase homework completion rates—namely, through after-school homework clubs or through tangible rewards. One teacher noted the importance of the homework initiative for increasing students' motivation, and two other teachers pointed out that homework was reinforcing their students' learning. In contrast, one teacher noted that while homework is a good idea in general, punishing students for not completing it "may be counterproductive" for some members of the student body.

The survey responses suggested that most teachers were taking the homework initiative seriously but that some still harbored misgivings about its usefulness. Furthermore, while Lindsa knew the results might be inflated by teachers' desire to say the right thing, she also believed there were enough negative answers to rule out the idea that teachers were only writing what they thought she wanted to hear. For instance, one teacher admitted that homework made up only 10 percent of his or her students' course grades. This was lower than what the action plan called for, but it still indicated that the teacher was accounting for homework, which was consistent with the spirit of the plan.

Lindsa shared the anonymous survey results with the department chairs and asked them to discuss the results in their department meetings. Overall, she felt that the evidence of implementation captured by the survey was consistent with the behavior she was seeing in classrooms. While she acknowledged that the 64 percent average homework completion rate that teachers reported was still not as high as it needed to be, she felt Community Academy had made notable progress in creating a more academic culture. The previous year, when homework was not assigned regularly, teachers reported that students turned in fewer than half their assignments. This year, by contrast, Lindsa observed that "kids understand homework is part of the lesson. It is taken for granted here now." This pattern suggested that, despite teachers' misgivings, setting higher homework expectations had prompted many students—and teachers—to rise to the challenge.

Although it appeared that the action plan was being implemented in most classrooms, the question remained of whether it was boosting students' learning. Anecdotal evidence from the teacher survey and from classes like Kennedy's geometry course indicated that students were indeed learning more material as a result of having to do academic work outside of class. Other teachers also noticed modestly higher achievement among students who complied with the initiative. For example, Chris noted that

a considerable share of his Algebra I and II students still did not do homework, but that pass rates on the chapter tests were higher for students who completed more than half of their homework assignments than for the students who did not. In his classes, Malcolm noticed that the "feel-good aspect" of recognition for homework completion seemed to motivate students to do more homework, but that it did not get all students to that "85 or 90 percent achievement level that I tell them all the time they need to reach."

Lindsa and the leadership team were eager for an objective measure of student achievement, but they knew they would have to wait until late summer for schoolwide results from the state accountability test. However, at Community Academy, several who had not passed the test in previous years were required to retake it midyear, and these students' performance suggested that the homework initiative may have been helping. Kennedy and Lindsa both noted that the pass rate that year for midyear retakes in mathematics was about 50 percent, as compared to roughly 20 percent in previous years. Given that fewer than 20 students took retests, both educators knew that the differences could easily be due to factors other than the action plan (including individual traits of the students who happened to be retesting each year), but they were cautiously optimistic that the action plan might have played a role in the students' success. They perceived an increased mathematical confidence in many of their students, and they hoped that their observations would be reflected in higher pass rates when more students took the state test that spring.

THE NEED FOR REFINEMENT

Despite the school's progress in fostering academic rigor through the homework initiative, the battle was not yet over. After several months of implementing the action plan and seeing early success, the staff realized that the daily challenges faced by the school were threatening to erode their hard-won gains. At Community Academy, these realities involved the steady influx of transfer students, many (though not all) of whom arrived involuntarily. During the fall semester, the number of transfers was steady but low. However, during the month of March, it was as if a floodgate had opened. Teachers reported that their class sizes roughly doubled during the month and wondered whether this phenomenon was related to the impending state assessment later that spring.

The problem was not that staff members were surprised by the new students or were reluctant to welcome them. On the contrary, student transfers had always been central to the life of the school. "This is always going to be a transitional community," explained Lindsa. "That is our mission. It is all about providing hope for these students."

Nevertheless, new students complicated the success of the homework initiative. As Kennedy explained, the reason was "about consistency." In describing his classes, he drew a clear distinction between low homework completion rates in his Algebra I class, which had received many new students throughout the year, and the high completion rates in his geometry class, in which enrollment had remained stable. He concluded that the difference was due to students' willingness to embrace the academic culture: "Those who joined in the middle . . . they want to be successful *without* doing homework. They

are not buying in." To deal with this trend, Kennedy proposed that each incoming student have a peer adviser for the first two weeks to help the student acclimate to the school's culture. Lindsa liked this proposal and suggested that the staff give it serious consideration.

Ryan also noticed shifting attitudes toward homework throughout the year: "The hard part about collecting data in this school is the cycles, with kids coming in and out. So how I would answer a question about homework completion rates two months ago is different from how I would answer it now."

Malcolm explained that his high-stakes homework system made it too easy for new students to falter:

> Every day you were handing a student a book. Everybody else was half-finished with it, and here comes the new guy. So what do you do? The nature of the program requires that you constantly make adjustments as you go along. The homework initiative had to be adjusted too, because some students were doing well, and then the new guy would walk in and say, "Wow, I can't do all of that. I want to, but I can't."

To help ensure that students new to the school could keep up, Malcolm ultimately decided to stop using the homework chart: "I took it down," he said. "I stopped the list." He continued to assign homework regularly, but in order to improve new students' chances of keeping up, he downgraded the weight of homework and "gave a lot more credit for whoever did the most in class." Because he had upgraded his weighting of homework to 34 percent in support of the homework initiative, his decision to weight it closer to 15 percent was still consistent with the action plan.

By April, several teachers pointed to a need for faculty to come together and problem-solve around the sustainability issue. Malcolm said, "This homework initiative—we have to revisit it as a staff. Now that we're in crunch time, it's going to be determined who passes and who fails for the year. You have students who are not doing homework or class work, and they're failing tests. The homework issue may be a minor point." His concern was that adherence to a homework policy for its own sake was not going to help the students who needed the most serious intervention. Malcolm believed that for students on the brink of failing or dropping out, whether teachers weighted homework as 5 percent or 30 percent of the grade was truly "a minor point." What mattered was that a trusted adult help them find a way to persist in school . . . or else they wouldn't.

It was indeed time to take stock of what was and was not working and to consider how to modify the action plan to make it more sustainable. The action plan had motivated students in many classes and had begun to show real promise for fostering a culture of achievement at Community Academy. How then could teachers adapt it to respond to the reality of student mobility?

Teachers offered some creative ideas. Malcolm, for example, believed that the school could help students who were falling behind by creating an after-school study hall where teachers would offer homework support. He suggested that such a study hall could be mandatory for students who had fallen behind academically and that it might help them stay on course. Kennedy felt that shorter courses might be the solution. Rather than year-long courses at Community Academy, he advocated breaking the curriculum into smaller chunks and offering each short course for only one academic quarter. To see how this approach might work, he began testing his ideas about curriculum restructuring with his Algebra I students. Ryan was thinking of suggesting a plan to the district in which transfer students would start on Mondays rather than at any point during the week. He reasoned that this might make it easier for staff members to plan orientation activities for new students. He also thought that whatever approach the school chose, the staff needed to come together to find ways to *sustain* the action plan the same way they had come together a year earlier to *create* it.

For her part, Lindsa was proud of her teachers, who had not only come together to hatch an action plan but had also implemented it, shared data about its implementation, and continued to think about how to make it better. She pointed out that the homework-focused action plan implementation was just one of several exciting developments that year, including the fact that 90 percent of seniors—28 out of 31 students—had a college to attend in the fall, and that the school's daily student attendance rate had risen that year from 69 to 85 percent. Lindsa knew that Community Academy was a school where progress was being made and that the homework initiative was an important component of that progress. Teachers were learning to work together to raise expectations, and many students were rising to meet those expectations. The school was well positioned for another run through the Data Wise improvement process.

✳ LESSONS FROM THE CASE

When implementing and assessing the action plan, *Data Wise* recommends that school leaders ask themselves four guiding questions: Are we all on the same page? Are we all doing what we said we would do? Are our students learning more? And where do we go from here? Community Academy's approach to these questions offers lessons for how to carry out the step toward which the entire improvement process has been building: acting and assessing.

1. **Take time to build trust.** As we have seen time and again throughout this volume, ongoing, carefully planned conversations among colleagues are essential for building the kind of trust that is needed for successful implementation of an action plan. If you are new to your school, or if there are clear rifts among your faculty, the importance of deliberately creating this trust is particularly crucial. When Lindsa came to the school as headmaster, she was determined to increase academic rigor in a school that had seen such initiatives come and go. But she knew that she would have to walk a fine line between tapping into her new staff members' push for tough standards and respecting the experience of the veteran teachers. Lindsa took two key steps to bring these groups together in conversation. First, she took care to include both new and veteran staff members in the leadership team. Second, she invited the entire staff to an off-site weekend retreat and made it clear that she was there not just to talk but to listen. Because every teacher played a part in devising the action plan, they could all feel invested in its implementation. When it came time to assess and modify the plan, the faculty could build on the trust that had developed as they designed it.

2. **Think carefully about scope.** Guiding colleagues toward the right-sized action plan is a critical task for Data Wise leaders. Should the plan involve all teachers in the building or a subset? Should it be designed to be implemented over the course of weeks, months, or even years? As you saw in chapter 6 from Two Rivers' process of choosing the scope for their action plan, how schools answer these questions depends on their unique goals and circumstances.

   At Community Academy, the instructional leadership team's decision to encourage the staff to come to a consensus around a homework-focused action plan was quite strategic. Because of the small size of the faculty, it was possible—and quite desirable—to involve every teacher in a meaningful way. The challenge was to find an issue that applied to teachers from a variety of disciplines. Homework is an issue that touches all classrooms, and it is potentially high-leverage because it can have a daily impact on how much students learn. By taking the broad issue of entrenched underachievement and cutting it down to a common, pragmatic problem of practice, the instructional leadership team made the lofty goal of raising academic rigor seem more manageable. Also, by allowing the plan to unfold over the course of a whole school year, they made sure there was enough time to give their solution a real try.

3. **Allow teachers room to make the action plan their own.** Even when teachers play a central role in designing an action plan, when it comes time to implement the plan, they will need flexibility to adapt it to their own individual classrooms. When the Community Academy faculty came together at the May retreat to lay out the nuts and bolts of the homework initiative, they arrived at an action plan that had enough teeth to make it measurable and unambiguous but was not so prescriptive that it stifled teachers' freedom to define assignments that matched their teaching style and their students' needs. Specifically, by stating that homework should be at least 15 percent of the grade, the policy clarified minimum requirements and sought to establish a school-wide norm of assigning homework. However, by allowing teachers the freedom to decide on the nature and frequency of homework (with a guideline that it be assigned daily), the policy made room for teachers like Kennedy and Ryan, who assigned their students problem-solving tasks every day, *and* for teachers like Malcolm who preferred to assign longer tasks and give students time to respond thoughtfully. You saw an acknowledgment of the importance of this lesson in chapter 5, in which teachers at the Murphy School described the need for establishing goals for consistency of implementation without requiring strict conformity to a particular script.

4. **Assess progress in multiple ways.** During many steps of the Data Wise improvement process, you and your colleagues may find it useful to draw on multiple data sources to "triangulate"—that is, to synthesize multiple kinds of evidence to understand what is really happening in your school. At Community Academy, Lindsa used various kinds of data to assess how well teachers were implementing the action plan. For instance, she conducted regular classroom visits to see that class time was used wisely and homework assignments were posted, and she developed and implemented a survey to assess teachers' attitudes and behavior regarding the homework initiative. While either of these measures is limited and subjective on its own, using them together can be valuable because each provides information that the other does not.

   As you saw in chapters 2 and 7, determining whether students are learning more also requires examining multiple data sources. Community Academy's teachers collected information on a range of factors directly or indirectly related to student achievement—including attendance rates, homework completion rates, grades, state test scores, and college acceptances—to get a handle on whether the plan they had worked hard to implement made a difference where it mattered most.

5. **Keep the faith.** It is almost guaranteed that some part of the plan you have worked so hard to develop will go awry. While you cannot control how many curveballs you may be thrown, you can control how you will respond to them. At Community Academy, some teachers feared that raising the bar for homework would discourage and overwhelm their students. But when they first implemented the plan, it turned out that many students rose to the elevated expectations. Instead, the real difficulty arose when the school experienced a major influx of transfer students partway through the year. For a host of reasons, the heavy focus on homework became problematic. Instead of chalking up the homework policy as a short-lived

initiative, however, the faculty began a conversation about how the school could modify the plan to adjust to what was happening.

Sustaining the action plan can be one of the most rewarding steps of the process because it is about building upon early efforts and strengthening collaborative ties among faculty members. Interestingly, in some schools that we have worked with, it is during the implementation phase that a collaborative culture really takes hold. Until that point, teachers may not quite believe that there will be real follow-through on their plan. When there are regular opportunities for teachers to check in with one another and the administration about how the plan is going and to make midcourse adjustments, they begin to have faith that there is indeed a new order. When schools arrive at this turning point, the full creativity of their faculty is often unleashed.

Time can threaten to erode gains at *any* school, not just in alternative schools with high student mobility. We have seen schools where promising action plans were sidelined due to heated union negotiations, high staff turnover, or sudden policy shifts in the central office. What marks a successful school is the ability to adapt the action plan over time to changing circumstances. The work of serving all students more effectively is never finished, but for dedicated educators like Lindsa and her staff, such knowledge is what keeps them pushing forward.   .

✳ QUESTIONS FOR DISCUSSION

1. Putting yourself in the position of the leadership team at Community Academy, what steps would you take next to revise the action plan so that it takes account of ongoing student mobility?

2. At your school, who will be responsible for measuring teachers' implementation of the action plan and for measuring how the action plan seems to affect student achievement? What processes might they use to gather the data, to synthesize and interpret the data, and to communicate the results to the faculty? What process might the faculty use to revise the action plan accordingly?

3. What circumstances at your school do you foresee as possible threats to the long-term sustainability of your action plan? Are there steps you can take now to avert or plan for those threats?

4. Think of a time when you or your school responded successfully to an obstacle that threatened an existing plan. What was the original plan, and what was the obstacle with which you were confronted? What do you think enabled you or your school to respond successfully?

Chapter 9

BUILDING LEARNING ORGANIZATIONS

BY USING DATA WISELY

Kathryn Parker Boudett

In a widely lauded, urban K–8 school, a seasoned principal worked with her staff to create a data overview that engaged teachers in a productive discussion . . . and now it is time to identify a learner-centered problem and find a way to address it.

✳

In a suburban elementary school, teachers dug deeply into a broad range of data sources to better understand the learning needs of their students . . . and now it is time to reexamine instruction to ensure that all students are encouraged to reach their potential.

✳

In an up-and-coming charter elementary school, teachers implemented and assessed two school-wide action plans . . . and now it is time to refine lessons that have worked and look toward a new school-wide plan.

✳

In a small, alternative high school, teachers designed and implemented an action plan for increasing homework expectations . . . and now it is time to modify the plan in a way that maintains high standards but takes account of shifting circumstances.

Data Wise stories are never over. There is always another step to the process, and even when you reach the eighth step, it is time to cycle back through the steps once again. Is this good news or bad news?

We have seen that, for schools that have truly embraced this approach to using data, cycling back does *not* bring frustration. Instead, educators at these schools find that when it comes time to create the next year's data overview or action plan, they have a great advantage. They can build on the strong foundation of assessment literacy and collaborative norms that they have worked hard to establish. They can analyze data more effectively, examine practice more critically, and brainstorm solutions more creatively than they did the first time around. Drawing on their collective experience in implementing the Data Wise improvement process, they can find ways to work faster, smarter, better. When this happens at a school, it is fair to say that it has become a "learning organization."

DATA WISE SCHOOLS AS LEARNING ORGANIZATIONS

Learning organization is a term that refers to an institution that has found a way to improve its practice continually. (Other terms that capture a similar idea are "professional learning community" and "community of practice"; see the list of selected readings at the end of this book for helpful writings on this topic.) The idea is that it is *the organization itself*—not just its individual members—that does the learning. By developing strategies for collecting data on its own

activities, interpreting this data, and then using it deliberately to improve practice, a learning organization is in a constant state of improvement. Perhaps most importantly, by systematically identifying and passing along best practices as they evolve, a learning organization ensures that it will continue to thrive even when faced with the inevitable turnover of its members.

There are many who argue that the only way for schools, businesses, hospitals, or government agencies to survive in an increasingly intense global marketplace is for them to become learning organizations. It comes as no surprise, then, that researchers are scrambling to figure out just what it takes to become a learning organization. People want to know: What is the secret to success? What regimen can my institution follow to transform itself?

The prescriptions from one domain to another vary somewhat, but they do tend to overlap in some key activities that can make organizational learning possible:

- Building trust

- Engaging *everyone* in the work of improvement

- Developing a process for encouraging diverse views and innovation

- Grounding collaborative work in evidence

- Valuing learning and making time for it

Does this list sound familiar? Indeed, throughout this book (and throughout *Data Wise* before it), we have encouraged school leaders to recast their roles in schools as focusing on building school cultures that engage in many of these practices. We have also emphasized the challenges facing Data Wise leaders. At the top of that list has been the challenge of building a community of trust, in which educators feel comfortable with the vulnerability that comes with admitting that they still have more to learn.

WHERE TO BEGIN?

You may believe that leading your school toward becoming a learning organization is a worthy goal. You may also feel that implementing the steps of the Data Wise improvement process would be a good idea. Yet chances are, you may be left with a nagging question: Does a school have to be a learning organization in order to implement the Data Wise improvement process, or can a school use the Data Wise improvement process to help it *become* a learning organization?

We have struggled with this question ever since we first began engaging with schools in this work. On one hand, we have found that having a collaborative culture and a strong learning orientation makes a school well poised to embrace the ideas of the Data Wise improvement process. For example, when we met the teams from West Hillsborough Elementary School and Two Rivers Public Charter School at the Data Wise Summer Institute, it was clear that each school brought to the work a strong culture rooted in educators learning together. West could draw on its powerful philosophy of "positive intentionality"—whereby years of building teams and sharing leadership gave all staff members confidence that everyone would act with students' best interests in mind.

Two Rivers could stand firm in its founding principle that good teaching required continuous investment in faculty learning. The sharp focus on a clear process for using data provided the "missing piece" that had eluded these high-functioning schools in their previous improvement efforts.

On the other hand, we have also seen that engaging in the Data Wise improvement process might actually be a first step toward *becoming* a learning organization. When Mary Russo first became principal at the Murphy School, the school culture was considerably less collaborative than it is now. Instead of starting with a major campaign to simply improve the culture of the school, however, Mary started with finding ways to engage teachers in talking together about *data*. By grounding collaborative work in real evidence of student learning, she was able to build momentum for change.

A focus on data also served as a useful starting point at Community Academy, where Lindsa McIntyre needed to find a way to involve new and veteran staff members in creating a more academically rigorous culture. By rallying teachers around the problem of students not internalizing what they learned in class, the school laid the foundation for a collaborative culture. When the faculty came together to develop and implement a homework policy, they saw what a unified approach to instruction might allow them to accomplish.

In schools like Murphy and Community Academy, methodically working through an approach like the Data Wise improvement process can offer a way out of "business as usual." We have discovered, however, that the chances that data can serve as a catalyst for organizational change are much higher when a few important conditions are met.

IS YOUR SCHOOL READY FOR DATA WISE?

If you are wondering whether your school is in good shape to take on the Data Wise improvement process, you may want to reflect on how you answer four key questions:

1. Is our principal committed to becoming a Data Wise leader?

2. Is there time for teachers to look at data collaboratively?

3. Is there someone besides the principal who can oversee data management?

4. Is there support for improving instruction?

Considering how the schools in this book answered these questions may help you think through your own situation.

QUESTION 1:
Is Our Principal Committed to Becoming a Data Wise Leader?

It probably comes as no surprise that for the Data Wise improvement process to work successfully at the school level, it is essential that the principal be on board. This means he or she has to be willing—it is probably no exaggeration to say *determined*—to develop into a Data Wise leader. If you are the principal, this means that you must commit to building a culture based on trust, in which teachers feel comfortable admitting what they don't know and confident that they will be supported as they strive to improve their practice. However, if you are a teacher, coach, or administrator, don't despair: you may well

be able to jump-start the process by testing it out with a group within your school. Showing your principal hard evidence that data can improve teaching and learning within your group may be a first step in having the process flourish throughout the school.

At the McKay K–8 School, Almi Abeyta's staff could see from day one that their principal was determined to ground the school's improvement work in data. Although she started off flying solo, Almi's understanding of how to use data collaboratively evolved quickly. By enrolling in a Data Wise graduate course with her McKay colleagues, she positioned herself as a learner and built a firm foundation of trust within her data team. By the time they had completed the class, they found additional staff members to join the team and to expand the scope of its work with data.

Like Almi, Principal Jen Price started her tenure at Newton North High School leaving no doubt that she personally would champion the cause of using data to improve instruction. Jen took the time to form a large and diverse data team and then to support that team in developing the skills they would need to use data responsibly and share their work with the faculty as a whole. Confident that Jen would do whatever it took to support their work, teachers were eager to take part in tackling a problem that had been troubling many of them for years: how to define and close the achievement gap at their school.

QUESTION 2:
Is There Time for Teachers to Look at Data Collaboratively?

If you are serious about implementing the Data Wise improvement process, you are going to have to make time for teachers to engage regularly in conversation about a wide range of data sources. This might mean that you need to rearrange your school schedule to ensure that teachers have ample common planning time. Or, it might mean that you need to rethink the way you use *existing* common time to ensure that teams can stay focused on talking about data and instruction instead of getting distracted by other things. In any case, you'll want to be sure that you develop a system for ensuring that the insights arising in small-group meetings can be shared across your entire staff.

Murphy K–8 School provides a compelling illustration of what can happen when teachers have regular opportunities to work together to improve instruction. At Murphy, common planning time involves much more than arranging for teachers of the same grade to have concurrent breaks; it also involves making sure that teachers have high-quality substitute coverage when they need to observe each other teach. Perhaps most importantly, it involves having a number of structures in place to ensure that common time is used most effectively. The six-step process for examining instruction and the classroom expectation documents provide teachers with the scaffolding they need to use their time together well and to initiate new teachers into *The Murphy Way*.

Mason School provides yet another powerful example of what can happen when teachers have ample time to work together to improve their practice. By guaranteeing teachers 90 minutes a week of common planning time, Principal Janet Palmer-Owens set her staff up for success. Strong teacher leaders like Hilary Shea could blossom in an environment where teachers were trusted to set their own agendas for this meeting time. When the data showed that Mason students were having trouble writing about what they'd read, teachers were able to hash out the issue together. Until they started talking to one another about reading response notebooks—a teaching strategy they had been using for years—they did not fully appreciate the extent to which this practice could be used to help students make real, measurable strides in their reading comprehension and writing skills.

QUESTION 3:

Is There Someone Besides the Principal Who Can Oversee Data Management?

To make collaborative time most effective, it is critical that someone at your school—ideally *not* the principal—take responsibility for managing the data and ensuring that they are shared with teachers in a way that draws them into the conversation. For many schools, freeing up a teacher or administrator to work part-time for a year to create a system for collecting, analyzing, and discussing data is an investment that pays off for years to come.

Again, the Mason School presents a useful example. Remember when Hilary first started working at the school? As a principal intern and later as a part-time data coordinator, Hilary was able to put into place a system for collecting and analyzing data. After that initial investment, she could maintain the system and bring new teachers up to speed while working full-time in the classroom. When Mason teachers gathered for their team meetings, they could use the data binders, templates, and reports Hilary had devised to make sure they got right to the business of talking about how to serve students better.

West Hillsborough Elementary School was similar to Mason in that it could draw on the talents of in-house data consultant and third-grade teacher Judy Pappas to ensure that when teachers got together, they were discussing data that was easy to understand and interpret. Although sometimes Judy developed sophisticated charts, at other times the reports she shared with teachers were quite simple. As was true at Mason, the person in charge of data at West was not a representative from a software company or a statistician from the central office. It was Judy—a teacher who, because of her day-to-day classroom responsibilities, knew exactly what kinds of information her colleagues would find most valuable.

QUESTION 4:
Is There Support for Improving Instruction?

Finally, if you really want all this data work to translate into real changes in classroom practice, it will be important that you think ahead about whether teachers will have somewhere to turn for creative strategies for improving instruction. Maybe untapped good ideas can be found within your school building itself, and it is just a matter of finding ways of unlocking the skills and knowledge of your own faculty. Or perhaps your school will need to draw upon district resources, such as math and literacy coaches, who can bring fresh ideas and perspectives. It could be that communities and other partners can play critical roles. The important thing is that teachers have access to support for improving their practice. Once

they begin to trust in the process, most teachers we have worked with want to do better by their students. It is only fair that they have access to the tools they need to do this.

At Pond Cove Elementary School, Principal Tom Eismeier built this connection to instruction in from the very beginning. By tapping Shari Robinson to spearhead the Data Enthusiasts, Tom ensured that the group would be directly connected to a powerful source of instructional support. As the media specialist at Pond Cove and one of the district's two facilitators for professional development and curriculum, Shari brought to the team deep knowledge about adult learning. Including the other district professional-development facilitator and two reading specialists on the team meant that there would be no shortage of good ideas about how to change practice in response to the data the Pond Cove team collected.

Two Rivers Public Charter School also took care to provide regular, high-quality opportunities for teachers to learn how to improve their craft. Jessica Wodatch and her leadership team drew upon both internal and external sources of expertise when planning professional development. They saw their teaching staff itself as a formidable resource, and they created regular opportunities for teachers to share their practice. They also took care to expose staff members to professional articles and embed conversations in a framework that could spark rich discussion. Finally, where appropriate, they pursued more formal professional development. The Data Wise Summer Institute is one of many opportunities they found for learning from external sources.

How does a school get ready for Data Wise? If you are feeling a bit daunted by the thought of following the example of the schools profiled in this book, that is okay. Remember, when each of these schools started out, they were daunted too. They took baby steps. Sometimes things took longer than they had expected. Sometimes they stumbled. But the key fact was: they didn't stumble alone. Because they embarked on the work of improvement as a collaborative effort, when they fell down they worked together to figure out what they could learn from the experience. And learn they did.

MODELING WHAT MATTERS

We opened this book by acknowledging the intense pressure to improve student achievement that many of us feel every day. Some of this pressure stems from accountability systems that punish schools for poor test scores. But it also comes from our evolving understanding that, if our children are to succeed in a changing world, *all* of them are going to need to master a set of skills that used to be demanded of just a few.

Richard Murnane, coeditor of *Data Wise* and Harvard economist, has explored this issue in great depth with his colleague Frank Levy. In their recent book, *The New Division of Labor*, they offer convincing evidence that there are two kinds of skills that people need today to get and keep jobs that can support a family: problem-solving skills and complex-communication skills. In writing *Data Wise in Action*, we have aimed to illustrate what it looks like when schools use data *not* to simply "teach to the test" but to improve instruction so that all our students are able to develop these critical skills.

It is no coincidence that using data for this purpose requires that, as educators, we work together to hone *our own* problem-solving and complex-communication skills. When we build these skills collaboratively and find ways to share our learning broadly, we may have the right to call our schools "learning organizations." But more importantly, we have the satisfaction of knowing that we are modeling for our students the approach to work—and life—that we believe will serve them best.

Selected Readings

The following readings have helped shape our understanding.

On the Data Wise Improvement Process

Boudett, K. P., City, E. A., & Murnane, R. J. (2005). *Data wise: A step-by-step guide to using assessment results to improve teaching and learning.* Cambridge, MA: Harvard Education Press.

On Leadership

Heifetz, R. A., & Laurie, D. L. (1997, January–February). The work of leadership. *Harvard Business Review,* 124–133.

Spillane, J. P., Halverson, R., & Diamond, J. B. (2001). Investigating school leadership practice: A distributed perspective. *Educational Researcher* 30(3), 23–28.

On Building Organizations Focused on Learning and Innovating

DuFour, R., & Eaker, R. (1998). *Professional learning communities at work: Best practices for enhancing student achievement.* Bloomington, IN: Solution Tree.

Garvin, D. (2000). *Learning in action: A guide to putting the learning organization to work.* Watertown, MA: Harvard Business School Press.

Tushman, M., & O'Reilly, C. (2002). *Winning through innovation: A practical guide to leading organizational change and renewal.* Watertown, MA: Harvard Business School Press.

On Internal Accountability and Trust in Schools

Abelmann, C., Elmore, R., Even, J., Kenyon, S., & Marshall, J. (1999). *When accountability knocks, will anyone answer?* No. RR-42. Philadelphia: Consortium for Policy Research in Education.

Bryk, A. S., & Schneider, B. (2002). *Trust in schools: A core resource for improvement.* New York: Russell Sage Foundation.

On Skills Needed in Today's Economy

Levy, F., & Murnane, R. J. (2004). *The new division of labor: How computers are creating the next job market.* Princeton, NJ: Princeton University Press.

About the Contributors

Kathryn Parker Boudett is Director of the Data Wise Project and Lecturer on Education at the Harvard Graduate School of Education. Co-editor of *Data Wise: A Step-by-Step Guide to Using Assessment Results to Improve Teaching and Learning*, her research and teaching focus on helping educators make effective use of a wide range of data sources to improve instruction and student achievement. She thanks Mike, Shannon, Dorothy, and Eliza for all their love and support.

Sarah E. Fiarman has taught grades 3–6 in Massachusetts and is a National Board Certified Teacher. She leads workshops for teachers and principals on how to build strong learning communities for children and for adults. Her current research focuses on teacher leadership. She thanks her family members for their patience, good humor, and apple pies.

Michelle L. Forman has worked in high schools as an English teacher, program coordinator, and researcher in New York City and Oakland, California. Her current research focuses on mobilizing faculties to increase organizational capacity in underperforming schools. She thanks her husband, Chris Herbert, for his valuable insights and his dedication to the teaching profession.

Trent E. Kaufman has worked in high schools in Washington, D.C., California, and Massachusetts as a teacher, administrator, and consultant. He researches school planning and performance-management processes and data-driven decisionmaking in schools and districts. He now serves as President of Education Direction, a scholastic research and marketing firm, and he thanks Rosie, JT, Isaac, and Kate for their inspiration and support.

David P. Ronka is a senior consultant at Public Consulting Group, Inc. (PCG). He works with school districts and state education agencies throughout the United States to implement organization-wide, sustained data-driven decisionmaking systems and processes. He thanks his wife, Ellen, for her loving support and creative editing and his colleagues at PCG for their shared commitment to school improvement through the use of data.

Jennifer L. Steele has been an elementary school teacher in Virginia and a high school teacher in California and has conducted research on teacher and administrator professional development in Massachusetts and Pennsylvania. She currently studies financial incentives for teachers. She thanks Rosie for her unflappability and priceless two cents.

Mark B. Teoh has been a history teacher in Houston and Philadelphia. His research focuses on issues of teacher quality and its impact on student achievement. He currently leads the program evaluation effort in the Boston Public Schools. He would like to thank the first educators in his life, his parents, Lily and Henry.

Rebecca A. Thessin has been a social studies teacher in Massachusetts and West Virginia. She also coordinated principal professional development, taught principals how to use data, and acquired principal certification while working in the Boston Public Schools. Her current research focuses on high school reform and using data to improve instruction. She would like to thank her husband, Jonathan, for his endless patience over the past year.

Thomas Tomberlin has been a high-school Latin teacher in North Carolina as well as an adjunct instructor of classics at Tulane University, Loyola University (New Orleans), and the University of North Carolina at Greensboro. He served as chairman of the leadership team of his high school as well as serving on school improvement committees at the district level. His research interest focuses on school improvement issues and educational technology. He wishes to thank Meredith for encouraging him to keep working and Nate for demanding he stop and play.

All contributors are doctoral students at the Harvard Graduate School of Education (HGSE) other than Kathryn Parker Boudett, an HGSE faculty member, and David P. Ronka, an HGSE alumnus.

Index   *Note:* Page numbers in italic type indicate the presence of figures or tables.